THE DEEP END

An Elite Swimmer's Struggle With
Alcoholism and Bipolar Disorder

Christi Vedejs

*Dear Katie,
I wish you the very best in life! Stay well!*

Christi Vedejs

Copyright ©2013 by Christi Vedejs

All rights reserved. No part of this publication may be reproduced or transmitted in any form or by any means, electronic or mechanical, including photocopy, recording, or any information storage and retrieval system, without permission in writing from the author/publisher.

Requests for permission to make copies of any part of the work should be mailed to the publisher at the following address:

Day & Night Media
P.O. Box 412
Chelsea, MI 48118

Published by Day & Night Media

www.DayAndNightMedia.com

www.TheDeepEnd.us

Library of Congress Control Number: 2013935176

ISBN: 978-0-9891423-0-4

Printed in the United States of America

Praise For *The Deep End*

"This book provides insight into the struggles with substance abuse and mental illness that many people of all ages endure. I find it a helpful resource when I am attempting to approach a person with these challenges in a caring, therapeutic manner. I would recommend it to primary care physicians and other health care providers."

-*Virginia L. Johnson, M.D., fellow ABFM*

"...Without at all blaming, which I think is unusual, Ms. Vedejs weaves in stories about her alcoholic family, her intimate friends, her teammates and her husband. This makes her, despite her status as an elite athlete, totally familiar, and makes her story that much more compelling and meaningful. *The Deep End* is a fascinating read."

-*Esta Grossman, Emeritus Co-Chair*
Department of Biology
Washtenaw Community College

"*The Deep End* is a frank and courageous account of the author's struggle and recovery from depression and alcoholism. Her amazingly detailed journey through what happened, what it was like, and what it's like now will give hope to those afflicted with mental illness or addiction, and will present a compelling reason for such individuals to *never give up*. This inspiring story helps us understand that mental illness *can be* controlled, addiction *can be* beat, and many who read it will come away thinking, 'If she could do it, I can do it. *I can recover!*'"

-*John G.*

"This book contains a message of hope by showing that change is possible at any time when dealing with addiction and its adverse consequences."

-*Kirk J. Brower, M.D.*
Professor of Psychiatry
University of Michigan

Praise For *The Deep End*

"I was blown away when I read *The Deep End*. Such honesty! Such brutal self-examination! I could relate to so many things in this book. At times it even made me cry, and that does not happen very often. I am grateful to have had the opportunity to read Ms. Vedejs' autobiography. This is an interesting and compelling story, well told."

-Kevin W., Engineer

"I already want to pre-order thirty copies for my patients (outpatient general psychiatry, homeless addicts program and state prison). Initially I was thinking only of the women, but men will relate as well. The descriptions of how it feels to be out of control, totally controlled and then balanced (Ms. Vedejs' balance) will be a lightning strike for those with compulsive achievement needs and psychiatric comorbidity. Persisting despite having both arms and both legs tied behind one's back is an ultimate definition of courage. This book is not perfect but much of it consists of the best perspective on living with conflicting needs I have ever seen.

"P.S. My conflicting needs involve the question, 'How do I get colleagues' help to buy these books?'"

-Mary Closser, D.O.
Adult and Addiction Psychiatry

"Three words came to mind when I read this book: acceptance, willingness and hope."

-Ann Byrne, Paralegal

Acknowledgments

Thank you to the following people for your editorial assistance and support. I truly appreciate your generosity in sharing your time and expertise. And a special thank you to Betsi Hill and Trudy Crandall for so much extra time and effort spent in helping me complete this book. I am most grateful.

Ann Byrne
Kirk Brower
Mary Closser
Trudy Crandall
Lori F.
Kim Fairley
Stacie Fruth
John G.
Esta Grossman
Betsi Hill
Virginia Johnson
Jon Margerum-Leys
Jacques Mersereau
Liz Shafer
Christina S.
Tracy Van den Bergh
Kevin W.

For Jacques,
My Best Friend and Soul Mate

Time present and time past
Are both perhaps present in time future,
And time future contained in time past.

T.S. Eliot, *Burnt Norton*

Contents

Acknowledgments   *iii*

Introduction	1
Brighton Hospital	9
Door B	11
Swimming	17
Danger	24
Scars	36
Self & Identity	46
Hawaii	63
Mom	79
Decisions	90
Olympic Trials	96
Michigan	105
Love, Reign O'er Me	128
Had Enough	143
Maggs and Jacques	165
Marriage and Codependence	185
The Beginning of The End	202
The Middle of The End	215
The End of The End	246
Wonder Woman	255
Hope and Faith	265
Epilogue	276

Appendix A: Source Notes   *279*

Some of the names in this book have been changed to respect the privacy and anonymity of the persons mentioned.

THE DEEP END

Introduction

I am Christi. I am a swimmer. I am also an alcoholic, among other things. Yes, I am one of *those people*. I am one of those people that walks among you, that lives and thrives and lives and breathes and sometimes bleeds the daily realities of my secret life. My nature is anxious. I bite my fingernails and have weird dreams. I have bipolar disorder. If you saw me at work, or in a café, or on the street, or in the pool I doubt that you would suspect. You would not suspect because I look just like you. I am a friend, an athlete, a wife, a partner. I am Christi the Swimmer. I am an alcoholic.

And I am a true alcoholic, true to the core. Because once I start drinking, once I have that first drink, I can't stop. Can't, as in *can't*. Can*NOT* stop. People who aren't alcoholics often don't understand this. They think of alcoholics as "weak," or lacking in "willpower."

"What do you mean you *can't* stop? What you really mean to say is you don't *want* to stop, right? That you *choose* not to stop."

Despite all the publicity and education about alcoholism and addiction there is still this pervasive image of alcoholics as weak, decrepit people – old unshaven men – bums clutching brown paper bags, dressed in filthy rags, stumbling down the street.

During my high school and college years I was an attractive, straight A student, a four-year high school State Champion and All-American swimmer,

THE DEEP END

Big Ten Champion and collegiate All-American swimmer, collegiate Academic All-American, multiple academic and athletic award winner, NCAA Finalist, and Olympic Trials Finalist, just to name some of my accomplishments. Few people who understand the intensity and rigors of the sport of swimming would have considered me "weak" or lacking in "willpower." There are many qualities that can be used to describe an elite competitive swimmer: hard-working, dedicated, committed, tough, strong, positive and *willful*, among others. We as a group certainly don't lack in personal fortitude. What we do lack is *balance*. Balance in our sport, in our work, in our personal lives.

These are also character traits that I have observed in many alcoholics I have met over the years. We come from all walks of life. Many of us are successful, high-functioning people. We have solid careers and good jobs, upstanding and respectable families. We have varied backgrounds and represent all socioeconomic classes. From outward appearances many of us seem to have it made, and everything is *fine*. That is how I appeared to the outsider and I still do: highly successful, high-functioning, and everything is *in control*.

The reality is that when we are drinking we are barely holding ourselves and our lives together. The outward appearance is just that: an appearance. We are leading double lives. One is the successful life – going to work, being productive, winning awards, making money, keeping our families together. The other is the alcoholic's life – terrible hangovers, the struggle to get to work on time, secret debts and financial difficulties, troubled children, guilt and remorse, and the never-ending obsession with drink. Alcohol dominates our lives in every respect. With every morning vow to never drink again comes the eventual overwhelming physical and psychological *need*. Before the vow is even a quiet whisper leaving our consciousness we are thinking about when and how we will get the next drink. Which store will I go to today after work? *I wouldn't want the clerks to notice that I drink every day, of course.* How will I be sure there is enough drink at the party? *Do I sneak a flask in my purse, hitting it during many trips to the Ladies Room?*

This is the real life of the alcoholic. And as time goes on things only get worse. Jobs are lost, finances are ruined, relationships and families are broken. There are drunk driving tickets, suspended drivers' licenses and often jail time. And there is the unending cycle of highs and lows, of intense productivity and happiness, followed by painful idleness, sickness, deep feelings of worthlessness, depression and hopelessness. Eventually there are no "highs;" the drink merely brings one back up to "normal," if it does that at all.

So then there is this matter of "personal choice." Why would anyone consciously choose the life of an alcoholic? And once mired in those awful circumstances, why would anyone choose to stay there? This is another aspect of the disease of addiction that many people don't understand.

An ex-friend of mine who is not an alcoholic used to say to me, "I don't understand this drinking thing. You're so miserable all the time. Why don't you just stop?"

Of course I *chose* to stop. I chose to stop many, many times. I was *desperate* to stop, but I couldn't. Truly, I could not stop. Alcoholism is a sneaky and seductive thing. There is social drinking, which is considered "normal." This is when a person is able to have "one or two" and then call it quits. Or maybe occasionally this person will get a tad more than "just buzzed," but then not think about alcohol again for weeks. There is also the moderate to heavy drinker, who drinks often and/or excessively and walks the fine line into "alcoholic drinking." Alcoholic drinking is when a person drinks in a compulsive and uncontrolled way, often, but not always, to the detriment of his or her health, relationships, occupation or ability to perform normal day-to-day tasks or to function socially. It is possible and common that a person can occasionally "abuse" alcohol, meaning "drink alcoholically," and still not be an "alcoholic." However an "alcoholic" cannot abuse alcohol and still go back to being a "normal" drinker. This is because an alcoholic has the progressive disease called Alcoholism, and for him or her, as time goes on alcohol becomes a psychological and physical *need*. It isn't just a simple *desire* for alcohol, like one might desire a bowl of ice cream. The alcoholic's body and brain are different from a normal person's body and brain. The alcoholic's body changes physically over time. It needs alcohol or it goes into withdrawal, a condition that is both very unpleasant (shaking, sweating, having headaches, feeling nauseous) and dangerous (having a seizure, dying).

Of course nobody of sound and rational mind would choose to become an alcoholic. Certainly I didn't want it! But as I said, the disease is clever, and it sneaks up on you. I like this simple metaphor for choice regarding alcohol or drug use in one's life: There are two doors, Door A and Door B. Each door opens up on the Path of Life, which starts as a beautiful, clean river flowing gently beneath a flawless blue sky. In both scenarios the rivers are edged with a deep green forest, which is flanked by rolling fields of golden corn. The start of each Path is the same. You are told that behind both Door A and Door B lie beauty, health, opportunity, possibility, success, hope, happiness and good times. However Door B is a trick. When you open it, the scene looks identical to Door A – beautiful, positive, happy. You are warned that Door B is a trick. You are told to be very careful about opening it, and that it might be best to not step through it at all. Because Door B offers something else, something that is harder to find on Door A's Path of Life. Door B offers instant gratification, instant satisfaction for your every desire, instant reward and instant pleasure. Door A represents a life free of drugs and alcohol. Door B represents a life that revolves around substance abuse, the life of an alcoholic or addict.

The opening backdrop as seen through both doors is identical. Both river scenes show beauty, promise, positivity and happiness. The rivers wind their way through the lovely countryside and eventually bend out of sight.

At the bend, River A begins to branch off, its waters spreading through the pastoral landscape into smaller rivers and channels that end in verdant swamps, fields and meadows, and crystal blue lakes of various shapes and sizes. The River is fed by healthy streams and rivulets created by deep underground springs and melting mountain snow. Its flow remains constant, steady and clean. Eventually, River A wends its way to its final destination, with its clear, fresh waters filtering through lush wetlands as they merge with the vast *Ocean of Life*.

River B branches off after the bend too, but not as often as River A. Instead, River B winds through cities and industrial zones, past shipyards and cone-shaped mounds, through dumps and landfills. River B is fed by acid rain, dirty canals filled with industrial waste, raw sewage and urban sludge. This river no longer flows gently beneath a clear blue sky. Instead, it is gathering speed and power as more murky water pours into the turbulent surge that is gushing onward under a smoggy metropolitan haze. River B is pounding along its deep bed now, frothing and foaming as its boiling waters approach its end: *The Falls of Death*.

Obviously River B is not where you want to go for a swim. But at first it's so inviting, is it not? It's clean and cool, like River A, and on top of that it offers the instant reward of intense pleasure without effort any time you want it, simply by using drugs or alcohol. For some, a small taste of that pleasure is enough. They are satisfied. Or maybe they see the bend approaching and either know or sense that something else lies ahead, something dark, desperate. Perhaps even something. . . evil. For these folks a brief dip into River B is all they need and want, and they are content to climb out quickly and slip gently back into River A's steady, comfortable flow.

For others, River B's pleasure is so intense that they are literally swept away from the start. Or they are continually blinded by its seductive beauty and return often to swim in its cool waters. They do not see the approaching shadow of the hazy sky or the darkness just beyond the bend. When they finally do see it, when they are bobbling in sewage and bumping up against chunks of urban debris, it is too late. The current is too swift, and most of the time they are swimming in the strongest part of the current, in the center. Every now and then they are able to struggle to the side and clutch at something on the River's edge, hoping to pull and claw their way out. But often the small branches break off in their hands, or are pulled out at the roots so they are sucked mercilessly, hopelessly back into the deep and turbulent swell. The waters become more brown and frothy as they surge toward *The Falls*, its rising clouds of spray now visible in the distance. The exhausted swimmer is so desperate she begs with all her heart and soul for help. One last, solid-looking tree approaches quickly on the Right Bank. If she can just paddle a little harder she can get to it in time. But will she still have enough strength to make it – to reach the low-hanging branch and lift her tired hand high enough to grasp it? She ducks her head and battles with every ounce of energy she has left...

In this metaphor there are only two possible outcomes. One is Door A, which represents a life path of making good, safe choices and leads to the *Ocean of Life*. Door B represents the life path of making poor or risky choices and leads to the *Falls of Death*. Some people are able to occasionally go through Door B and make a risky choice or two, and then return to the safety and health of the path that Door A offers. Then there are those who go through Door B, make a poor or risky choice or two, and are swept away by the dark river as in the story and barely make it out before it is too late, if they make it out at all.

Regardless, the point is that at the early stage of drug or alcohol use *one is able to make a choice: either use, or don't use.* Some people are able to use drugs and/or alcohol occasionally and still *choose* to stop, to return to River A. Some can do this their entire lives and never have a problem. But then there are those who, by making poor choices too many times (by staying in River B), ultimately destroy their ability to choose. They have become addicted, and can no longer *choose* to stop using at will. For these people, who are treading madly in the chaos of River B's whirling, swirling waters, there are only two

Introduction

possible outcomes: quit using, or die (by failed health, overdose or suicide). Because the ability to choose to quit using has become so badly eroded, it usually takes some sort of intervention or an extremely desperate situation to enable this addicted person to quit. This is what the term "hitting rock bottom" refers to, and it can mean different things to different people.

For one person it might be a brush with suicide. For another, a drunk driving incident and jail time. Yet another person's "rock bottom" might be feeling sick every morning and going to work with a hangover. Whatever the "bottom" may be, it is usually necessary for an addicted person to finally arrive there in order to quit using alcohol or drugs. And then, sadly, there are those who don't make it, who are never able to quit. For those people the outcome is very dire.

For me, River B was too powerful from the start and I was swept away immediately upon entering it. In my case it would have been better never to have crossed Door B's threshold at all. But I was young and naive. I didn't think I would be one of *those people*, the ones who try a drug once and are immediately hooked. I am fortunate that I was afraid to try the hard-core street drugs, like crack cocaine, heroin and methamphetamine, to name a few. Based on my experience with alcohol I knew that I would be addicted to those powerful drugs immediately, so I smartly avoided them. I feel it necessary to point out, however, that when I started drinking at age fourteen those drugs were nowhere near as common and easy to get as they are today. It is very frightening that in many communities a sixth grader can buy heroin or prescription drugs in the playground at school. In many cases it is much easier for an underage person to obtain street drugs and prescription medications than it is to obtain alcohol.

And so that's how it is. And I *am* one of *those people*. I walk among you. I live and thrive and live and breathe and sometimes bleed the daily realities of my secret life. I am a friend, an athlete, a wife, a partner. I wrote this book so that I could share my life, so that maybe someone out there reading this story might find some commonality, some identification, and might benefit from the experience, strength and hope that I have to offer. I wrote this book for me, and I wrote it for you. I am Christi the Swimmer, a recovering, bipolar alcoholic. I chose Door B, and this is what happened.

Brighton Hospital

"That is *not* my mother!" I sputtered in hysterics. "Did you see that?! I swear I saw a... demon! It's like she's possessed. Oh my *God!!*"

"Yeah, I saw." Jacques shuddered as he backed slowly out of the narrow parking space.

"I can't believe we left her like that, in that wheelchair." I sobbed frantically as we drove away. "That *room!* That horrible, horrible room. And did you see her eyes? That *color*... that... that *look*. I've never seen her look so... gone. It's like she's not even here anymore."

I wiped my nose with the back of my sleeve as I rifled through my bag for tissues. Jacques, my husband, sat up straight, gripping the wheel and looking forward intently. He took one hand off the wheel and grasped mine, pulling it against his thigh and holding it tight while I cried and my body quivered, the pain coming in waves, emanating from some dark place deep inside me.

It was the day after Christmas, 2008. We had just left Brighton Hospital, a detox and rehabilitation facility for alcoholics and drug addicts. Earlier that morning we had picked up my mother at the ER in a hospital near her home where she had spent the night in the intensive care unit. She was there because I had pleaded with the doctor to keep her until morning.

"Please," I had begged through my tears, "If she goes home nothing will change. It will be just like all the other times. She's going to die! Isn't there *anything* you can do to keep her overnight? Please! Can you at least *try* to talk with her about rehab?"

I waited on my end of the phone, staring at the dingy linoleum floor and pacing back and forth in our tiny kitchen, wiping my tears with shaking hands. After what seemed an eternity he said that yes, they could keep her and he would have someone from psych come talk with her about starting a treatment program for her alcoholism. *Oh, thank God.* I realized I had been holding my breath. I exhaled long and took deep, heaving breaths as I put down the phone and sank to the floor, sliding my back against the cabinet under the sink. I was utterly, completely spent, drained to the core of my being. I was so tired of watching my mother dying, so exhausted from everything that had happened, and so sick of seeing my own slow death unfolding before my eyes. I sat down and put my hands on both sides of my throbbing head, leaning forward with my elbows on my knees. "Breathe," I told myself. "Breathe. . ."

Door B

I had my first drink when I was fourteen years old. Or, more accurately, I had my first *drinks*, at the much-anticipated "State Party" following our State High School Swimming Championships. I had been hearing about this party from my older teammates throughout the eighth grade.

"Just wait 'til State Party!" they'd said. "You're going to get *soo* wasted!"

I heard about it many times during our short high school swim season too, and began to look forward to it as much as I feared it.

I knew a lot about alcohol and drug use, after all. We had learned about it in school. I knew that it was dangerous, and that a certain percentage of people would become "alcoholics," or worse, "drug addicts." During our sixth grade health education class one day we were told to look around at our classmates and think about the fact that one in every ten of us would grow up to have an alcohol or drug problem. We were told that if you had a person or people in your family who were alcoholics or addicts that you were even more likely to become one yourself. And the scariest thing to me was this: that there were people who could try a drink or a drug just one time and *Bam!* They would become addicted. *How is that even possible?* I scoffed at the idea. I just couldn't wrap my eleven-year-old mind around that concept, but I feared it all the same.

So there I was three years later in a dimly lit, nicely finished basement room, in the process of getting drunk for the first time. "Soo wasted," as my teammates promised. I remember how my first drunk felt. I remember it because it was the feeling that I craved and sought from then on, every time I drank.

At first the beer tasted horrible. It was awful and bitter and it made me gag. I had to chug a plastic "glass" while everyone cheered, "Chug! Chug! Chug!" I held my breath, squeezed my eyes shut and downed the horrible foamy liquid, imagining it was orange soda. It left an acrid aftertaste in the back of my throat. "Ugh! Why do people *like* this?" I thought. Someone handed me another and the "Chug!" chant started again. I shook my head no – I was still near puking from the first one.

The second I drank more slowly, and then the third, and the fourth. I was feeling relaxed and warm all over, and smiled happily as I moved through the darkish, crowded basement, beer in hand. I had always been shy, painfully so, but alcohol erased my inhibitions. I was actually able to mingle with people I barely knew: some of the boys' team swimmers and their friends. It was a magical experience and I loved it. The more drunk I got, the more drunk I wanted to be. I was alive! I was no longer counting my beers. *This is perfect!* I thought.

I don't remember the end of the party or when I passed out. I do remember waking up the next morning with a pounding headache and the stabbing pain behind my eyes that goes with a raging hangover. We had slept at the party host's house so, thankfully, I was not at home. Everyone was grinning at me and calling me "Crash." That soon became one of my nicknames in high school: "Christi Crash."

From that moment, that very morning, I knew I was different. In my entire drinking career I have never been in denial. I knew I had an alcohol problem from Day One. That fateful morning I buried myself under a blanket and held my hands against my aching head.

"What have I done?" I groaned to myself. I was always so obsessed with my health, my diet, with being strong and fit and prepared to be a superstar athlete.

"Oh, God," I vowed, "if you will get me out of this mess I swear, I *swear*! If you will take away this hangover I swear I will *never drink again!*"

The memory of that first hangover is strong to this day, but it wasn't strong enough at the time to keep me from drinking. My vow forgotten, I drank again several weeks later, with the same result. I got completely and totally, blasted drunk. I was the classic binge drinker. Unable to just "have a few" and drink socially, I always drank to get obliterated. I drank to relax, to feel good, to celebrate or to forget. I drank when I was happy, I drank when I was sad. It didn't matter the occasion or circumstance, alcohol was always the soothing lubricant, the magic elixir that made the machine run quiet, smooth, easy. For me it was the perfect relief-valve for stress, and it gave me a calming, gentle feeling of numbness. Alcohol took away my pain, my shyness, my loneliness, my feelings of inadequacy and fear, my confusion about my sexuality, the feeling that I had always had that I was different, that I was *weird*. Alcohol allowed me to fit in, to feel "normal."

The obsessive-compulsive streak that enabled my success in swimming and academics extended into my drinking as well. I was extreme, wild, over the top. I was a heavy drinker for nearly thirty years. Alcoholism wrapped its insidious tentacles around everything I did, everything I thought and everything I was. When I drank it dominated me. When I wasn't drinking alcoholism lurked in the background, attacking my identity and robbing the light from my soul, replacing it with blackness. How could this happen, I often wondered? How could a super successful, attractive, straight A student, All-American athlete and model teenager succumb to this destructive, self-made hell?

Here is an actual entry from my diary, written when I was fourteen:

"Things have been going really well so far this year (school year) but now it's time for the New Year and some resolutions. I'm not going to list all my resolutions here. This page is just for swimming. My other resolutions I will write later. My main resolution in swimming and life right now is to stop drinking alcohol or learn to control it. I know this will be hard, because I love it (and hate it) and it's a lot of fun, but this is what I must do this New Year. I must also learn not to be afraid. . .

Over All Goal (Swimming):
    Make Nationals in 100 and 200 Breaststroke
    What I need to do to get there (general):
        1. Physical
            -stop drinking alcohol or control
            -train hard in pool, don't miss practice, use time well
            -lift weights daily, challenge myself in weight room
            -sit ups, stretch, shoulder rehab every day
            -don't overeat
        2. Mental
            -decide to go for it, and do it!
            -be confident. Believe in myself!!
            -learn to accept myself
            -learn to be patient, not to give up
            -get obsessiveness (alcohol, food) under control
            -channel obsessiveness into swimming. Control!!
            -relax. Make it fun
            -learn not to be afraid
            -be aggressive/confident
        3. Health
            -control or quit drinking
            -"eat to win" Eat less. Have a better diet
            -don't smoke pot
            -get rest, try to meditate, try to sleep!!
        4. Weight
            -keep around 140
        5. Compete aggressively. Don't be afraid!!!"

Three decades after I wrote that diary entry I sat in a low-ceilinged room in the basement of a church at a meeting of Alcoholics Anonymous, my steaming mug of coffee in front of me on the long, rectangular table. Sitting with me were people I recognized from previous meetings, a few I didn't know well and a couple of good friends. There was the usual din of conversation and laughter that preceded every meeting in that place, where most everyone knew or were at least familiar with each other.

It was the typical pre-AA meeting vibe – light, companionable, cheerful. Then in walked an unfamiliar young woman. She was tall, thin, with long blonde hair and a striking face. Model beautiful. I thought she was maybe in her mid-twenties for her poise and graceful appearance. It turned out she had been sober for less than a week and was a newly recovering alcoholic and addict. Apparently her best friend had died the week before of a heroin overdose. It surprised me that she wasn't more shy and fearful, this being only her third meeting ever. But in a controlled manner and with a steady tempo to her strong voice, she shared her story, of what had happened and how she ended up here, with us. Later I found out that her friend had been sixteen years old, and "X" was only seventeen.

"Wow," I thought. "How sad for her, but how lucky she is! How fortunate that she managed to get herself to a meeting at her age. I hope she stays."

I meant "stays" as in "comes back" to more meetings and, most importantly, stays in the Program and stays sober.

I felt a slight twinge of envy. How lucky indeed! By age seventeen I had spoken to two different school counselors about my drinking problem. It took enormous courage and strength for me to do that, being trained as I was to not admit to having problems or to seek help. Both counselors had shrugged off my concerns as simply "typical high school-age behavior."

"Oh, don't worry, you can't be an alcoholic," they had said. "You're too successful. You're too strong. All you have to do is say no. Just don't drink."

What a laugh, I remember thinking as I slunk from their offices, still quaking inside from the sheer trauma of the experience. I was far too shy and obedient to question their assessments. But not so several years later when I found myself in a similar situation in a counselor's office my sophomore year at the University of Michigan. That time I looked the man square in the face, the anger in my older, more confident voice loud and clear. "You idiot! If I could 'just quit' I wouldn't have a problem!" I stormed from his office. After that disappointing session I was so disgusted with psychologists that I didn't ask the medical profession for help again for nearly fifteen years.

Swimming

When I was very young, despite my asthma and long before the days of hypoxic training, I was able to hold my breath underwater for long periods of time. I had learned to relax every part of my body and to go into a semi-hypnotic, meditative trance. In this condition everything moved slowly and effortlessly, like the long, wispy green grasses that sway gently in the current of a small stream.

I loved to sink down to the bottom of the pool, especially in the deep end, and hang out there as long as I could. The other kids ignored me for the most part, which is exactly what I wanted, but the lifeguards hated it. I wasn't trying to earn any points or win any contests. My objective was to escape, to get away from everything in the "above" world and go to my own, private sanctuary. I loved the feeling of weightlessness, of sitting on the bottom ever so lightly, the subtle currents swishing my hair and moving my body from side to side. I would put my goggles on, take a deep breath and then pull my legs together, making my body a needle, and stroke slowly upward, moving my body downwards. The noisy din of joyfully shrieking children would suddenly stop and lessen the deeper I went until, eventually, there was no noise at all except for a slight hum. Sometimes I could tell that it was the hum of equipment – strange and frightening machines with creepy, curvy pipes hidden behind the locked Pump Room door. Other times I wondered if it was the hum of my own brain, the hum of my Life Force itself.

Down at the bottom mysteries were revealed to me through my countless hours of study there. I watched tiny oval water bugs with paddle-shaped arms wriggle against the side of the pool. Clumsy looking and slow, they zipped away with lightning speed when my hand came close. They were almost impossible to catch. I also observed how the sunlight danced and formed odd, magical shapes in a myriad of colors as it bounced along the bottom and up and down the sides of the pool. Blowing bubble rings and seeing them undulate and grow as they neared the surface was a never-ending source of amusement. But mostly my pleasure came from the pure joy of being truly, untouchably alone. Nobody could hurt me there at the bottom of the pool, and no one could see me cry.

I can't remember when I first learned to swim but I know that my parents taught us to be comfortable in the water from an early age. We were outdoorsy folks and spent many weekends camping in remote places that always had a lake or river. My brother Mike, two years older, and I would be turned loose and left to our own devices, free to explore the water and surrounding marshes. We captured frogs and snakes, lizards and salamanders, turtles, minnows, crayfish, even leeches. We were fascinated by the water and everything in it, and knew no fear.

As a competitive swimmer I started slowly. I didn't truly learn to "swim" until my parents moved to a new, upscale neighborhood when I was six. The neighborhood had a members-only pool, The Hill Farm Swim Club, and we were fortunate to be able to join it almost immediately. It was there that I took my first formal swimming and diving lessons.

Like most of the other kids, I was enrolled in just about every program the Club offered: swimming lessons, swimming team, diving lessons, diving team, synchronized swimming, synchronized swimming team and so on. I discovered that I didn't like synchro and was afraid of diving, so I limited my endeavors to lessons and swim team. These sessions were held in the morning, and afterward all the kids would go home for lunch, then come back and spend the rest of the day playing Marco Polo, Sharks and Minnows, racing or just goofing off in the pool (or in my case, sitting on the bottom in the deep end). For me assimilating with the other kids was difficult. We were new to the neighborhood, the school and, more importantly, new to The Pool. We had a weird last name that no one could pronounce and I was painfully shy. I had asthma, which was considered "icky" by some of my teammates, and to top it off I was a tad overweight and not a very good swimmer. Some of the kids would pick on me, which is why I spent so much time in my underwater hideout.

I desperately wanted to be accepted and to have friends. Like everywhere, there were cliques. At our pool it was a group of girls who were the Good Swimmers, and I ached to be a part of their little club. But workouts were hard and I was always in the way or being passed. I couldn't keep up, and was reminded often that I was "slow." I was a C level swimmer and the Good Swimmer cadre had all made their A level time standards. I was always on the C relays and had to spread my towel and belongings alongside the other C swimmers at meets. It was painful to be an outsider and I tried hard to worm my way into the Good Swimmer club. I soon discovered that in order to do that I had to become a Good Swimmer myself. This was difficult. Not only was my asthma crippling at this stage of my life but the workouts were tough and no fun at all for us "slow kids."

Many years later when I was coaching I had a parent of a young age-group swimmer tell me that she wanted her daughter to become a national caliber swimmer and possibly make the Olympic Team, and could I offer some advice. What I *wanted* to say was, "Yes. Get out of it while you still can and get her to like tennis. At least she'll be able to make some money." (This was before one could be a professional swimmer). What I *did* say to her was this: "Yes. You have to be willing to allow your daughter to be tortured, and she has to love it. More importantly, she has to love it more than she hates it."

I always had a love/hate relationship with swimming. At first it was almost entirely a "hate" relationship. I hated the practices because they were painful and I couldn't keep up. I hated not being able to breathe and having the other kids tell me I was "icky." I hated my big thighs and being called "fat." I hated being on C relays, going to C meets and not being accepted into the Good Swimmer Club. I hated being shy, and I hated being afraid – of the workouts, of losing, of being teased, of everything. But somewhere, somehow and despite all of this, deep inside me a seed of competitiveness was growing. I realized that in order to be accepted by the Good Swimmers I needed to not only beat everyone else, but I needed to beat them too.

By the time I was in the nine-to-ten year old age group I was starting to become a decent swimmer, but I still hadn't made my A cuts and I still didn't win anything except the occasional heat, which would earn me a Heat Winner ribbon. I was now swimming year round, as a member of the neighborhood team in the summer and the Badger Dolphin Swim Team the rest of the year. Swimming for the Badger Dolphins was much more serious than the summer club and the practices were even more challenging. I struggled to stay motivated and to not quit. Even though I was starting to become a good swimmer, the practices were very difficult for me and I still felt like an outsider. But I kept at it and slowly, ever so slowly improved. I started to win races, and the other kids started to notice that I was becoming a good breaststroker.

But then catastrophe struck. When I was ten years old my parents divorced. We were one of the first families in the area, or at least that I knew about in my circle of friends and acquaintances, to split up. The divorce came as a total shock to my brother and me. We had no idea it was going to happen; the news was just dropped on us one day like a bomb. I was devastated. Not only was I fearful about what would happen to me, I was afraid that this would make me even more of an outsider in my already shaky ten-year-old world. I feared that I would be looked at with pity and talked about in audible whispers behind my back. I was now one of "those kids." I felt totally and completely alone. My brother, who had been my best friend growing up, was no longer interested in hanging around with his little sister. I had a few friends at this age but nobody ever asked me how I was doing or how I was feeling. One time one of the girls on the team told me that she felt "sorry for me" and that I "looked sad all the time." I hated that. I hated to be singled out, hated the pity, hated to be noticed in that manner. But it was true – I *was* sad much of the time and I did cry a lot, my tears hidden behind my goggles and my sobs stifled underwater as I struggled through practice after torturous practice.

By age eleven I knew there was something more seriously wrong with me than the obvious explanation for my depression, that I came from a broken home. I still felt deeply sad and just couldn't shake it. I also suffered terribly from insomnia. When I did get a few fleeting hours of sleep I was plagued by horrific nightmares. My parents knew this but I think they attributed it to the lingering effects of a hard and ugly divorce, and figured I would outgrow it. At any rate, they clearly didn't know what to do about it because nothing was ever done. I was never taken to the doctor or to a counselor. The only thing that gave me relief – oddly – was swimming. During workouts I could "get away" from myself and the awful feelings of loneliness and despair. These feelings were never talked about – not at home, not with coaches, friends or anyone. For one thing, I didn't want to be looked at as any more "weird" than I already was, so I didn't talk about my problems with the other kids. Also, as competitive swimmers we were trained from an early age to be "tough" and to "rise above the pain." We were also told to "leave our crap at the door." No negativity was allowed in the pool. Essentially we were not allowed to express pain or discomfort of any kind, but taught to gut it out and to do the best we could all of the time. As such I didn't feel like I could tell anyone how I was feeling or ask for help. So I did what I had to do to survive, and stuffed my emotions deep down inside where they couldn't hurt me.

This I did best when I was swimming because there was nothing to do except focus on the work at hand. But I dreaded going to practice. I knew it would be hard and would hurt. I also knew that somehow it was my salvation. So I worked, and worked, and I worked. I wanted to not feel, and I wanted to be accepted. I also wanted to win, and wanted it badly. I pounded my feelings away with every painful lap, and tried to keep my focus on how good a swimmer I would eventually become.

Every so often it would become too much, as my teammates and I worked past the point of exhaustion. I remember one time I was slacking off and my coach, Jim, stopped me mid-pool.

"What the hell is that?!" he screamed.

"I'm so tired," I said, panting, "I just can't do anymore."

He bent down and glared at me. "DO YOU WANT TO BEAT *DENISE SUTTER?!!*" he bellowed, his loud voice reverberating off the walls. Denise was my main competitor at the time.

"Yes, I. . . . . "

"DO YOU *REALLY WANT TO BEAT DENISE SUTTER??!*"

"Yes!" I sputtered back, my rage starting to build.

"*WHAT DID YOU SAY?!*"

"YES, I WANT TO BEAT DENISE SUTTER!!" Screaming this time.

"THEN SHUT UP AND GET THE HELL GOING!!!"

And so I went, and I swam, and I swam faster, and he cheered and urged me on, stomping up and down the deck alongside me and waving his arms.

"Come on!! Come *ON!!* *Work* it!! You can *DO* it! Let's *GO!!* Let's *GO!!* *MOVE IT!!*"

And I did. Later, at the end of the set as I clung to the gutter gasping and heaving, totally spent, he reached down and took my hand.

"Good job!!" he said, smiling. "Now that's my girl! That's what I want to see."

My heart was filled with joy. Few things are more gratifying to a young swimmer than really busting it out, taking yourself beyond what you think you can do, and having the coach, whom you worship, acknowledge your success. I was ecstatic.

My desire to win was deep and intense. I wanted it more than anything. Jim told me one day during a meet that I had what it took to be great.

"You know why?" he said, "Because you have *DESIRE*. You have desire like few people have. It will make you great if you let it."

I was thirteen at the time and was now one of the Good Swimmers. And as the pain that I stifled went deeper into the dark recesses of my mind, a new love was starting to grow and blossom. Swimming began to bring me joy, and it began to evolve into what would ultimately become my first true love.

Danger

I met Caroline Watts on the pool deck when I was fifteen and she was thirteen. She was a tall, lanky kid with long arms and legs and a shock of curly, unruly hair. Quick to smile, she always had a mischievous gleam in her eye, as though she found everything somewhat amusing and fun. Caroline was from England so had a heavy but pleasant British accent. Her parents were quite well-to-do and she lived with her family in a stately mansion on the east side of town. I have many fond memories of the time Caroline spent with our team, both from practices and meets.

Caroline was a distance swimmer and so trained even more insanely hard than we, the "middle distance" swimmers, did. She was the only female swimmer on our club team who trained in the same lanes as the college men, and she routinely beat them in practice. Sometimes our coach would have Caroline and one of his top male swimmers race a five-hundred yard freestyle at the end of practice. They would push each other to break specified times (and of course not to lose). If they made the times we would all get out early. This type of event really brought the team together and we cheered wildly for both the poor souls who had to endure this additional ordeal at the end of an already grueling workout. But the pressure was on and both participants loved to race. I can't remember if Caroline won these competitions, but I do remember that we almost always got out of practice, and the two exhausted swimmers were heroes for the day.

At meets Caroline was fun to watch because she almost always won her events. Also because her mother provided countless hours of entertainment from the pool deck. Small in stature and wiry, Mrs. Watts either wore a dress or skirt and button-up blouse combination. She had the same curly hair as Caroline (though slightly better styled) and a pair of round, wire-framed glasses. In her unmistakable British accent she would stand up in her seat and cheer loudly whenever Caroline swam, her shrill voice cutting through the deafening din that echoed around the pool.

"Gooooooooooo Caarroollliiiiiiiiinnnne!!" she would scream from the crowd.

Caroline's father was much more sedate, leaving the cheering to his wife, who dominated the stands and left no uncertainty as to who was her daughter.

In the pool Caroline was strong and beautiful, with a perfect stroke and a long, sleek body that sliced through the water. On land she was somewhat gawky and awkward, as many teenagers are at that age. She ate lots of junk food and I, who was ever concerned with my healthy diet, couldn't understand how she could swim so fast on a diet loaded with crap. I recall big bags of chips and candy devoured during the long rides to swim meets. She would also consume massive quantities of salty, greasy snacks, her face stained orange from various cheese-flavored delicacies. I remember one hilarious incident in particular when we were carpooling with one of our coaches in his new car to a three-day regional meet in Minnesota. Caroline had her usual assortment of junk food but this time she also brought along a one pound bag of peanut M&Ms. She tried to open it like a bag of chips, grasping the middle edges and pulling hard. Suddenly the bag ripped wide open, spewing peanut M&Ms in all directions, the multicolored candies disappearing into every nook and cranny of our coach's spotless new car. Being teenage girls, we had already been giggling throughout most of the trip, but this sent us into a wild frenzy of uncontrollable laughter. Our coach's unhappy and pitifully resigned reaction made us giggle even more, as we tried to smother our laughter while picking up handfuls of the colorful little orbs.

Caroline swam with our club for several years between extended trips to England. She made two British Olympic Teams and ended up attending the University of Texas in Austin, where she helped the team win five consecutive National Championships. I lost touch with Caroline during those collegiate years, not only because of the distance between us but because I was older and had already started to pull away from the sport and lose touch with many of my former teammates.

Many years later, after social networking became an essential part of my life, I "ran into" Caroline through a mutual friend on Facebook. To my surprise she had changed her name and was living in southern California. We became Facebook "friends" and exchanged a few notes. I was intrigued by her name change and what she was up to. From the Facebook posts I gathered that she was involved in some sort of organization to help prevent abuse (both sexual and nonsexual) of athletes of all ages and in all sports. I also learned – much to my shock and disgust – that she had been raped when she was fourteen by her Olympic coach and suffered through years of sexual and emotional abuse. She later founded a non-profit organization whose mission is to promote awareness of abuse and to provide guidelines of safe conduct for clubs, parents and coaches.

Caroline is one of many former swimmers around the world who have now come forward with allegations of abuse. At first, United States Swimming was reluctant to admit how widespread and serious the problem was and was even accused of a massive sexual abuse cover-up, a scandal on par with that of Penn State, according to reports by ABC News. One of the more well-known and much publicized cases is that of former coach Andrew "Andy" King, who coached in San Jose and other places along the west coast. King was accused and convicted of sexually abusing multiple teenaged girls over a nearly thirty-year period, and in 2010 was sentenced to forty years in prison. USA swimming has since created specific guidelines for appropriate coach-to-athlete conduct and definitions of what constitutes abuse. It has also established a formal vetting process for new coaches that includes a criminal background check. Over sixty coaches (listed on the USA Swimming website) have been banned from the sport for life. This is only a partial list according to USA Swimming, so one can reasonably assume that the list is much larger. Because of Caroline's and others' courage in coming forward there is now much more awareness about the problem and, hopefully, there will be fewer occurrences in the future.

But my personal opinion is that the sport has a long way to go to ensure that athletes are safe from sexual predators and from other forms of abuse. By its very nature swimming is an abusive sport. From the less serious programs to the top-notch, elite programs expectations are high for both the physical work done in and out of the pool as well as the time commitment. In order to be a good swimmer one has to dedicate oneself to hours and hours every day of intense, difficult training. The schedule is generally two swim workouts per day on most days, plus weight training and other dry land exercises. To be an excellent swimmer with big ambitions, like making the National and/or Olympic Teams, the expectations are even higher. It is a relentless, year-round grind with little rest and few days off. Regularly scheduled competitions are another important part of the sport, not just to gauge one's progress, but as important aspects of training and practice.

Depending on the program and the coach, the sport can cross a critical line. There are progressive coaches who believe in rational training hours with recovery days, healthy dietary habits and some personal time for outside social activities. These programs also allow opportunities for good communication between coaches and athletes. Athletes are allowed to express concerns about their training and other elements in their lives that may be troubling them or creating emotional stress. Then there are the "old school" coaches who run their programs in quite a different way. In these programs often every aspect of an athlete's life is under scrutiny and control: what and how much they eat, what they are allowed to do outside of practice, how much they weigh, what is their body fat percentage and so forth. Practices are extremely hard. Nobody is allowed to question the coach or complain during workouts. Communication about personal problems, emotional problems or other concerns is nonexistent. The attitude is "positive thoughts only" and "no negativity allowed on deck or in the pool." If you have a problem you work it out or keep it to yourself.

I consider all serious swimming programs to be "hard" and even potentially "dangerous." Individual sports have a high level of stress and anxiety because the attention is focused solely on the athlete and his or her measured performance. It's not like a team sport, where, although individual performance is also important and measured, the pressure is spread about amongst the team members. Swimming is a pressure cooker. It is an ideal breeding ground for all kinds of abuse, partly because the athletes are trained to never question the coach. The coach is often feared and even worshipped by the athletes. In some programs parents are not allowed on deck or in locker rooms. Things happen in swim programs that rarely happen in school settings. For example, overweight athletes are often singled out and humiliated in front of the team. Athletes are chastised or yelled at for not performing well in practice or for complaining about being exhausted. Profanity is not uncommon. Athletes may also be subjected to various forms of punishment for poor performance or behavior. I'm not saying that these forms of abuse are unique to swimming, and most everyone who reads the news or takes part in serious sports knows this. What I *am* saying is that despite the increased awareness of what goes on in practices and elsewhere, I believe abuse is still widespread in the sport of swimming.

Again, I consider serious swimming programs to be potentially "dangerous." I mean that from both an emotional and a physical standpoint.

Emotionally the swimming life – even for athletes who aren't training at the elite level – is a very unbalanced life. Between swim training and school there is little time for anything else. The workouts are strenuous and require substantial energy expenditure. Even if there was time for other activities most kids simply would not have the energy. Then there is the element of parental pressure to succeed. I was fortunate that I did not have that, at least not in an overt way. I did feel (rightly or wrongly) that I was expected to succeed in everything I did, however, not just swimming. But in reality I believe I put this pressure on myself, and I *did* succeed. My parents never had to push me to work or to be focused. Other kids on my team endured much more overt parental pressure.

Most important is the pressure that athletes put on themselves – the need to validate all the time and money spent by both the athlete and the parents, the need to see progress after so much effort has been given and so many sacrifices made, the need to succeed to please parents and meet one's own expectations, the need to please a coach, the need to live up to teammates' expectations and so on. This pressure is intense and it comes at a vulnerable time in a person's life, i.e., before and during puberty. Emotions are running high just as the sport is trying to control and stifle them. The strain from both the pressure of life at that age and the sport is often too much and there is no built-in relief valve. So what does the athlete do? Many swimmers can't take the strain anymore and quit at this point. Others turn to self-destructive activities to regain "control" and reassert themselves as individuals. Still others go to extreme measures just to "have fun and blow off steam." This is when the danger starts and we begin to see problems such as drug and alcohol abuse, anorexia, bulimia, depression, anxiety and even suicide.

Then there is the physical aspect of swimming. When most people think of dangerous sports they usually think of football, hockey, rugby, skiing, rock-climbing etc. Swimming has its own set of injuries. By the time I was eighteen just about everyone on my team had some sort of overuse injury, usually in the shoulders or knees. Swimmers do a lot of weight and dry land training in addition to water training so there are short and long-term repercussions from those activities as well: tendonitis, bursitis, torn rotator cuffs, torn muscles, strains, sprains, arthritis – pretty much the same types of injuries that are seen in most "on land" sports, but overuse injuries are the most common in swimming.

But dangerous? Yes. Temporary physical injuries heal, and some are even beneficial, in my opinion, because they can make a person appreciate good health and therefore become mentally stronger. More serious physical injuries can last a lifetime and that's no fun, but are they actually "dangerous?" Not all are (tendonitis, for example). And one can live with the chronic injuries associated with swimming, although they can limit one's life in many ways (arthritis, for example). What I am talking about when I say "dangerous" are the emotional repercussions caused by the sport of swimming. Wounds that are so deep and sometimes so serious that they take years to heal, if they heal at all. The trauma of sexual abuse is but one example of that.

At this point the former swimmers reading this will either agree with me wholeheartedly or disagree with me strongly and call me a quack. Sexual abuse is an extreme example, is it not? and not that common, they will say. But I believe I can state with assurance that many people leave the sport of swimming with one or more psychological problems, some of which I already mentioned above, and some that are very serious. I recall a conversation with a good friend of mine, a former national champion distance freestyler who swam at the University of Southern California. One day over lunch we were discussing the psychological effects of being an elite swimmer and talking about how nearly everyone we knew who was "good" had some sort of "problem." And so we debated the question: does a person have to be somewhat nuts to stay in the sport of swimming or does the sport itself make one "nuts?" I believe that the answer to that question is both. It definitely takes a special type of person to endure the requirements of the sport, but those same requirements take a heavy physical and psychological toll.

Some people handle it just fine and leave as healthy, balanced individuals ready to take on the world and move gracefully into the next phase of their lives. Not every football player comes away from the sport with a collection of concussions, after all, and not every former ballerina or figure skater is anorexic. But there are others who are not so fortunate and find the transition into the "normal world" much more difficult. Those are the ones who *did* suffer from concussions or broken bones, serious impact and overuse injuries, anorexia or bulimia, drug and alcohol abuse or other physical and psychological problems. Needless to say, I was in the latter group.

For me the transition into the "normal world" was rough. For one thing, I had amassed a fair assortment of physical injuries. I had extensive wear in both shoulders which caused "looseness" and chronic pain. Both knees had cartilage damage which also caused chronic pain. When I was a freshman in college I developed a somewhat rare and very painful condition called Sternal Costochondritis, which is inflammation of the cartilage between the sternum and ribs. This was the worst injury from which I had suffered up to that point in time. It is caused by overuse: too many bench presses, too many pushups, too many tosses with the medicine ball. . . exercises meant to strengthen the chest muscles, which are important for breaststrokers.

I first noticed the injury just before Christmas Training began, the two to three weeks of "Hell" that everyone dreads. There was a difficulty in swallowing that felt like an acid reflux problem. I thought at first that this might be happening because I ate so much. But it became worse and worse as I kept training and eventually got to the point where I couldn't swallow anything – not food, water, saliva – nothing. When I swallowed it felt like a spiked ball was lodged in my esophagus in the middle of my chest. It became difficult to breathe because every time my chest moved I was wracked with pain. By then I was no longer training and had to sit and watch my teammates from the pool deck. I could hardly eat and drink so I lost weight, which was the last thing I needed, being already very lean and almost devoid of body fat.

The injury never really "healed," as cartilage injuries generally don't, but the inflammation lessened with the help of medication. I was eventually able to train again and finish the season, though I endured pain in my chest the entire time. The summer following my freshman year I was forced to take time off for several months – an eternity for a competitive swimmer at the elite level. But it did help and I was able to come back my sophomore year, although the pain never totally went away.

When I left the sport at age twenty-one I was obsessed with exercise and physical activity. I had so much hyper, manic energy, and was so accustomed to many hours a day of hard training that I simply had to keep moving. This was a psychological experience as well as a physiological one. Psychologically exercise was an important part of my daily routine, a way to maintain structure and order, a way to stay organized and to avoid chaos, a way to stabilize my mood, and a compulsive habit. It was also a way to stay lean and fit, physical attributes that to this day remain extremely important to my overall self-image.

I would rise early in the morning, hungover or not, and go for a vigorous bike ride. Then I would either swim later in the day or take a long run in the evening, jogging through the woods along the Huron River and up into the surrounding swanky neighborhoods. The job I had before I graduated was physical too. I worked at the pool as part of the maintenance crew, mopping, scrubbing, cleaning, carrying and so on. As an older adult I had a variety of occupations that were also physical and strenuous, and these took a heavy toll on my body as well.

Physiologically exercise was a chemical *need*, a "fix." My brain and body were used to being infused daily with massive amounts of naturally created substances, such as endorphins and hormones. These potent chemicals coursed through me, through my brain cells, organs, muscle fibers and nervous system, causing profound physical changes to the structures themselves as well as to the electrical-chemical mechanisms that occur at the cellular level. These mechanisms are responsible for every metabolic task of the body, from energy creation and transfer, to hunger and appetite, to sexual desire and arousal, to feelings of pleasure and pain. Of course I didn't spend hours pondering exercise in quite that way on a daily basis, although I did write a well-researched paper once titled *'Runners' High' and the Competitive Swimmer*. So I was somewhat educated in the subject and keenly aware from that and my own experiences that intense exercise results in chemical and hormonal influences leading to changes in the brain and body. On a practical level, and in my daily thoughts, exercise provided a certain amount of pleasure and pain relief. Most importantly, it helped control my mood swings, which by my collegiate years were becoming quite severe.

The bottom line is that when I eventually "retired" from the sport I had amassed a collection of chronic physical injuries and emotional problems. Physically I now suffer, at the age of forty-seven, from arthritis in nearly every joint. It is particularly bad in my lower back, which significantly limits what I can do. I have had major surgery to rebuild my right shoulder while the left one remains loose, weak and painful. I have had knee surgery on the left side to repair cartilage damage and need the same procedure done on the right. My *sternal costochondritis* has never healed so I have constant pain in my chest, sometimes mild, sometimes severe. I have chronic pain from nerve damage (neuropathy) throughout my body, and am treated with several pain medications daily. When I wake in the morning it takes a good ten minutes to move around in bed before I even try to stand. I get dressed half sitting, half lying because I am unable to stand or bend to put on my clothes. From there I make my way to my recliner, where I sip coffee as I loosen up. It sounds like a little old lady's routine, doesn't it? Unfortunately this is my daily reality. And despite the pain I continue to exercise and do physical work. Not a lot – I am no longer able. But I need my daily endorphin "fix" or I feel, as I say to my husband, "wonky." It takes about an hour of mild-to-moderate aerobic exercise every day to get loose and make me "feel right." Then I can enjoy a productive, positive day. Rarely do I take a day off from my routine – I am compelled to exercise and need it, like I need food, air and water.

So this brings me to the next part of my story, the emotional scars left from swimming. Before I get into that, however, I would like to make one point very clear. When I was a competitive swimmer in my prime I absolutely and totally loved the sport. I thrived on training like a deranged person despite the dread and pain. I was always nervous about competition but I craved it, especially the winning part. Swimming gave me confidence in my ability to endure most anything and to be successful in every endeavor I undertook throughout my life. It taught me how to set and achieve goals and gave me an extraordinary work ethic. It provided a structure for my life and it helped frame and build my identity. Swimming gave me a sense of belonging. Even though I struggled through periods of burnout and often questioned my level of motivation, there was nothing, absolutely nothing in the world that would have made me quit. Swimming was my life and my passion. It filled a void in my Self that brought light and joy to the root of my soul.

At the end of my junior year in college I made my first US National Team. I can still recall the excitement I felt as I tore through the two gigantic boxes full of Team USA gear that arrived via UPS. None of my housemates were home so I spread the contents all around our living room. It was like living my dream-fantasy Christmas, opening those thick cardboard boxes. There was everything a swimmer could want, all in red, white and blue and emblazoned with "USA": shoes, socks, shirts, towels, caps, dress clothes, shorts, baseball caps, pins, racing suits, a robe, and of course the coveted, beautiful Team USA Warm-Up Suit (which I slept in that night). I was dancing on air for days. My dad even took a day off from his busy schedule to come visit and see all my new "loot." I'll never forget the thrill of walking into the Athlete's Village of the World University Games, held in Zagreb, then Yugoslavia. The Opening Ceremonies and the format of the Games are just like the Olympics, except that all the athletes are university students. I loved the village, the facilities, exploring the city, watching the various events and hanging out with my new USA teammates. Along with the 1984 Olympic Trials and my wedding, that trip remains one of the highlights of my life.

~~~

Two months after returning from the Games, in the summer of 1987, I marched purposefully into the old Matt Mann Pool building at the University of Michigan and walked toward Coach Jim Richardson's office. It was the day before classes started, my senior year. I was Co-Captain of the team. I paused briefly before the door, my heart hammering against my chest. Jim's door was always open, and there he sat at his desk, staring transfixed at the computer screen.

"Hi Christi," he said as he turned around and smiled at me.

"Jim," I said with a slight quiver in my voice. "I have to tell you something. I just dropped all my classes, and I've decided to quit."

There was a pause, a moment of complete silence and stillness in the air. He looked at me intently. Slowly he nodded his head.

"Are you sure this is what you want to do?"

"Yes," I said, starting to cry, "I've given it a lot of thought."

"OK," he said. "It's alright. But sit down for a minute and let's talk. . ."

Scars

It would be remiss to examine the emotional damage caused by swimming without also delving into the subject of my alcoholism. The two are cleverly intertwined – swimming the firm but rocky ground with robust wooden fence posts; the disease of alcoholism encircling them like wild, sinuous grape vines, twisting around each other as they slither up and outward. For me swimming was my bedrock, my foundation. It was larger-than-life. Swimming gave me an identity but it also controlled it. As much as it gave me confidence, poise and friendships, it also enabled me to hide my deep, inner self and stifle my adolescent feelings. By constantly pushing myself to the point of physical and mental exhaustion I was able to ignore my feelings of loneliness, self-doubt, worthlessness, "weirdness," pain and fear. Swimming allowed me to circle around these feelings rather than go through and *experience* them. I didn't have to question my identity or values because swimming told me who I was and what was important. It filled a spiritual and emotional void that nothing else could touch. Except alcohol.

I was never in denial that I had a problem with alcohol. I avoided using the term "alcoholic," however. When I was young and in high school, I still felt that it was possible to control it. I would tell myself, "I know I have a *potentially* serious problem with alcohol. If and when it turns into a big problem, I will go to AA and quit." Every now and then someone would actually tell me that I had an alcohol problem and that I should go to AA and quit. This would be a friend who was equally drunk at the time, and we would laugh as we staggered around with arms around each other's shoulders. The issue of going to AA and quitting would be a joke between us, but deep down I wondered – and worried. I suspected I was an alcoholic, and I was terribly, painfully ashamed.

After that infamous State Party where I had my first taste of alcohol I continued to binge sporadically whenever an opportunity arose. This usually happened on Saturday nights because we rarely had morning workouts on Sundays, so I didn't have to get up early. I was always very concerned about my diet and health and how they affected my swimming. I wasn't stupid – I knew that alcohol was bad for me and that it would affect my performance negatively. So I would set specific periods of time when it was "OK" to drink, for example not closer than "four months to a big meet" like Nationals or an important regional competition, or "never two nights in a row." As time went on these self-imposed regulations became less stringent and were often broken. Four months became three. Two nights in a row became acceptable, but never three, and so on. This is a commonality among alcoholics – the constant setting of self-determined rules in the vain attempt to control one's drinking, the constant breaking of these rules, and the inevitable self-disgust and self-loathing that comes as a result.

The summer after my freshman year the drinking became more intense. I was fifteen and now training with our club's senior team, which consisted of college men and women and a small crew of high school students. Despite my alcohol consumption I trained very well and almost always won my events or placed high in major competitions. As such, I started allowing myself to drink more frequently, rationalizing that I could "handle it" and still be successful. The older members of the team partied a lot and we were invited to attend these team parties. At the time, the legal drinking age in Wisconsin was eighteen and it wasn't that strict yet. We had no trouble getting into bars, asking older friends to buy us alcohol and even sometimes buying it ourselves. Because we trained so hard as athletes, our motto was always "work hard, party hard." It was almost like a badge of honor to party until the wee hours and still make it to morning workout, where we knew we would get our butts kicked. Some people would show up still drunk and years later I would do that too, but in high school I mostly just went to some morning practices with terrible hangovers.

There were also high school parties thrown by the older kids. These were sometimes held in houses when parents were away, but usually they took place in dark, secluded spots like golf courses or shelters in woodsy neighborhood parks. The beer was free and seemed unlimited. The parties often became quite large and loud, with lots of parked cars and small groups of high school kids milling around. Neighbors invariably called the police so these parties were almost always "busted." When that happened the kids would scatter in all directions, crashing through the underbrush or running to their cars, hoping to be the lucky ones to get away. My friends and I rarely drove to these parties ourselves because it was too dangerous. This was not because of the inherent risks of drunk driving, but because of the possibility of being caught by our parents. So we either hitched rides with other friends, walked or rode our bikes to these events.

I was deathly afraid of being caught drinking by my parents. I didn't know what they would do to me, but I knew it would be bad. I think it was easier for me to hide my drinking than for some of my friends because my parents were divorced so there weren't two inquisitors waiting to greet me when I came home. Also, my brother Mike was rarely home in the evenings. He was either working his job at the Coca-Cola company or out partying with his friends, so that threat was gone as well.

My mom was extremely strict about curfew and other household rules. Like many mothers and daughters, during high school we had a stormy relationship and generally tried to avoid each other. Finances were tight and

Mom worked long hours, so she was often not at home when I returned from workouts or dates. My freshman year I rarely "went out" on weeknights except to study at friends' houses. As I got older and started dating my curfew was ten o'clock. This was a self-imposed rule as well as mother-imposed, because I usually had to get up at five in the morning for workout and needed to sleep. Because I suffered from terrible insomnia I had to be diligent about my sleep habits or there would be almost no chance of sleeping at all.

I think I got away with a lot of drinking in high school for several reasons. One is that I tried to follow the rules and maintain the outward appearance of being obedient. Even when drunk I would be home before or by my curfew. My mom smoked and also drank so I was able to hurry past her without her smelling the alcohol. Since we didn't get along we didn't want to sit and talk anyway, and she understood that I needed to get to bed. I would try to walk straight and not say much when she would meet me at the door, and then go right to my room. Gripping the handrail as I swayed up the stairs, I would breathe a sigh of relief that I had "gotten away with another one."

Another reason I was so adept at "getting away" with drinking was that my parents trusted me. Even though my mom and I didn't get along and often fought, I was considered a "good kid." I was a top-notch swimmer who got excellent grades and was most likely going to get a full scholarship to a top university. I dressed nicely and kept my room neat. I did my homework, had nice friends, and listened to "pleasant" music. I was in bed most nights by nine o'clock and up at five. What more could a parent want?

I believe the most important reason that I was able to so successfully hide my drinking was *denial*. One time I was so drunk that my good friend Dina refused to take me home.

"But I'll be late for curfew!" I slurred as we drove around and around in the cool evening air, me in the back seat with my head hanging out the window.

"That's too bad," she said. "I can't take you home like this. You've gotta sober up."

"But my mom will *kill* me if I'm late!"

And sure enough, as we finally arrived at my house there was Mom, sitting on the front steps smoking a cigarette. My curfew was eleven o'clock. It was eleven fifteen.

"I'm dead," I said, still drunk, "Oh my God, am I ever dead meat!"

As we pulled into the driveway my mom stood up slowly, her hands on her hips. I could see that she was very angry.

"Where the hell have you been?" she said as I opened the car door and stepped out.

"We were at Dina's house." Dina was already pulling out of the driveway.

"Well you're late and I am *really* pissed!" she said.

I tried hard not to stagger as I trudged up the front walkway toward the steps. Suddenly I tripped and fell forward, landing face down on the damp cement. "This is it," I thought as I pulled myself to my feet, "I'm really in for it now."

"Have you been *drinking?!*" she asked, in a low and threatening tone.

"No, Mother. Of course not! I'm just really, really tired."

There was a short pause as she looked at me severely.

"OK. Well get to bed right now and don't you ever be late again."

I was also successful in hiding my drinking from my dad and for the same reasons – obedience, trust and denial. I remember once I had been out on a date on a night when I was sleeping over at my dad's house. My curfew there was also eleven o'clock and I was slightly late. He wasn't waiting at the door, but he was awake in the den watching television. I had to sit for a few minutes and talk with him, though I desperately wanted to get away and go to my room. I was drunk, and it was all I could do to not slur my words. I still find it difficult to believe that he couldn't tell I was loaded. But he never said anything about it, not then and not since. He did tell me once that if I was ever drunk or with drunk friends and needed a ride to call him, and he would not be mad. He also said, in a stern voice, that if he ever knew that I had been driving while under the influence that he would be very, *very* angry. I was always a little afraid of my dad and his anger, but this didn't stop me from occasionally driving drunk. It was fortunate that I never owned a car while in high school or college. My mode of transportation was usually my bicycle, and I was quite skilled at riding it in all sorts of conditions, be it rain, sub-zero temperatures or extreme drunkenness.

As my drinking accelerated my alcoholism became more apparent to me. I no longer called myself a "problem drinker." I knew I was truly an alcoholic and that my drinking was out of control. I despised myself for my inability to get a handle on it. I knew that alcoholism was a disease and, from reading about it, knew that by definition the *problem itself* is the inability to control the consumption of alcohol. I had mixed and confusing feelings about the control issue. On the one hand, I hated the fact that once I started drinking I couldn't stop, and this always resulted in the same thing – getting very drunk, being hungover the next day and hating myself for that, hating myself for things that happened when I was drunk, feeling embarrassed about my behavior, feeling remorseful, regretful and guilty. I felt especially guilty about betraying my parents' trust. My self-esteem always took a big hit "the morning after" and I punished myself with my intense self-loathing.

On the other hand the loss of "control" was one of the things I sought and one of the reasons I loved to drink. I had really built a complicated cage in which to live, and was very obsessive/compulsive about certain aspects of my life. Everything had its time, its place and its purpose. For example, I was so busy with schoolwork and training that I would make lists and daily schedules to map out my time. Sometimes I would even draw calendars with grid marks in fifteen-minute increments. These I would fill with the various activities that occurred throughout my day: training, classes, study time, eating time, social events, rest time, etc. I made sure that not even a single minute was wasted.

My schoolwork was important to me and I felt pressure to get good grades. This was partly due to family expectations as well as my own. My friends were all excellent students and, as always, I wanted to "fit in," so I had to be a straight A student too. Swimming, of course, brought its own set of pressures and stresses and was by far the largest contributor to my overall level of anxiety. This was because my physical and emotional investments in the sport were so high. There had been years and years of training, many competitions, past goals reached and goals not reached, friendships courted and gained, friendships lost. Current goals were often lofty and sometimes seemingly unattainable. My sense of "fitting in" was totally dependent on my identity as a Good Swimmer and good student.

My parents' investment was substantial too, not just in the financial sense but in the time and energy spent. This weighed heavily on my mind. All of these things combined to make my life – which I had carefully constructed in order to meet my own goals – extremely rigid and strict. As such, I loved the feeling of getting drunk and losing control. I loved getting "wild and crazy" and doing irresponsible and impulsive things when drunk. It was a tremendously effective pressure-relief valve and one of the main objectives of my drinking.

When I said earlier that competitive swimming is dangerous from an emotional standpoint I was not trying to criminalize the sport itself. Competitive swimming can be and is, in a lot of cases, a healthy sport that provides good exercise, good daily structure, good social experiences and teaches an excellent work ethic with a positive self-image. What I am criticizing is the unbalanced, unhealthy life that goes along with competitive swimming at the very serious or elite levels. For me this unbalanced lifestyle was particularly destructive. Why? Because, just like alcohol, the swimming life allowed me to stifle painful feelings and emotions. In fact, it encouraged it. Swimming was so intense both in the time commitment and the energy spent that it was all-consuming. There was little time or energy (physical or mental), left to pursue other social or nonsocial interests and activities. In the teen years, most young people have similar emotional issues: feelings of pain, loneliness, awkwardness and being uncomfortable in their own skin, among others. I went *around* my emotional problems and avoided them by suppressing and burying myself in my swimming and schoolwork, rather than by experiencing them and finding ways to work them out.

Swimming, like alcohol, was also isolating. Even though I was in a team situation swimming by its nature is solitary. One is surrounded and embraced in a cocoon of water, the outside world temporarily forgotten. You can choose how much you interact with your teammates in the pool, and if it becomes unpleasant, you can bury yourself by working harder in the next set or by simply going underwater, as I did when I was younger.

Alcohol does the same thing. Whether drinking by myself or with other people I often felt very lonely. Alcohol formed a protective veil around me by enabling me to push my real emotions down deep and not feel – I mean not feel *real intimacy or closeness* with other people. The "openness" that I thought I was experiencing while drinking was a false sense of connecting with others. This is evident by looking at the friends I had and still have. Those who I was "close" with as drinking companions or during my heaviest periods of drinking are generally gone from my social picture now. Although there are a few exceptions, most of my "drinking buddies" were just that – drinking buddies. Outside of that, even though we felt a common bond and lots of "friendship" at the time, there was little depth to the relationships because neither of us allowed ourselves to get close. There was always a "firewall" that existed somewhere between us, somewhere hidden deep in our individual selves.

For me swimming was similar. Again there are exceptions, but by and large the "many friends" that were my teammates are not close friends now. I understand that most relationships ebb and flow and we all drift away from a certain percentage of once-close people in our lives. But truly deep and intimate friendships tend to last throughout one's lifetime. I have friends from my childhood (and a few from my swimming life too) that I may not have seen for a decade or more, but when we get together it's as if no time has passed at all. When I was drinking, alcohol blunted my ability to open up to everyone, my best friends included. It was like a thick wool blanket that enabled me to disguise my true self, my deepest, darkest self, from others. In that respect swimming and alcoholism were the same. At the beginning of my swimming career, when I was very shy and before I became "good," I hid and stifled my emotions by retreating to the bottom of the pool. As I improved and training became more difficult I learned to bury my shyness and true feelings by working hard and stuffing those feelings deep inside. There was no place for "emotional bullshit," as one coach put it, in training and competition.

Like everyone else, I learned that some consequences of closeness are pain and fear: of being shunned or treated poorly by others, of losing a friend or family member, of the destruction (by divorce) of one's family. This was not a subconscious idea for me. One time when I was young I was hiding in my underwater sanctuary, having just been teased by the other kids for some reason I can't recall. I remember clearly thinking, "I have to build a wall around myself. I can't let them in anymore to hurt me." Swimming helped construct and cement that wall because it let me escape from reality and keep people far from my "center." Alcohol helped numb the pain and fear I had when those feelings emerged.

Both swimming and alcoholism enabled me to engage in "isolationist" behavior. This is exactly what it sounds like: being alone, distant, solitary, separated from other people. As I said earlier, swim training is a solitary activity. Sure, there are social activities based around it and relationships with teammates, but when you get right to it swimming is done alone. You are by yourself when you step on the block to compete. Nobody can do anything for you except cheer, sometimes curse or urge you on. In reality you are on your own in training and competition and this is what I sought. I loved the "aloneness" of swimming. Looking down at the black line and swimming countless laps, back and forth, back and forth, my mind drifting and flowing freely, like the current in a river. Working hard, to the point of total exhaustion, and knowing that the fruits of this labor would be almost entirely of my own doing gave me immense happiness (I must give fair credit to coaches and parents). Training and competing were so rewarding for me, so seductive and filled with such satisfaction and pleasure, that they became more important than anything else, including family, friends and school.

Isolationism is a behavior pattern that I have struggled with my entire life (granting that most of my adult life I have been a heavy drinking alcoholic). To this day I still struggle with this behavior and am still learning how to overcome it and have more "normal" social experiences.

Between swimming and alcoholism I had two very powerful addictions wreaking havoc on my vulnerable, developing brain. Both were huge contributors in shaping my identity and in the dictation of my life's course. It is difficult to sort out which emotional scars that I still have today are a result of swimming and which are a result of drinking. As I said at the beginning of this chapter, both became highly intertwined as I entered my adolescent years. Both swimming and drinking were persistent, intense, extreme, isolating, obsessive and compulsive. I could use those same words to describe myself today. I also suffer from bipolar disorder, a mood problem not formally diagnosed until I was in my mid-forties. This plagued me terribly during my swimming years, causing me to vacillate between periods of hypomania, mania and moderate to severe depression.

So what are the emotional scars left from swimming? Which are from alcoholic drinking? Which are due to my then untreated bipolar disorder? And are these scars, these character traits that I have today and often struggle with, traits that I was born with, that I would have anyway, or were they caused by swimming and/or drinking and/or being bipolar? And if I was born with these character traits, were they enhanced or exacerbated by these other very strong and influential facets of my life?

Self & Identity

I continue to clarify my thoughts about my self-image and identity. Even now, for all the consideration I've given this subject, all the talking about it with friends, therapists and fellow AA members, it can be such a tangled morass. I am introspective by nature and, while this is sometimes beneficial, it can also cause me to obsess about my complex and often conflicting thoughts and emotions. It's difficult to sift through this mumbo of mind-jumbo and be able to say in a short sentence or two, *I am this.*

But *why* is it so difficult for me to think about self-image and identity? Do I fear discovering and facing up to some secret part of myself, making it "real" by acknowledging it? Or is it my compulsive need to have my thoughts organized all neat and tidy, fitting snugly into small cushioned boxes? Is it fear of a perceived duty to define and quantify my life, to judge it and place it on a certain level in the hierarchy of things? Or is this difficulty simply a carryover from my alcoholic thinking patterns, my deeply ingrained habit of avoiding painful subjects and burying those complex feelings under the thick, hazy shroud of drunkenness?

I have always had a conflict with how I feel others see me vs. how I feel inside – outside appearances vs. inside actualities. As I've written several times already, I have often felt that I am "different" and "weird." Throughout my life I have tried to hide this feeling of weirdness. I became very good at camouflaging other aspects of my *Self* as well. For example I learned to hide my shyness. I cloaked my thoughts about my body image and my perception of myself as masculine. I suppressed my fixation with food, my confusion about my sexuality, the feeling that I was never "good enough," my anger and rage at my family, and finally, my anger and rage at myself.

Hiding aspects of oneself is not constructive when one is recovering from alcoholism and being told to learn to be open and honest. Even today I struggle with my conflicting views of myself and the "me" that I present to the world. I also struggle mightily with acceptance and forgiveness – acceptance by others of me and acceptance and forgiveness of myself.

In order to look at my self-image and identity in an organized manner I had to find some way to break it down into manageable chunks. Since swimming has always been such a huge part of my life it made sense to break it down as follows: Before Swimming, During Swimming and After Swimming. "Swimming" here is defined as "Competitive Swimming" since I still swim recreationally, and am certain I will continue to do so for the rest of my life.

"Before Swimming" is the short period of time from when I was born until about age six or seven. During that time, family played the most important role in building my self-image and identity. I was born and spent the first eighteen years of my life in Madison, Wisconsin. My family is small. I have two parents, now divorced, and one brother, two years older. Mike was born with several birth defects and spent much of his young life in hospitals, with many corrective surgeries and doctor visits. I remember countless trips to the children's hospital in Chicago, being terribly bored in waiting rooms, and watching hours of exercises as he did rehab with our dad in our tiny living room. By necessity Mike was always the focus of my family's attention, not just because of his physical problems but because he was the firstborn, and the son. There was a tremendous financial burden on my family because my brother's medical care was expensive and my parents initially had no health insurance. My father was a grad student in chemistry at the time and my mom worked to help support the family. After I was born my dad got a fellowship to Harvard and Mom became a full-time homemaker. While I don't remember it, I have been told that there was always considerable stress over finances.

My parents are both immigrants from Latvia, a small country nestled between Estonia and Lithuania on the Baltic Sea and bordered by Russia to the east. Both of their families fled Latvia as World War II was drawing to a close and the Iron Curtain fell across Europe. The consequences of staying in Latvia were dire for people of their social status: either be shipped to Siberia to work in labor camps or be shot. Hundreds of thousands of civilians were murdered under the Stalinist regime, and I heard about this evil often as I was growing up, mostly from my grandparents. Both families spent several or more years living in refugee camps as they waited for an opportunity to emigrate to the United States. My mom's family of two parents and four children was eventually sponsored by a Baptist Church and settled in Forest City, North Carolina. My dad's family of three consisted of my grandmother (her husband had abandoned the family during the war) and his brother, who were sponsored by and lived with three separate families in Fort Atkinson, Wisconsin. Like millions of war refugees around the world, they arrived in this country with nothing more than their suitcases and so had to start over from scratch.

The children grew up in their respective homes and eventually both sets of grandparents moved to Grand Rapids, Michigan, where there is an active Latvian community. My parents met in the Latvian Club and Chemistry Department while attending and graduating from the University of Michigan. My dad was a chemist and ultimately became a Professor of Chemistry at the University of Wisconsin-Madison. My mom's role, initially, was to be a housewife and mother to my brother and me. Later, after the divorce, she taught art classes at a Madison community college for eight years and also worked a variety of part-time jobs. Eventually she became the Art Director and Advertising Manager for a sports medicine company near Madison.

From early on I learned from my family that one of the most important character traits that one must have is a strong work ethic. Given their history and what happened after the war it's totally understandable that a person would be very concerned about financial security, and the only way to attain this after losing everything was through hard work. My grandmother would often take me aside and tell me, "Christi. . . life is hard. It is a lot of work, and work is *good*. You must work and save so you have enough money for your future." This idea was deeply ingrained in me from an early age, not just because my grandmother told me, but because I saw it at home – both parents were successful, hard-working and demanding. These were the examples and standards my brother and I observed, along with the unspoken expectation that we, too, would work hard and be successful.

I was extremely shy when I was a small child, and very thin. My grandfather used to joke that he was afraid to look at me because I might "blow over." I was terrified of strangers and especially of men. There was an incident one Christmas when the neighborhood Santa, a supposedly friendly, burly man who really did look like Santa Claus, came to our house to wish us a Merry Christmas and entertain us kids. I screamed, cried and howled as I had to sit on his lap. I can't recall ever sitting on a Santa's lap at a shopping mall or parade again after that terrifying experience.

I was jealous of the attention my brother got when we were young. Even so, we were best pals and spent countless hours playing and romping together, both indoors and out and with the other kids in the neighborhood. Both of us were picked on, bullied and teased by some of the kids, especially Mike because of his physical problems. Mike handled it a lot better than I. I believe this was because he learned from early on not to let what other people think bother him, or at least to not show it. I'm not sure what it was about me – perhaps my shyness – but the other kids seemed to sense my inner insecurity and this I think caused the bullying, which hurt me deeply. I was, and have always been, a very sensitive person, and have felt like an outsider for as long as I can remember. It was only at home with Mike that I felt safe and cared for. Of course I felt cared for by my parents as well, but the jealousy issue and extra attention Mike received were ever present. I must have been around five years old at the time, but I clearly remember consciously thinking, "I have to decide if I'm going to be good or bad. I need more attention." I mulled this over for a while and after a period of time decided that it was better to be "good" and that I was going to be "so good that they will *have* to notice me."

My memories of my "Before Swimming" years are mostly of my brother and our time together. We were creative kids and loved to play outside, as well as with our multitude of art supplies, chemistry and biology sets, stuffed animals, Star Trek models and dolls, Lego blocks, erector sets and other "hands on" educational toys and gadgets. Our parents encouraged us to play on our own and be "free" with our creativity. But they didn't know all that this freedom brought! In our basement "laboratory" we secretly melted candles and experimented with burning various items to make different colors of fire. We melted small glass tubules that came from Dad's "real" laboratory and made delicate curly sculptures. We took apart shotgun shells so we could melt the lead and pour the hot liquid in water, making exotically shaped castings. In those days chemistry sets actually had real chemicals and one could make disappearing ink, bubbling "volcanoes" and even small bombs, if one knew how (as Mike did). We hunted through dumpsters at the local doctors' office to find thermometers and syringes (this was before the days of AIDS and concern about medical waste). Back at home we would break the thermometers to get the mercury, with which we would then experiment, dropping it and watching it splatter, dispersing into tiny balls and then rejoining again in a big, molten metal glob. We played Cops and Robbers (mostly Robbers) and built our own private, elaborate kids' world of secret games and languages, of hideouts and forts, of Lego cities with a complex array of characters, of good behavior and bad.

Self & Identity

For the most part our parents left us alone. My dad's work kept him away from home a lot, between time at the "Chem Building" and traveling. My mom had gone back to graduate school to get her MFA as a painter when I was about six, so she was often buried in her work in her studio. And of course they had their own problems and issues to sort out, as we found out later when they abruptly announced that they were getting divorced. Had they known our secret antics I think they would have been much more involved in our young lives, but as it was, we had a lot of freedom and a lot of opportunity to explore, learn and get into mischief on our own.

Growing up I was a tomboy from the start. I loved to play with my brother and some of his friends, and had few female friends of my own. I hated playing with dolls and doing "girlie" things. My mom used to make me wear dresses and other horrific homemade "girl" clothes until she finally figured out that I wouldn't wear them, that I wanted to look like Mike. So she compromised and made me shorts and shirts but with semi-girlish patterns in the fabric. I also loved to go shirtless in our yard, like my brother, and this brought a shriek of laughter, pointing and teasing from any neighborhood kid who happened to see it.

As I got older my brother lost interest in playing with his little sister and I started to make female friends. They were all tomboys too and we engaged in "boy-like" games and activities. I had a bit of an identity problem from early on because I didn't like being female. I thought it was unfair that Mike was treated differently, that because he was the "first born son" he received more attention and gifts than I: silver cups and even a gold coin from my grandmother. I thought life was unfair being a girl. I really wished I was a boy when I was a young child, and this created a certain amount of confusion at the time.

I was now well into the early part of the "During Swimming" years, age around ten/eleven, and swimming was beginning to shape and build my identity. I was still slow, a tad overweight for a swimmer and had a big gap between my two front teeth. I was often teased about these things. I wore my hair short and dressed in what would now be considered "gender neutral" clothes. I was still a tomboy but I no longer wanted to *be* a boy. I wanted to be a girl, but I wanted to be myself too. I was confused about what exactly that was, especially because of what I heard from the other kids. I was often called "ugly" and "fat," even though I was not. Going to the bathroom in public places, and even sometimes at school, was an intimidating experience because I was often accused of being a boy, and I hated that. It only added to an inner turmoil that was developing about my sexuality. I was a girl, but I looked and acted like a boy, and every now and then I still *wanted* to be a boy. Was there something wrong with me? I worried.

But when I entered the sixth grade I started having crushes on boys. This was a huge relief. Prior to that I saw them only as friends, and actually had a "crush," of sorts, on one of my female friends for a short period of time. My first boy crush helped solidify my feeling – and hope – that I was, indeed, a real girl with real girl emotions. But the confusion over my sexuality continued as I got older because, for one, my body began to change in more masculine ways than feminine.

Between the sixth and eighth grades swim training really intensified. My teammates and I were swimming every day plus Saturdays and twice per day several times each week. The training was grueling, demanding, and often excessive. We were also lifting weights and doing other forms of dry land work. I loved being one of the Good Swimmers. We worked hard to an extreme and were proud of our work ethic and what we accomplished in practice. Other values became important too, like dedication, commitment and sacrifice. By this time I was winning races and was invigorated by that and my overall progress in the sport.

My body became hard and muscular. I was lean and fit, with wide shoulders and narrow hips. As far as self-image and identity go, it was at this stage in my life that my body image began to play a major role in my perception of myself. Inside I felt like a young woman, but outside I looked like a teenage boy (as my brother sometimes reminded me). In high school my teammates called me "Biceps" in addition to "Christi Crash." During my freshman year a young woman sitting behind me in one of my classes always picked on me. She would pull hairs from my head and say, "Your hair is so white it looks like glass. I could break it if I hit you on the head." Nearly every day she told me "You look like a boy. Maybe you really are one, disguised as a girl." She was smaller than I but I think she felt challenged by my size and presence. I had gained confidence in myself and it showed in my poise and self-assured mannerisms. My troublesome classmate tried to egg me on by poking me in the back with pencils and even pushing me in the hallways between classes. I tried to ignore it, but one time I ran into her alone in the bathroom and she started in on me, calling me names and poking her finger in my chest. I was big and strong and sick of being the victim. I grabbed her by her shoulders and shoved her smaller body roughly against the wall as I pushed my full weight against her. My face was inches from hers. "Don't you ever mess with me again or I swear to God I'll beat the living shit out of you!" That was the last time she ever made fun of me.

 I was proud of my toughness in training and my tough-looking body. I looked like a body-builder with well defined, "cut" muscles and six-pack abs. I used to look at myself in the mirror and flex every muscle, to make sure I looked good and fit. No matter how hard we had worked during practices I almost always came home and did more in the evenings, alone in my room: pushups, situps, elastic cord exercises and so on. Then I would examine myself naked in the mirror, admiring the parts I liked and thinking about how I could improve the parts I didn't like. I was essentially flat-chested except for my pectoral muscles and I didn't mind that. I really didn't want to have breasts and was glad that mine were so small.

 Generally I was very pleased with my body image, unlike most high school kids. It was one of the positive results of swimming – being lean, strong and fit. But this notion of body image has also haunted me throughout my life. It has been such a large part of my overall self-image that I have continued to work hard to preserve it. Somehow I feel that if I am less than fit, if I'm not pounding on myself, then I am losing a part of "me." It has become a compulsion to be fit and this has been very tough on my body, with many resulting injuries as evidence. So this positive result of swimming, the compulsion to be fit, has also turned into a negative, both an "emotional" and a "physical" scar. I am obsessed with exercise and staying fit to this day, even if it means injuries, pain and surgeries. The amount of exercise I do, about an hour a day because that is all I can manage, is miniscule compared to what I did in training. I wish I could say that I have found a comfortable balance, but I have not. I still feel an inner need to beat on myself even though it's limited. Is this an emotional scar left over from swimming, this need to "beat on myself?" Whether it is or isn't, the fact is as I get older more parts are breaking down. Rather than being pleased with doing less and not looking quite as fit, I feel that I am being forced to give up what has always been such a major part of my identity. I have yet to come to terms with this inevitable and frightening reality.

<center>~~~</center>

During my freshman year in high school I was consumed by swimming, school, my body image and my growing identity as "Christi the Swimmer." It was also the year I started drinking, as I have already written. My bipolar disorder was also worsening, although I didn't understand it or why I had such agonizing periods of depression and mania. Other things were going on as well, serious issues that my young mind and developing sense of identity were having a difficult time coming to grips with. I found myself again attracted to a woman. She was older than I, and went to our school. She was also an athlete.

The attraction was more emotional than physical. I was totally infatuated and fascinated by her. She was funny, confident, self-assured and cheerful. She had an outgoing personality, laughed often and made friends easily, traits that I wished I had. I felt electrified when I was near her and thrilled when I received attention from her. Every now and then I wondered what it would be like to kiss her, but I quickly shut down and smothered those thoughts. That would mean I was gay. It would be horrible to be a lesbian, I thought, and I definitely did NOT want that. I was very confused about my attraction to her. I did not see myself as gay because I was also attracted to boys, and this was a very strong physical attraction rather than an emotional one. Yet I worried that I might be bisexual, which would also be horrible. But how else to explain my attraction to Sherrie? My solution to dealing with this conflict was to not think about it. I would look in the mirror and tell myself sternly, "Do *NOT* think about this. This is a distraction from swimming. You *MUST NOT* think about this." And so rather than trying to resolve the conflict or discussing it with others I quashed it by disciplined thought, by losing myself in my training – and by getting drunk.

I did have a few boyfriends when I was in high school. These young men were also athletes and alcohol always played a large role in the relationships. For one thing, I always dated guys who drank. I didn't think about this consciously but on some level I suppose I was choosing boys who drank because I wanted to be sure I could drink too. I was still very shy and would be terribly nervous before a date. My sophomore year I actually had a bottle of booze, Galliano or some other sickly sweet liqueur, stashed in my room and I would take a few belts from it before being picked up by my date. The alcohol burned as it slid down my throat and I still had to shut my eyes and hold my breath so I wouldn't gag. But I loved the feeling of warmth and fire once it made its way to my stomach. The warmth spread throughout my body and I could feel the tension slipping away. Almost immediately it gave me the sense of being more relaxed and happy. It alleviated my nervousness and made me outgoing and fun. At this stage I wouldn't say I *needed* alcohol in order to go on a date. There were plenty of times when I didn't have any, when my bottle had run out and I hadn't yet found someone to buy me another. Now and then I actually went on a date with a guy and we *didn't* drink. On those occasions I simply went out and usually ended up having a decent time, though I really had to wrestle with my anxiety and shyness.

This precedent proved to be very important for how I handled relationships and problems with relationships in the future. I viewed alcohol as a necessary part of dating and having a serious relationship. It was the lubricant that dulled my anxiety and dispelled my nervousness. It made me more comfortable with myself and my conflicting emotions about my sexuality. And while I didn't have intercourse when I was in high school, I did date boys where making out would become sexual. But I never had sexual relations of any type without being drunk. I simply couldn't do it without my "best friend alcohol" along for the ride. Alcohol enabled me to perform and was a crutch for blunting my emotional difficulties with sex (like the discomfort and fear I felt about my sexuality) as well as the stress of feeling that I might not be "good." So from the start of my dating years I came to rely on alcohol as an essential component of a relationship, to help me deal with the emotional aspects of it and to enable me to have sexual relations.

My involvements with young men in high school and my early college years never lasted long because I always ended them. As a relationship began to get serious I became more and more uncomfortable. With this discomfort came more drinking and I knew that I was sabotaging myself. As I've said, I knew I had a serious alcohol problem from the very first day. Usually by drinking during dates I would break one or more of my self-imposed "rules" about how often I could drink and/or how close to a major competition. Then I would feel regretful and disgusted with myself that I couldn't maintain my own commitment to my training and health. That was one reason why I broke off relationships. Another reason was that I felt that having a boyfriend would take too much time and emotional energy and would be a distraction from swimming.

I became more bothered by my conflicting views about my sexuality. I definitely thought of myself as a woman as far as how I felt inside, but I also looked at myself as androgynous because of how I appeared on the outside. When I dressed up and wore makeup I usually felt that I was attractive and feminine-looking. But this apparently was not how the world saw me. I endured a lot of criticism over the years about how I looked. I was often accused of being a "dyke," "lesbian," "bi-freak," or worse, "fag." I avoided public bathrooms as much as I could because I was almost always told, "Sir, you're in the wrong bathroom," or "Excuse me, sir, but the men's room is that way." I remember attending a family gathering for a good friend, a renewal of his and his wife's vows, when I was thirty-three. His father, an elderly man, had been staring at me for a long time. I had dressed nicely, was wearing makeup and really felt that I looked beautiful. But all of the sudden, out of the blue, this elderly gentleman announced in a loud voice, "You look like you could rip heads off with those arms." Needless to say that remark didn't help me feel pretty! Many times I would go to the counter in a store or gas station and be called sir. I even heard, on several occasions, "May I help you sir, or. . . ma'am, or. . . whatever you are?" I confused small children the most. They would stare at me and either hide behind their parent's legs, eyes wide with wonderment, or boldly ask, "What are you? Are you a boy or a girl?" After a while I started to answer, "I am a space alien. Boooooo!"

These types of comments hurt me deeply and made me question my self-image even more. On the one hand, privately I loved my muscular, toned body and felt good about myself from a physical standpoint. On the other hand, I was constantly being told that I was either a lesbian or a man. Could I be transgendered? I explored that possibility for a while when I was in college and rejected it. I *did* feel like a woman inside, after all. I endured these types of remarks often, even when I was well into my thirties, and occasionally even today. They have added to my feelings of "weirdness," and have fostered a negative view of myself and my body that has been hard to accept. As always, I have dealt with conflicting "outside appearances" vs. "inside actualities" and these conflicts continue to be difficult. This is an example of how I wrestle with acceptance. There is my own acceptance of myself, my body and my physical self-image. In contrast is my perception of the acceptance or non-acceptance of myself by others.

Like many young women, when I was in middle school I became obsessed with food. Women as a group are constantly bombarded with the idea that in order to be beautiful one has to be model-thin and eat next to nothing. This idea is everywhere in the media (magazines, billboards, advertising) and in many peoples' homes: criticism by parents or other family members (or in my case, by other kids) that one is "fat" and therefore "ugly." Since swimmers wear only small swimsuits, our bodies are always exposed and therefore our physical condition can be easily judged and compared. Also, many teams have regular weight checks and body fat percentage tests, which add to the pressure to be thin.

By the time I was in high school I was very lean and had dangerously low body fat. For several years I didn't get my period because my body fat percentage was so low. But this wasn't because I regulated my food intake by starving myself. Quite the contrary. Our training was so intense and extreme that I couldn't eat enough to maintain energy and a healthy weight. There was a large genetic component to this too, as my family on both sides is naturally lean and fit. My eating was disgustingly excessive and, much to my mother's dismay, expensive (I often heard her say, "between you and Mike I can barely keep up with cooking!"). It was normal for Mike and me to polish off a huge casserole meant to feed six, coupled with a large salad, bread, and then finish off the meal with an enormous milkshake complete with vitamin powder, a raw egg, peanut butter and chocolate chips blended in. Other people would comment on how much I ate, and it became an expectation and also a source of pride for me that I could eat so much and stay so thin. I never had a problem with bulimia or anorexia, which are common disorders among competitive swimmers, especially females. But I definitely was obsessed with eating, and this did become an issue for me later.

Keeping up calories by eating enormous quantities of food is not uncommon among competitive swimmers. The sport requires a substantial caloric intake, for some people more than others. Then there is the truism that swimmers tend to be competitive in everything they do, and eating is no exception. We would keep an eye on each other and sometimes even have outright contests. The idea, of course, was to be able to eat more than anyone else but still stay thin. I fell into this mentality easily because eating had already become an obsession, even though I didn't have a weight problem. And despite my physical need for a lot of calories, for me eating turned into another potentially harmful activity, for which the negative ramifications came much later in my life. This was because I hadn't learned how to balance my life in healthy ways. Everything I did was always to excess: working out, eating, drinking, working. The concept of "moderation" rarely entered my reality, and I have always cared about looking fit and healthy, as well as being able to perform well in physical activities and work.

I took pride in my body but knew that my excessive drinking and eating would ultimately destroy it. But rather than moderate my eating (which I didn't want to do) and control my drinking (which I *couldn't* do), my answer to all my problems was to exercise more. Ate too much? Go for a bike ride. Feeling edgy? Rollerblade. Pissed off? Run. Depressed? Swim. Any or all of the above? Drink. Extreme activity or extreme drinking became my solution for just about every emotional problem or uncomfortable state that I was in. I simply hadn't learned how else to cope with most situations, difficult or not, so I responded by either pounding myself with exercise or smothering my feelings with alcohol.

Another way I coped with discomfort either within myself (i.e., my bipolar disorder) or due to situations, was to do reckless, crazy things that involved *both* exercise and drinking. These activities escalated after my swimming years were over, when I was in my twenties and thirties and no longer as concerned about getting injured. I needed some way to fill the void once the thrill of competition was gone and I loved the rush of adrenaline that dangerous activities provided. For example I loved to drink beer while rollerblading, the more steep hills the better. I had a large fanny pack that held eight cans of beer, which I would fill with Miller Genuine Draft and then head out at night for a long, fast skate (the darkness added to the thrill). I would put on my safety gear – I didn't want to get injured, after all – and my headlamp, and skate easily along the bumpy roads in our small town until I got to the main road that was long, fairly smooth and hilly. Then I would slam beers as I skated hard, tossing the cans into the tall, grassy scrub alongside the road. Usually by the time I got to the biggest hill I had a good buzz going, both from the adrenaline of skating and the alcohol, so I was especially fearless. I would bomb toward the hill as fast as I could, getting a good head of steam going as I crested the top, until the steepness of it would take over and I would start to accelerate. At that point I would crouch down into a ball, hugging my legs together tight and squeezing my head down into my shoulders, to increase my speed. In this manner I would fly down the hill like a bullet, the wind deafening in my ears. At the bottom, in order to slow down, I would stand up with my arms spread as I carefully braked, letting my body's resistance work like a parachute. Sometimes, if I felt particularly energetic, I would make the long climb back up and do it again, sometimes several times, before skating back home. By the time I returned I was exhausted but giddy and higher than a kite. Then the serious drinking would begin.

 I also enjoyed windsurfing in all sorts of conditions, even more so when I had a good buzz going. The town in which my future husband, Jacques, and I lived was next to a large, all-sports lake. We had a mild early winter one year and the lake was still ice-free in December. One day we had a nasty, howling blizzard. The snow was coming down like mad and blasting around like thick smoke in a hurricane. Jacques wasn't home, so I decided it would be fun to go windsurfing (he would have argued strongly against this plan had he been home). I gathered all my gear and donned my wetsuit, neoprene cap, gloves and booties, drank another beer and headed out.

Despite all the other insanely reckless things I have done over the years I have to say that this one ranks as one of the craziest. My windsurf rig at the time was expert level, and liked stiff winds in order to perform at its best – high up on plane with little more than the rear skeg, or fin, of the board actually in the water. I was sailing crazy fast in the vicious blizzard, the sail taut and rigid and held back at a steep angle as my butt skittered on the water's surface and the board skipped crisply over the waves. I was terrified and exhilarated as I hung from my harness, gripping the boom with all my strength, slicing smooth curves in the black, frothy water. Visibility was maybe twenty feet as I zoomed along through the thick haze of snow, enjoying the sheer ecstasy of the experience. I don't know how I was able to find the launch site when I finished, but I remember the terrible hypothermia that followed. That unpleasantness aside, sailing on that blustery day remains one of the most fun and memorable adventures I've ever had.

In 1998, when I was thirty-two, I made yet another serious attempt to quit drinking. I had fallen so far and my life was in such a shambles that I truly felt I was at the end of my rope – the "jumping off place" as we say in AA. I was depressed and suicidal, separated from my husband and living in a small side room attached to the office at the shop where I worked. My brother Mike and I ran a marine fabrication and mechanical service business there. I designed and built enormous steel and canvas structures for large boats, covers, tops, upholstery and all sorts of miscellaneous items used in boats and cars. Mike performed mechanical service on boats, cars and anything else that would fit on the lift in our shop. We kept the building meticulously neat and clean but it still smelled like a garage. The odors of oil, solvents and gas permeated everything, including the small room where I slept and did my office work.

I had pulled out all the stops to quit drinking this time and had even enlisted the help of a therapist, who immediately recommended that I see a psychiatrist because she thought I needed to be on medication for my depression (incidentally she was the first person to suggest that I might have bipolar disorder). She also told me that she couldn't work with me unless I went to AA and didn't drink. I had never been to AA before and was reluctant to go, and scared. But Mike, who is a recovering alcoholic himself and had been sober for quite a while, assured me that it would be good for me and that I might even like it. He also told me that he thought it would be "easier for me than for some people to stay sober because I liked to do so many things. I could keep myself busy and my mind away from alcohol." I agreed with him that I had a vast array of interests, but worried inside about keeping my mind away from alcohol. This was, of course, because I rarely did anything *without* alcohol. Would I have the guts to rollerblade down a hill at over thirty miles an hour in the dark if I was sober? What about going windsurfing in a wetsuit in a raging blizzard? Or kayaking in January at midnight in the foaming water under one of the dams of the Huron River? Then there was the terror of going to parties and other social events and actually conversing with people. How was I going to do these things sober? How would I ever have *fun* again?!

Hawaii

When I was sixteen, at the start of the second semester of my junior year in high school, I attempted my first "geographical cure." In AA parlance a geographical cure is when one either moves, changes jobs or makes some other sudden, drastic change in their life in the hopes of controlling or quitting drinking. In my case the motive was two-fold. One, I wanted to go "somewhere else" to train, as I thought that doing so would enable me to train at an even higher level and improve my swim times even more. That was my stated reason. I was also desperate to control my drinking, and I thought that moving to a new place and hanging out with new people would help me do that. That was my secret, unstated reason. Other unstated reasons included the fact that I wasn't getting along with my mom, so life at home was often angry and turbulent. Also I was suffering on and off from depression, and thought that a change of scenery might help to alleviate that awful feeling of deep sadness that I sometimes felt, that I worked so hard to hide.

Our club team's head coach, Jack, suggested that I go to Hawaii, to train with the Punahou Swim Team and attend Punahou High, an outstanding private school near the University of Hawaii in Honolulu (incidentally, Punahou is the school that President Barack Obama attended). Jack recommended both the school and the coach, Steve Borowski, who was a personal friend of his and a former champion swimmer himself. The plan was that I would live with a family there, attend Punahou for one semester and train under Steve's excellent coaching and guidance.

The idea sounded beyond great to me but I thought the odds of it happening were almost zero. It had been made clear to me by both parents in subtle and sometimes not so subtle ways that my swimming fees and the costs of attending meets were a financial hardship. This was especially true of regional competitions, where we had to stay in hotels and there were transportation and meal costs, and trips to Nationals, which usually included airfare costs as well. I was well aware of the problems with financing my swim meets and often felt very guilty about it. The knowledge about what everything cost produced added pressure on me to perform well, as I felt my parents would be upset if I did poorly after they had invested so much time and money in me and my sport. So I was surprised when my dad said he thought that going to Hawaii was a good idea and even more surprised when he offered to pay for it.

My dad is a tall, slim, handsome man with dark hair, brown eyes and a guarded smile. He is an intense person, with a stately, somewhat aristocratic bearing that exudes confidence and success, and sometimes can be intimidating. He is quiet and mild-mannered, not in a shy way, but rather in a serious, thoughtful way. He is comfortable in his own skin, modest and likes to be in control. Cautious and careful, he doesn't do anything rashly, but takes his time considering all angles of a problem or question before addressing it. My husband once complained that it was maddening to play chess with him, not because he was a better player, but because "he wins because he takes so much time between moves that he puts the other player to sleep."

When my parents were still married we used to go on all kinds of outdoor adventures. Everyone in our family enjoyed camping in remote places, canoeing, looking for and exploring caves, hunting for nuts and berries, searching in old quarries for prehistoric fossils, looking for agates, geodes and crystals, hiking, skiing, biking and so on. I have many recollections of the good times we had with my dad both before and after the divorce, when he would take Mike and me on extended trips "out west" to explore the mountains, deserts and many famous parks and landmarks. As usual, we were often turned loose to discover things on our own, searching in woods and brambles for antique beer cans and other priceless treasures while my dad played his guitar by the campfire or went on more difficult hikes than we kids could handle. After the divorce he remarried and Mike and I acquired a stepmom, Pat, a stepsister, Jesikah and, later, an adopted sister from Korea, Julia. My "new" second family was kind and seemed very "normal" to me, by my sheltered and directed teenaged-life standards. We got along well and continued to undertake various adventures, though these lessened as time went on and our lives became more hectic.

My dad is an avid skier and enjoys outdoor adventures, which may be where I inherited my zest for risk and challenging physical activities. He loves nature and creatures of all sorts and is interested in just about everything. He is also a serious man who has spent his lifetime – as long as I've known him – devoted to his work in the field of chemistry. I remember when I was young sometimes being afraid of him when he would come home for dinner. He was often tired from a long day at the chem building and had no patience for chatter and noise from us. He rarely spanked us when we misbehaved but he did employ a sharp knuckle-blow to the head to keep us in line. This punishment was more humiliating than painful, and I dreaded it. My dad would also give us *The Look*, as Mike and I called it, when he was angry or displeased with our behavior. The Look is a very severe, steely-eyed and scathing glare that penetrates deep inside, almost as if he can see right through to the core of one's soul. As I got older I came to believe that the whole point of The Look was to manipulate – to express his displeasure by silently being critical and judgmental, thereby attempting to control our behavior. It was like an emotional "spanking" rather than a physical one, and it enraged me. I hated and resented being the recipient of The Look and did my best to avoid it.

But my dad is a kind and gentle man and is only *not* when he gets angry or frustrated. I was devastated when my parents divorced. I worried about who would take care of us kids and also about what the other kids would think. I worried that we would be harassed and teased because we were among the first families in our neighborhood to break up. I feared that we would be shunned by the others, and that I would be even more alone. When the divorce became final and the assets divided, my mom, Mike and I moved into a smaller house with a huge yard a few blocks from where we had previously lived. My dad moved into a house a mile or two away. I was ten at the time and became very sad and depressed, and I buried these feelings in my swim training. We saw my dad one evening each week and on the weekends. The other nights I would cry myself to sleep because I missed him, and because I felt that life had treated me unfairly in general.

I was surprised that my dad agreed to send me to Hawaii for several reasons. One, he tended to be austere and reserved when it came to spending money. I didn't think he even *had* the money to pay for me to live and go to school in Hawaii for eight months. I was also surprised because I was under the impression that he wasn't all that keen on certain aspects of my swimming. This was more a feeling I had than a direct statement from him, although he did make remarks now and then that angered and confused me. One time he told me that I should get a job at McDonald's so I could "learn what hard work is." At that point I was training twice a day in the pool plus doing dry land exercises six days per week in addition to being a full-time, straight A student. I couldn't imagine working harder than I was, and really resented comments like that. Another time when I was in high school he told me my "values were all screwed up." I never understood that one, except that maybe he felt I didn't spend enough time with the family.

These sorts of things affected my self-image because they added to my deep-seated feeling that I was never good enough, that I could never quite measure up to both my mom's and my dad's high expectations. It seemed that no matter what I did, no matter how much I tried or how successful I was, there was always some sort of criticism. By my junior year I was having relationship troubles with both parents, a phenomenon not at all unusual for a high school student. I did have people to talk with about this – my friends – but there was still a lot of pain and anger toward my parents, with which I had a hard time coping. I had different issues with my mom, but I felt that my dad didn't understand the role swimming played in the delicate equilibrium of my life. At the time I felt that he didn't realize how much it enabled me to have friends and be accepted, to have confidence in myself, poise, and – most importantly – to manage my emotions and keep my depression and mood problems at bay. I also felt that he didn't care much for my swimming because he never really said that he did, and I needed to hear that, in words, and often. But these issues aside, my opinion of my dad changed a lot when he sent me to Hawaii. I absolutely loved it there, and was deeply grateful to him for the opportunity. Not only that, it was definitive proof that he really did support my swimming and was serious about helping me reach my goals. I always felt that I needed his support and approval – it helped me feel good about myself and what I was accomplishing. Just like when I made my childhood vow to be "good," I still craved the attention and affirmation that only my dad could give.

We left for Hawaii two weeks before Christmas in the middle of my junior year. My dad came with me, to meet the family with whom I would be living, meet the headmaster of the school, the coach, and basically to make sure that I was set up well and that everything was to his liking.

We spent the first few days meeting people and being tourists. It was great fun to explore and go snorkeling in the crystal clear water of one of Hawaii's most famous attractions, Hanauma Bay. We saw an amazing assortment of multicolored fish swimming in and around the coral-encrusted lava formations. It was a spectacular place and we sported spectacular sunburns afterwards. We also drove around the island to take in the sights and do some hiking.

I had a blast just walking the strip at Waikiki beach, looking in the colorful shops and examining all the "tourist trap junk," as my dad called it, that lined the street in the various, grass-roofed vendor booths. People-watching was also great fun. I was quite "green" at age sixteen and had never been to a place quite like Honolulu. There was so much to see that dazzled my young imagination. Later, after I'd lived there for a while, I would spend countless hours exploring by bicycle the local fish markets, surf spots, shops and other places that didn't cater to tourists.

After several days my dad returned to Madison and I was on my own. The family I lived with was terrific: two parents and two daughters, one my age, Sandra, and one two years younger, Cindy. We lived in what would be considered a "modest" middle class house in the States but in Honolulu was considered wealthy. It was a 1960s-era two-story home set up like a condominium. We inhabited the upper floor. This consisted of three smallish bedrooms, two bathrooms and a large open space that was the living room, kitchen and dining area. There was also a long balcony that provided an incredible view of the ocean bordered by the strip of tall white hotels along Waikiki, as well as the city of Honolulu, which was spread out before and below us in all directions.

Honolulu is a long, narrow, sprawling, crowded city bordered on one side by the deep blue Pacific ocean and on the other by jagged green mountains. They don't call Hawaii the "Rainbow State" for nothing! There really are incredible rainbows every day, as it rains often in the mountains and the sun is always shining everywhere else. While it is dry, hot and desert-like down in the "flats," in the hills where it gets more rain it is lush and green. Higher in the mountains the vegetation is truly a tropical jungle because of so much rainfall. We lived in the foothills of the mountains so it was hilly everywhere, the streets were narrow and the houses were packed tightly together, built into the steep terrain. I was amazed at how it *smelled* in Hawaii. It seemed that everywhere I went the aroma was sweet and fragrant, like flowers, with a tinge of sea salt in the clean, fresh air. Downtown Honolulu was the exception. There, when the air was still, were pockets of diesel bus exhaust, auto fumes and smog mixed in with the smell of the ocean and coconut sunbathing oil. The beach was pleasant with the cool, cleansing ocean breezes but inland the fumes from the constant stream of autos were often overpowering and asphyxiating in the hot sun.

Our house overlooking the city had screens on the windows but sometimes the doors to the balcony were open so all kinds of critters came and went at will. I shared a room with Sandra, and the first night as we were getting ready for bed I pulled back the covers only to see a small cockroach go scuttling away under the sheets. Horrified, I found it and brushed it off.

"Oh, don't worry, you'll get used to them," said Sandra. "And that one was puny. Wait 'til you see the ones in the kitchen at night. They're like rats they're so big! Be sure you turn on the light first if you go in there at night!"

We had parakeets and other tropical birds visit us, and it was common to see small geckos, some bright green, others various shades of brown, climbing the walls, stuck to the ceiling or poking their heads from behind the wide, comfortable couch. The cockroaches were, indeed, ridiculously large and I eventually did get used to them. When I would see one on the floor I would just kick it, its hard, shelled body making a "thwack" sound when my foot made contact.

As for the people, I was very nervous when I first arrived in Hawaii and had all my usual fears and concerns. Would I get along with my new "family?" Would they like me? Would the other kids like me? How would I fit in with the team? Would I be accepted right away or shunned and treated like an outsider? How would I be treated at my new school? As nervous as I was, it didn't take long to realize that most everyone was friendly and quite eager to get to know "the new girl."

My new family was a relaxed, laid back group of folks and I felt comfortable living with them. It took a little while to open up with Sandra and Cindy but I attribute that more to my shyness than to any reluctance on their end. They were fun, outgoing girls, especially Sandra, and they joked and laughed a lot with their parents, who were very tolerant and kind. Unlike at my house, there didn't seem to be any strict rules, and everything had that calm, "hang loose" feel about it that was so prevalent everywhere I went while I was there. It was a pleasant living arrangement and also quite interesting. The family dynamic was so different from mine, with the parents seemingly on a more even par with the kids. I really enjoyed listening to the happy, joking and often sarcastic banter that was always going on between them.

Another nice thing about living there was that we were within walking distance of Punahou, my new school. Punahou was incredibly beautiful and looked to me more like a ritzy, small college campus than a K-12 school. There were many small-to-large, well-maintained buildings for the various classrooms and no hallways because none of the buildings were connected. To get to classes one either walked on paved or wood-chip walkways or on the neatly trimmed lawn. There were rich green, multi-limbed trees and lush, tiered gardens everywhere, benches for studying or taking a break with classmates, fountains and stone landscaping around gardens for sitting. The athletic facilities were top-notch and most of them looked new, as if a major renovation of the athletic section of campus had recently occurred. I was stunned by the absolute beauty of the place, and couldn't believe how lucky I was to be there.

Of course my primary interest was the pool, and it did not disappoint. The entire facility, from the deep, eight lane, fifty meter competition pool, to the weight and dry land exercise room, to the spotless locker rooms, was first rate. I remember my first workout with the team when my dad was still there. Everyone gathered around us as my new coach, Steve, introduced me. I recall that I was terribly nervous and shy, but once I got into the water the anxiety began to melt away and the water soothed my fears as it always did. I adored Steve from the moment I met him. He was friendly and kind, with a warm, outgoing nature that exuded a calm confidence and strength. The team was receptive and welcoming too, and I started to make friends almost immediately. This is typical of being on a swim team – everyone is doing the hard work and sharing the pain so camaraderie and friendships develop quickly.

And with those friendships came the parties. It didn't take long to figure out who the drinkers were, and even less time to fit right in with them. I discovered that this team was just like my team back home. There were a fair amount of parties, especially in the summer after school had ended and there were college swimmers on the team as well. During the school year there were often parties on the weekends and as is typical there were a few kids who drank more than most. I was in that group. Despite moving halfway around the globe, and attempting my "geographical cure," my drinking behavior hadn't changed one bit. I still drank to alleviate my anxiety, fear and that ever-present feeling of loneliness and "weirdness." I continued to binge drink as I always had, unable to stop after that first drink and continuing until I was thoroughly drunk.

It's an interesting feeling, that first drink. My mind would seem to "let go" and start to unwind before the alcohol even hit it. There would be the ever-sought-after feeling of pleasure and happiness that comes at first, and once that happened it was like a switch flipped deep inside my brain. I could almost feel it. The switch would flip and suddenly the desire for pleasure would be much more, and the logical thought would be to drink more, but having more didn't necessarily increase the pleasure, it only increased the drunk. I sometimes felt that the best part of drinking was the feeling I got after the first several drinks. That was the feeling I often sought: the gentle warmth, the release of tension in my body, the feeling that my anxiety was melting away, the overall calmness, lightheadedness and happiness. But after those first few drinks there would be absolutely no control and my drinking would just escalate. Sometimes I thought I could maintain that initial buzz as I kept drinking, that feeling of calm, looseness and happiness, but it usually didn't work that way. That feeling wasn't there anymore. The "high" wasn't like it was at first. Often it was more intense, more "wild," more erratic, as if my mind was starting to spin up like a computer's hard drive, getting ready to perform some complex or meaningful task but just spinning and spinning, faster and faster, but not moving forward, just stuck, spinning. Most times I *liked* that feeling, of losing control. I knew it would happen, could feel it happening, and looked forward to "losing myself." I often craved the excitement of the "super high" – that mega-happy, manic, reckless me that could come out with hard drinking. Other times I wanted the "mellow" me, and the eventual sweet oblivion of simple, mind-numbing drunkenness. In between those extremes I liked the long, slow, happy sense of gradually easing into inebriation, not getting completely wasted to the point of passing out but drunk enough. But regardless of the effect, for me it was always "more, more, more," and that's how my alcoholism worked. My brain seemed to lack the necessary chemical response to the alcohol to say, "*No* more. That's *enough*."

Schoolwork at Punahou was difficult and competitive, much like it was at the school I attended in Madison. I took it very seriously and made good grades, but every now and then the intensity of school and swimming was too much and I needed to blow off steam. Again my alcoholism and penchant for reckless behavior was my pressure relief-valve. Sandra, Cindy and some of the other girls would take me body surfing at various local surf spots and we had loads of fun. I loved the feeling of catching a wave just right, of being quickly lifted up and then slicing down its face as the powerful wave thundered toward shore. I even liked the feeling of being hammered at the finish, when the wave broke, and being caught up in the frothy, soupy mass of currents and sand as the water gushed back out to sea. Sometimes, rather than pull out early, I intentionally let myself ride a wave to its end, where I knew I would be slammed as it broke. I loved that feeling of having absolutely no control, and of being a little afraid too. It was exhilarating and great fun – an excellent way to relieve stress in a healthy way.

But as always I had to take that fun to the next level. I had a male friend on the team who also liked to drink to excess. One day we decided to take a cooler of beer and go bodysurfing at a local beach called Sandy's. It was appropriately named because the waves nearly always broke close to shore, so no matter how well one caught and rode the wave there was the inevitable crash at the end, and the pounding of the sand-filled, swirling surf as one's flailing body was driven almost onto the beach. I didn't particularly like this surf spot because of that, but my friend lived close by so we went there anyway. By mid-afternoon we were both feeling pretty buzzed and were ready to go back into the water. I was wearing my favorite one-piece suit, the kind that wrapped in front so there was a diagonal slit where the fabric overlapped in the middle. I caught a good wave and was having a nice ride until I got pounded on shore as usual. But this time, somehow my suit, which was essentially open in front because of the overlapping fabric, filled with sand and I ended up on my butt and sliding as the retreating water tried to take me back out to sea. I looked like I was pregnant for all the sand, and my friend by now was standing on shore watching, and laughing hysterically. I couldn't stand because of the extra weight, and the current was so strong that there was nothing I could do but be pulled back out as the next wave came roaring in. I held my breath as wave after wave slammed me into the sand, each time filling my suit a little more and pulling me deeper into the frothy water. My initial feeling of hilarity quickly turned to genuine fear. Meanwhile my good friend was crawling on the ground on all fours, laughing his head off. If not for my being such a good swimmer and therefore able to hold my breath for a very long time I might well have drowned. Finally he came in and rescued me, by essentially turning me over as the next wave clobbered us, scooping the sand out of my suit underwater and then dragging my exhausted body back to shore. After that we went to his place and proceeded to get smashed.

This experience was typical for me in terms of my alcoholism. Not only was it yet another example of the fearless, risky behavior that often accompanied my drinking, but it was another time in my life when I experienced a total "blackout." "Blacking out" is not the same as "passing out," which is when one is so drunk that they fall into a deep, drunken sleep. A blackout is when one has drunk enough and/or the disease of alcoholism has progressed enough, that after a certain point of drunkenness is reached one literally "blacks out," and doesn't remember anything that happens during the blackout phase. During this phase one appears completely conscious and awake, and can be busy cleaning house, socializing at a party, dancing in a club or – most frighteningly – driving.

Blackouts are common among alcoholics, and nearly every alcoholic I know has had one, or many, at some point in time. What is significant is that having blackouts generally means that one is well along the road in terms of how serious and how far the disease has progressed. It is common knowledge that the disease of alcoholism progresses regardless of whether the alcoholic is drinking. A person could be sober, for example, for ten years and then start drinking again, and he would be in the exact same place as when he quit drinking, or worse. Having blackouts indicates that the disease has gone beyond a certain point, past a critical line. One can no longer say, "I am a heavy drinker and sometimes it is a problem." Having a blackout usually means one is an alcoholic, that his behavior has moved him past the fuzzy line that separates problem drinking from serious alcoholic drinking.

That night I don't remember what we did at my friend's house, or how or when I got home, only that I woke up the next morning in my own bed naked and dry, my sandy suit crumpled on the floor. "Oh, God," I worried. "Did we have sex? Were my 'parents' awake when I got home?" I agonized over my fears about the previous evening and tried desperately to piece it together despite my raging hangover. I had had another serious blackout. It didn't take a genius to know that my alcoholism had moved into a new phase. I was scared.

That memorable incident happened in the summer, after school was over. Like with my team in Madison, more parties and drinking events were held in the summer because there was more time and because college swimmers joined the team. If the coaches were aware of these parties they didn't show it. We had team meetings where we were lectured about our health, but these meetings didn't focus on alcohol and I don't remember the team ever being chastised or punished for partying. Rather, the meetings focused on diet, weight, body fat and overall fitness, as well as how to deal with various emotional issues and the stresses of the sport. Every now and then we had a guest lecturer, a sports psychologist or someone of the sort, and we did spend a fair amount of time talking about emotional balance and working on our respective fears, troubles and anxieties. I'm sure that somewhere along the line we were told about how destructive alcohol is to the body, and were lectured not to use it. But I don't remember this as a dominant theme at our meetings and, as I recall, there were no team rules about drinking.

Our head coach, Steve, was fit and lean. An avid surfer, runner and weight lifter, he was very athletic and looked like a natural body builder. He was serious about his physical condition and insisted that we be serious about ours as well. From the moment I met him I was enthralled with him. Steve had a calm serenity about him, an inner peacefulness, as though he was totally content with himself and the world. He had large, gentle, caring eyes and smiled broadly and easily. Steve also had a long, hooked nose, which years ago had earned him the nickname, "Ski." He had a magnetic personality that drew me to him immediately.

As a coach Steve was what I would consider "progressive" and ahead of his time when it came to how he trained his athletes. Our workout schedule was essentially the same in Hawaii as it was back home: six days per week with two-a-days on Monday, Wednesday and Friday plus weights and dry land exercises. We worked hard under Steve, but the training rarely crossed the line into "excessively abusive" which I thought it often did at home. Steve was a firm believer in putting in the work, but he also understood the value and necessity of recovery days in the workout schedule. I thought this was a revolutionary concept at the time because the prevailing mentality in the United States (and the world) was to push, push, push and constantly beat the crap out of the athletes. Nobody could argue that this type of training didn't produce results, however, as times were constantly getting faster and world records were being broken. But the progressive coaches, like Steve, were having great success also, and the price the athletes paid was not as hefty. I myself thrived under Steve's training program. In competition I nearly always won my specialty events, the one-hundred and two-hundred meter breaststroke, and often set records as well. My times in my "secondary" events improved too, and overall I was very pleased with how I was swimming both in training and in competition.

The other element that I liked about Steve's coaching was that he was concerned with how his athletes were doing on an emotional level. He told me right from the start that his office door was always open and if I ever had a problem or concern to come talk to him. It could be about anything, not just swimming-related. I took advantage of this invitation because by then I really needed someone to talk to. I had a mountain, it seemed, of "emotional garbage" (as I once heard a coach say) built up inside me. In reality I needed to be seeing a therapist on a regular basis but back then that wasn't really "done" and I was still reluctant to ask for help. But I did try to talk with Steve about my issues, although I was afraid to bring up my concerns about drinking. I was afraid to talk about them for a couple of reasons. One, I respected Steve very much and was deeply ashamed of my alcoholism. I thought if I told him about how bad my drinking was that he would be judgmental and think poorly of me. The other reason was that I worried that he might feel it necessary to involve my parents, which I did not want, or punish me in some way. So I didn't confide my fears and concerns about my drinking to Steve but I did talk with him about other things, mostly swimming-related – how to handle the pressure of competition, how to endure the relentless practice schedule and stay positive, how to deal with my fear of failure, my fear of success and my fears in general.

One time Steve told me, "Christi, you know what your biggest problem is? You're afraid. Of everything! *Don't* be afraid." From then on he would always say that to me, when I would go into his office or right before a competition, "Don't be afraid. Christi. *Don't be afraid.*"

I was sixteen at the time and totally in love with Steve, but not in the way you might be thinking. I had a very strong physical attraction to him but it wasn't sexual. There were no sexual thoughts, feelings, desires or fantasies about Steve. But there was something about him that just drew me to him. I yearned for his touch, and loved it when he would put his arm around my shoulders or pat me on the back. When he would touch me I would feel a jolt of electricity that would fire my nerves and travel throughout my body. I think my attraction was due in part to the fact that he had personality traits that I admired and wished I had – calmness, serenity, confidence, empathy. He also seemed to have boundless compassion and concern for others, and just pure love of life, of humanity, of everything. I was deeply enamored and infatuated with Steve. I worked especially hard in practice because I wanted to please him, and this was also a big motivation for me to perform well at meets, which I did. If ever there was an instance of an athlete worshipping a coach it was me with Steve. I just adored him.

This brings me back to what I wrote in an earlier chapter about sexual abuse and/or inappropriate behavior by coaches toward their athletes. There was never any improper touching or language between Steve and me. He was just a good person and a great coach and somehow we connected on some higher metaphysical plane. But I can totally understand how easy it would be for a coach to take advantage of a situation like this and abuse his or her athletes. I'm certainly not the first swimmer to worship a coach, and I'm sure this type of adoration happens all the time and in all sports. Yet this is such a potentially dangerous situation for a young person. I believe parents should keep a close eye on their young athletes' relationships with coaches and mentors, and make sure the lines of communication are always open. Had there been any sort of improper behavior between Steve (or any coach) and myself, I think it would have been extremely difficult to discuss it. This is because it was so difficult for me to discuss *any* emotional issue, and I certainly was not unique in that regard. So I believe that parents' observations and involvement are critical in ensuring that their athletes are not being abused, sexually or emotionally, or treated in any improper manner. Having someone to turn to and talk with, someone to trust, is so important for the adolescent, especially one like myself, who had such a problem with communicating.

Mom

The person that I trusted and turned to for help and support was my mother. Even though we weren't getting along well when I was in high school I always felt that she was there for me, and that I could talk with her and get her advice if I had a problem with my schoolwork or a friend, and occasionally an emotional issue. This was difficult, however, because I struggled so much internally with opening up and discussing my feelings, even with her. I always felt a strong need to please and to live up to what I perceived were her high expectations, not just of my performance as an athlete and a student, but of me as a person. I still felt that gnawing sense of "weirdness" and "aloneness." Somehow I felt that I was trying to be something or someone that I wasn't, in order to please my parents and others, and that if they knew the *real* me that they wouldn't like me. The fact that Mom and I weren't getting along didn't help matters. That made it even harder for me to feel free to express myself, to talk about my fears, for example about my sexuality, and also to talk about my periods of depression, which confused and frightened me.

Several months into my eight-month stay in Hawaii I gathered my courage and decided to call my mother to tell her about my drinking problem. I rationalized that because I was halfway around the globe she couldn't get angry at me or punish me. I remember how scared I was when I picked up the phone to make the call. My hands were shaking so hard I could barely dial, but I did, and as planned (we scheduled our talks because of the time difference) she answered the phone.

I don't recall any of the conversation except for the part where I told her that I drank, and that I drank a lot, and that I was worried because I knew I had a serious drinking problem. She listened in silence as I told her, through my tears, about the failed attempt to get help from the school guidance counselor. I told her about all the partying, the binge drinking, the reckless behavior, the drinking on dates, the bottle that I still had stashed in my room in Madison. I told her about my sneakiness, my lying, my deception. I told her about the hangovers, the puking, the blackouts, the regrets. I told her everything. Then I held my breath as I waited for her response. I was certain that she would be very disappointed, and I think I feared that more than her anger. But to my surprise she was not angry at all, just extremely concerned. She told me that she had no idea that I drank and was shocked to learn it. I reminded her of the time when I was so drunk I fell flat on my face right in front of her and lied that I was tired. To that she responded that it didn't surprise her that I was that tired, because it was late and because she had seen it before: like the times I was too exhausted to ride my bike home after practice and she had to come get me, or when I was so fatigued from working out that I could barely make it up the five steps to the back porch.

Apparently I had done an excellent job of hiding my drinking, because she truly had no idea. Her response was of deep concern and worry. She told me something to the effect that, "I don't know what I can do to help. This just doesn't make any sense. You're always so concerned about your diet, your body and your health, and then you choose to destroy it with alcohol. It doesn't make any sense." And indeed, it didn't make any sense, but there it was. We talked for quite a while about my drinking problem but I don't remember coming away from the conversation with anything except the advice to "not drink" and that I could call her anytime I needed to talk or if I needed to be "talked out of drinking." Of course I never called for that reason. I was deeply ashamed of, and felt guilty about my alcoholism. I was relieved to have told my mom about it but at the same time felt terrible. Now I knew that *she* knew. I knew that she would worry, which I felt bad about, and I thought that she was as disappointed in me as I was in myself. But I did feel better after having that conversation. At least I was no longer being dishonest about such a major part of my life, and that in itself was a big monkey off my back.

My mom and I hadn't always been at odds with each other. We only started to not get along when I was perhaps in the seventh or eighth grade, at about the age when most kids start having problems with their parents. I felt that she was domineering and controlling, and exacting to a fault. She was such a perfectionist – everything had to be "just so," and I was starting to rebel against that. The other thing that became a wedge between us was her smoking. At that time she smoked in the house and was nearly a chain smoker. I absolutely *hated* it. I hated the smell, hated that my clothes stank of smoke (I was even accused at school once of smoking because of the smell), and hated how she looked with the cigarette dangling from her mouth. Mostly I hated that I was breathing in poison, and that the smoke was damaging to my lungs and therefore hurting my performance in swimming. She used to angrily accuse me of hiding her cigarettes (which I never did) and we used to have terrible, screaming fights about that and her smoking in general.

But before those tumultuous teenage years began I had a mixed relationship with my mom: mostly good, but sometimes bad. I was very needy as a youngster in addition to my shyness. I needed a lot of hugs and cuddling and most of the time she was available for that. But I do remember some times when I was begging for attention and she would lock me out of her studio so she could work. I now understand the need for private space in which to focus on painting (or writing), but at the time this was extremely painful and it sticks out in my memory. There was one incident in particular that I remember clearly where I was locked out and crying while she was on the phone. Finally she came out in a rage and spanked me so I would stop. I don't remember if that worked, but somehow I doubt it.

When I was young my mom was tall, slender and extremely beautiful. She had shiny light blonde hair and a sleek, athletic body with long legs, wide shoulders and good muscle tone because she swam nearly every day. She had a big smile that would light up the room, and she was always the center of attention. Mom had a lively step and walked with confidence and poise, her shoulders back and head held high. She had a certain presence about her in addition to her natural beauty, and she turned heads wherever she went.

Mom and I were complete opposites when it came to personality. As a child I was shy and timid, and that is still often the case today, although I have learned to hide my shyness even without the protective shield of alcohol. My mom was outgoing and vivacious, and loved to be around people. On a crowded dance floor she would be the one in the middle, laughing and dancing with a gaggle of admirers surrounding her. I would be the one leaning against the wall, watching from the shadows, and hoping like hell that nobody tried to get me to go out there. When I was drinking it was a different story. With alcohol firing through my veins I could handle most social situations, even dancing, though I generally preferred watching, hanging around near the bar and talking, or playing drinking games.

My mom used to tell me stories about when she was growing up, after her family immigrated to the States and they were living in North Carolina. She lived in a small town that had one high school, and she had lots of friends and was one of the Popular Girls. She would show me her yearbooks from school. There are pictures of her everywhere: Head Cheerleader, Captain of the Champion Basketball Team, Debate Team, Glee Club, Student Council, Journalism Club, Most Artistic and Wittiest, National Merit Finalist. . . My mom was a dynamo and everyone loved her, and it was obvious by looking at her and knowing her why that was the case.

Mom

From an early age I felt awed by my mom. I looked at all of her accomplishments, heard her stories, and felt that I was expected to accomplish many things too. I worried that I would not be able to do it, that I wouldn't live up to her expectations. I thought about this a lot as I got older. I was a smart kid, but I knew that I didn't have the same personality as my mother. Head cheerleader? I would die first!

Mom was always busy doing something and she was good at everything she did. She was a talented artist and an excellent painter. She received her MFA degree just as the divorce became final. Occasionally she would jokingly lament to me about how she had had to give up her dream of being an artist in order to take care of us kids. I never thought that was funny – there was definitely truth in the statement and it made me feel bad to hear it. But by and large she was a very positive person and we got along pretty well when I was young.

Mom was creative and fun and the neighborhood kids loved her. When it was her turn to drive the carpool she would occasionally take the five or six of us girls to the McDonald's on campus after practice. We would follow her like a string of baby ducks following their mother as she led us through the Union Terrace, around fountains, up steps, over benches and under balconies. She always found a way to make routine activities fun, and everyone looked forward to the nights when she was driving. Everyone except me, that is. I was embarrassed by my mom's outgoing, devil-may-care behavior. I didn't want to be noticed, and certainly not with my mother, who did crazy things like sing to herself in the grocery store and smile and talk with strangers.

Every now and then I tried to talk with my mom about my depression, which I didn't understand and which was getting worse as I got older. As a young child, as young as five or six, I remember periods of sadness and lots of crying. Later, after my parents divorced, I also had long periods of deep sadness but I told myself that this was because of the divorce and that I needed to work my way out of it. My mom would say, "You need to get over it and move on," or, "Christi, are you working yourself into a depression again?" I was confused by how I felt and got no sympathy at home. Apparently I either hadn't made the case that my "sadness" (I didn't yet call it depression) was that bad or my mom just didn't know what to do about it. I don't think she didn't care; I think she was just unaware of the severity of the problem.

Around the same time that my depression worsened, in late middle school, I began to notice another side of my as yet undiagnosed bipolar disorder, the manic side. At first this phase was characterized by having excessive energy, being super productive and feeling naturally "high" and happy, and I enjoyed it. But I also felt edgy, tense and uncomfortable inside myself, as though I wanted to flee from my own skin. As it worsened my thoughts began to spin around at a hundred miles per hour and I was unable to concentrate. My insomnia became much worse too. Sometimes I would experience both the negative effects of the manic side and the depression at the same time. This is called a "mixed state" and it was a particularly awful place to be. I tried desperately to make it go away. Mostly I pounded on myself even harder in practice to try to "beat my way out of it." Later in high school, to ease the pain, I self-medicated with alcohol. I also contemplated suicide. But usually the intensity of my training kept the manic side of the disorder somewhat controlled and, as such, the eventual switch back to depression wouldn't be as severe either. And there were long stretches of time when I felt almost "normal," when my swimming seemed to control both sides of the disorder and I would be on somewhat of an even keel mood-wise. Generally the manic side would become more evident and uncomfortable during the short breaks we had from training, when I wasn't expending the necessary energy to control it.

Excerpts from my diary when I was seventeen illustrate my confusion when being in a "mixed" state:

April 28

"I don't know what to do, but I want to do something nuts. I've got tons of energy and I'm bored, and depressed. I could read a good book or do my homework but I can't read for *fun* knowing all the work I should be doing. I think I'm starting to wig out!! I'm bored, bored, BORED and there are a zillion things to do but I can't for a number of reasons. I am stuck here.

Maybe I'll talk to Mom. No, we talked so long last night, she'll think I'm crazy. Maybe I am?? Maybe it's genetic or maybe it's the Devil. God, life can be so scary! Well, at least I've learned drinking's not the answer – it only makes me feel sick and hate myself. And suicide wouldn't work, 'cause I still don't know what lies beyond. I don't want to die now anyway. There's too much good in life. It's just so damn frustrating! I can't stand this feeling. I hate myself."

May 3

"I wish X would call. I wish my dad would call. I guess I wish I knew what the fuck I'm doing here and why. I wish I had the guts, or nerve, or stupidity, to just pack it up and say 'fuck it all.' Would I regret that? I'm sure at some point I'll know what all of this is for, but I sure as hell wish it would be soon. I feel like doing something drastic. I feel like going bonkers – but not alone! I feel really alone right now. I could write a letter to Dad (funny how weird that sounds) but I'm really not in the best state of mind for that. God, I am so confused today. My brain is going 90 miles/hr. and in a zillion directions."

May 5

"This stuff is all fucked. I mean useless. Sure education is great blah blah but the useless stuff is just fucked. What a crock. Why do I always have to prove something to someone? It sucks! I'm tired of having to prove myself all the time. I *know* I can do things well – why prove it to thirty million people? Does it really matter? How in hell am I supposed to know what does matter? I don't know what I want to do, be etc. – same old story – why isn't it easier? I am 17, I would think I'd know something about myself by now. OK, I do know that I'm depressed as hell. That's not hard to figure out. But why?? It's not like I don't try, and search for the answer to this incredible sadness. I'm the most happy when I'm swimming, or partying, but I know that's not the answer. Maybe I'm looking too hard, or in the wrong places? I know I've got a lot to be thankful for, and being here, and "nice things" etc. for what we can do, which has not been easy. But oh, great – I'm a shithead for not being able to be happy/thankful right now. So what to do? God I have the urge to just smash that window to bits – or dive through it – or something. I have so much energy I think I am going to explode! Help! Maybe if I take a walk I'd feel better but it's late and it's so unsafe. I may be freaked out, but I can still be a chicken shit."

In addition to depression/mania I had a terrible problem with insomnia. According to my parents I always had trouble getting to, and staying, asleep, starting when I was born, and this problem has tormented me my entire life. There were times when I would literally go for days without sleeping. This was especially awful before and during swim meets, as I knew that good sleep was essential for peak performance. In order to get to sleep I needed absolute quiet and I often tried various meditation and relaxation techniques, which usually didn't work. I don't know how I survived living in the dorm my freshman year at the university. We had to be up at five-thirty for morning practice and go to bed early. Everyone else in the dorm stayed up late. There was constant noise, plus my roommate was very social so we would get phone calls and knocks on the door at all hours. I rarely slept more than a few hours, if I slept at all. It was an unpleasant experience living in the dorm and I was ecstatic to live in an apartment with only two other teammates my sophomore year.

I also suffered from horrendous nightmares. This started in middle school, around age eleven, and continued until I was in my mid-thirties. These dreams were very scary and very "real." I called them "Scream Dreams" because I would awake from them screaming bloody murder at the top of my lungs.

The first time I had one of these dreams I remember my mom telling me how she came charging up the stairs to my room, not knowing what was going on and thinking something horrible was happening to her youngest child. Another time, during the summer when the windows were open, my brother told me he heard me screaming from several blocks away as he was riding his bike home. The dreams seemed to happen more often during times of intense anxiety or stress: the night before an exam, before or after a major competition (if I fell asleep at all), after a fight with my mom, or during a particularly stressful period of time in our home.

There were several themes to these nightmares. There were the "Falling" type of dreams that everyone seems to have, where one is falling and suddenly catches oneself and wakes up. Those didn't make me scream, they were just alarming. Then there were the "Falling On Me" dreams that did make me scream. These were when I would be looking up, as though awake, and all of the sudden the ceiling or some other large, suspended object would come crashing toward me, and sometimes land on me. Another category was the "Leaping Out At Me" dreams. These screamers happened when some horrendous, cloaked *thing* would come flying out of my open closet door or from a dark corner of the room, with blurry arms outstretched as it reached for my throat. But the two scariest varieties of scream dreams that I had were what I called the "Locked In" dreams and "The Spectator" dreams. These were by far the most horrible and terrifying.

One time I was spending the night at my dad's house sleeping in the guest room. He had a small, dark brown leather sofa with a pull out bed which was up against the wall under a multi-paned window. I remember tossing and turning for a long time, as usual, as I tried desperately to fall asleep. Eventually I dozed off and found myself, as though fully awake, inside a musty old garage. My dreams were always very vivid and detailed, and even included sounds and smells. The garage was filled with all kinds of dirty, dusty junk. Objects were hanging from the ceiling, tools and boxes were piled against the walls and heavy equipment was on the floor in the small, jammed room. Everywhere was dust and long, stringy cobwebs, just like in a horror movie. Next to the big garage door was a regular door, the upper half consisting of a multi-paned glass window. As I recall I was locked in this garage and couldn't find a way out, and I was terrified. Suddenly I saw a person, someone unrecognizable to me, walking by outside. I started yelling and screaming as I banged on the door, trying to get this person's attention. Finally I put my hand through one of the glass panes as I screamed, "Heeeeelp!" In reality I had punched through one of the real panes of glass, in the real window above the sofa bed. I remember my dad barging into the room, very alarmed, and holding me until I stopped screaming. There was blood on my palm and the sheets from putting my hand through the window. That terrifying dream had crossed the line from imagination into reality, and I still bear an inch-long scar on my hand today.

The other extremely frightening dreams were from what I now refer to as the "Spectator Series." These were infrequent, but particularly realistic. Usually the dream would be very simple. I would think I was awake, lying in bed with my eyes open, and there would be a blurred figure standing right next to my bed. The figure wouldn't be doing anything, it would just be standing there watching me. For some reason I was especially terrified of this "person," and would wake up screaming my head off. Occasionally the Spectator dreams were more complex. One time I had a dream where I was being chased through an old house with dark, creepy hallways going from room to small room. The doors to these rooms were always closed, so I had to stop each time to struggle with them as the phantom came closer. I was screaming "heeellp, heeellp!" the entire time as I ran, desperately trying to escape. In this dream, unlike all the others, at one point I stopped and turned toward the apparition. "Who are you? What do you want?!" I cried. In a cold, stony voice it replied, "You know who I am. You have always known. I am the Spectator. I am for *you*."

When I lived in Hawaii I continued to have vivid dreams but I don't recall having "scream dreams." Even though there was pressure from swimming and schoolwork I didn't feel the kind of stress that I experienced living at home in Madison. For one, swimming under Steve with the Punahou team was much less intense, both in the way he coached and in the way we were able to talk with each other, as we worked on my fears and anxieties. "Don't be afraid!" he continued to say. Steve was a great mentor and really helped me develop a better attitude about myself and how to deal with the stress of competition. Another big factor was that home life in Hawaii was much more relaxed and comfortable, as the family dynamic was totally different with everyone getting along and having fun. The relatively stress-free environment certainly played a large role in my overall calmness, although I did still suffer from periods of depression, hypomania and, occasionally, mania, due to my untreated bipolar disorder.

I returned from Hawaii at the end of the summer in 1983, just before my senior year in high school. The trip was planned so that I would compete with the Punahou Swim Team at Nationals and then fly back to Madison with my Badger Dolphin teammates. My performance at the meet was adequate, but more so I remember the crazy party afterwards, and the horrific post-party hangover. That was my homecoming after the eight wonderful, successful months I spent living in Hawaii. I was hungover, sick, and bleeding inside from lack of self-respect. *Why, I thought again in anguish, can't I control my drinking?*

Decisions

During my senior year my mom's and my relationship improved dramatically. I'm not sure if it was because of the time I had spent away or because we both had matured. We still had the occasional argument but by and large we related to each other more like friends and got along well. I still had some problems with depression and mania but I didn't talk about these. I dealt with them like I always did: by burying myself in my training and pounding the crap out of myself to try to keep "centered." This was easy to do (pounding the crap out of myself) during my senior year because I was by then training for the Olympic Trials, which were to be held in June of 1984.

It's a big deal to qualify for the Olympic Trials. The time standards that one has to make are very difficult, even harder than those needed to qualify for Nationals. Only one other young woman on my team – my friend Ann – and I made the Trials, so we had the same training schedule. The rest of the team was focusing on a later "final meet" of the season and was at a different stage of training for much of the time. Ann and I would swim with the team in the mornings, then would be coached separately in the afternoons. Since we swam different events (she was a freestyler and I a breaststroker) we didn't train together in the same lane. I was often by myself with my coach, Steve Roush.

Steve was a great coach but he was tough. His workouts were especially hard, and he expected a lot from me and the other athletes he trained. In the afternoons and on some mornings he would coach me by myself, which added to the pressure. There was no joking around with teammates between sets, no camaraderie and no way to "slack off" because he was always watching me. I was getting better about my shyness but I still felt nervous being "watched," especially so intently. This made me uncomfortable, but as usual I was able to bury this emotion by focusing on the work and putting everything I had into it.

Steve was good at pushing me to my absolute limit, and then getting me to do a little more. Often I would think we were at the end of a grueling workout and then he would give me an additional challenge: "Swim a two hundred-yard time trial and make X time, and I'll take you to Dairy Queen for a banana split after practice." Sometimes I was so exhausted I would start to cry when he would say this, but I never had the opportunity to say "no," of course, and would never even think of it. You didn't question the coach; you just did what he said. I both dreaded and enjoyed these extra swims, as much as they hurt. I almost always earned the banana split or whatever the prize happened to be at the time. The real treat, though, was simply being rewarded by my coach, who I respected tremendously, for a job well done.

Throughout my senior year my dad was on sabbatical in Germany and my mom carried the burden of supporting me and my swimming. It was always stressful at our house. Mom worked many hours in a demanding job as Art Director and Advertising Manager for a growing sports medicine company. There were always tight deadlines for the various magazine and catalog advertisements, packaging designs, publications and so forth. Mom walked a tightrope of stress most of the time, and that was the atmosphere at our house. Between that and the intensity of my own training I was always exhausted, both mentally and physically. I loved the swimming and thrived under Steve's training program. My times during the winter were improving and I was feeling confident as the Olympic Trials approached. But the strain at home was often very taxing. Occasionally my mom would come home so "wrapped" and worn out from the demands of her job that she would be "unable to cope," as she would say. Sometimes I told her to lie on the living room floor and I would give her a massage to try to ease her tension. She helped me in the same way, listening when I needed to talk (I was getting better at that) and helping with rides home from practice when I was literally too fatigued to walk, let alone ride my bike home.

My mom had become my hero. Even though I secretly called her a "bitch" (as she did me, jokingly and openly), I had enormous respect for her. She worked harder than anyone I knew and mostly managed to hold everything together. She worked insane hours at her job and still managed to cook large dinners for us – usually creative and delicious casseroles that she made early in the morning so we could heat them up later. She kept a neat and tidy household. Granted Mike and I had chores, but Mom did a lot of the house and yard work just because she was "like that." The house was small and nicely decorated with artwork, plants, flowers and an assortment of artsy bric-a-brac. Everywhere one looked it was beautiful. The yard was glorious too, with a brimming vegetable garden and small, colorful flower beds surrounding the house and garage. Mom liked things to be "just so" and kept herself busy, always doing something whether it be job-related, house or yard-related. One Christmas I gave her a long, narrow, rectangular plexiglass paperweight. I was proud and happy when she opened the gift. Imprinted in bright orange were the words, "Wonder Woman Works Here." She placed it on the windowsill above the kitchen sink, where it stayed for many years.

I was mostly happy during my senior year. My bipolar disorder was largely under control, I believe because of the excessive training, under which I thrived. I was swimming well and fast, and won nearly every race I swam, which really bolstered my confidence and overall self-esteem. We had won our high school State Championships for the fourth year in a row and our team was ranked number one in the "mythical" National Championships. I was a four-year State Champion and All-American in multiple events, and was being heavily recruited by many top universities around the country. I even received a recruiting letter from Harvard, which, much to my mother's horror, I didn't even look at twice but rather unceremoniously tossed in the trash. They didn't have a top-notch swim program so *of course* I wasn't interested. By and large I had my choice of where I wanted to go to college and at most places I would receive a full scholarship for swimming.

We had the usual gangbuster of a party after the State Championship meet. During the fall high school swim season I had been to quite a few parties and had done my share of drinking. I was even more concerned about how my drinking was escalating because I now had very few self-imposed "rules" and I often broke the few I had. I had basically given up on following the rules during the first half of my senior year, because I knew that if there was a party or an opportunity I would go and drink. Because I was swimming so well I rationalized that "drinking on Friday and Saturday nights isn't hurting my swimming" so I continued with my pattern of extreme bingeing. I now often drank during the week as well, regardless of whether I had morning practice. If I had a date or another opportunity to go out I would take it, and I would drink.

Alcohol had taken on an even more important role in my life and was now influencing how I made major decisions. I had narrowed my choice of universities that I wanted to attend down to a handful. I was looking for a large school with an excellent swim program and facilities and an outstanding academic reputation. I was seriously considering The University of California-Berkeley, The University of Minnesota, the University of Michigan-Ann Arbor and Northwestern University. One school that was not on my list was the University of Wisconsin. I felt bad about this because I felt that I was being disloyal. The coaches at the UW were the head coaches of our club team and had had an enormous role in my progression and success as a swimmer for many years. I was heavily recruited by them too, to attend the University of Wisconsin, but I flat out said no, that I wasn't at all interested. I was ashamed and felt guilty that I couldn't tell our head coach, Jack, why. My main reason was that I wanted to try, yet again, a "geographical cure." I reasoned that by getting away from Madison and the partying mentality that maybe I would have a chance at controlling my drinking. I knew that if I stayed in Madison my drinking would become even more out of control, and that worried me tremendously.

Ironically, at the same time I was only looking at universities that *had* a drinking atmosphere, and rejected those that didn't. For example I loved Northwestern. I loved the campus, the atmosphere, the coach, and the new pool facility that was almost complete and being built right on the shore of Lake Michigan. I loved that it was close to Chicago and also close to Madison, so it would be easy to come home to visit. I had a great recruiting trip there and really liked the team as well. But then I found out that Northwestern was a dry campus in a dry county. Sure, there were parties at the frat houses, but by and large it was a hassle to get alcohol and partying was not high on the list of the team's priorities, or so it seemed to me. So I nixed Northwestern, with its excellent reputation and all the plusses of going there, because of alcohol, or the lack thereof.

When I was eighteen I had a fake ID that claimed I was twenty-one and I must have looked the part because I never had a problem buying alcohol. During some of my recruiting trips I purchased the alcohol so that my hosts (who were usually freshman and therefore underage) and I could drink. After visiting the other three universities on my list I finally decided to attend the University of Michigan in Ann Arbor. At the time it didn't have a new swimming facility and the team was in the process of "rebuilding," but I liked the people I met from the team and was overall very impressed with the campus and the school in general. I liked the coach, Pete, a lot too, and felt that the school and swim program were a good fit. Plus there was alcohol aplenty and the team seemed to like to party. I was mired in contradiction with myself because on the one hand I desperately wanted to control my drinking. On the other hand I didn't know how I could live, how I could be social and have *fun*, without it.

So I decided to compromise: I would try someplace new and make a vow to myself to learn to control my drinking. If I couldn't control it, I vowed (again), then I would have to figure out a way to quit.

Olympic Trials

My mom had always been supportive of me and my swimming. She came to meets whenever she could and never missed the big ones, like Nationals, when they were close by. Fortunately, at the time the most modern arena for swim competition was in Indianapolis, and that's where Nationals and the Olympic Trials were held in 1984. Because this was fairly close to Madison – just a five hour drive – my mom was able to afford to attend both meets.

There was a big buildup to the Olympic Trials. Swimming in Madison was a popular sport and always received a lot of press coverage. Since Ann and I were already "stars" in the Madison sports world we had several nice write-ups and photos in the newspaper as the event approached. Both of us were long shots to make the team but Ann had a better chance, being higher ranked in the country than I.

I had been even more disciplined about my training and daily regimen leading up to the Trials during the second half of my senior year in high school. For over four months (that was the current self-imposed rule) I managed to not drink a drop of alcohol, and for this I was very proud and happy. I thought that maybe this meant that I *could* control my drinking. I had done it, so therefore I had proved it. Hadn't I?

I also had been strict about my sleep schedule and my diet. By necessity

I still had to eat enormous quantities of food but I was trying to change how I felt about eating and therefore be less compulsive about it. I tried not to think of food as a "pleasure" or a "competition" but rather as "fuel" to enable me to train hard to reach my goals. I was careful about what I ate and made sure that most everything was healthy. Even the huge ice cream shakes I made every night had raw eggs and vitamin powder blended in. It was obvious to me that I had a growing problem with how I viewed eating and so was trying to change my attitude toward it to one of planned indifference, except for its usefulness as fuel. Like my very early thoughts about alcohol I felt that my eating habits had the *potential* to turn into a serious problem later. Again I thought to myself, "if this becomes a problem someday then I'll do something about it and change my behavior."

As we began our taper, the "fun" stage of training where the workload is greatly reduced and the focus is on speed and rest, I was feeling very good about my overall condition. I had trained extraordinarily well for a long time, had really put in the work, and was confident about my preparation. I was lean, mean and the most fit I had ever been. I looked fantastic and was pleased with my physical appearance. My sleeping had even improved with my strict schedule, and I was doing a better job of meditating and working on controlling my anxiety with relaxation techniques. I was swimming fast and felt great in the water. All of these things together gave me a sense of calm and readiness – I was nervous, but confident at the same time. I felt ready to go.

It was the middle of June, 1984, a month before the Olympics. Just walking into the natatorium in Indianapolis one could feel the excitement. The building was new and state of the art, the largest and most modern indoor swim competition facility in the country. One entered the facility and walked up a flight of stairs to a wide hallway that bordered one side of the building. It had glass observation windows along the pool side, so one could observe the action by looking down at the pools below. The air had that familiar smell that I had grown to love, and which always started the butterflies in my stomach and a tingling in my body that originated from deep within me. It was fresh and clean, with an ever so slight tinge of chlorine and that unmistakable "new building" smell, slightly plastic, like a new car.

Down below and surrounded by beautiful new, clean tile were three pools: at the far end of the natatorium was the large diving well with the springboards and ten-meter platform. This pool was twenty-five yards wide and had lane lines put in so it could be used for warming up before or cooling down after a race. A wide walkway next to the diving well separated it from the main competition pool. Here were the starting blocks and the four chairs set up behind each lane, for the backup timers and lane officials. The competition pool itself had eight lanes and was fifty meters long by twenty-five yards wide. The pool had a reputation for being "fast" because it was deep and had wide lanes, which minimized turbulence and underwater currents. At the far end of the building was a glass wall that separated the main pools from yet another six-lane pool. This pool was used for warming up or cooling down during the competition, when the other pool(s) were in use. Along the entire length of the building on both sides, next to the diving well and competition pool, was a huge grandstand that could seat over six thousand people. On one side, under the grandstand, were the spotless locker rooms and control room offices.

The entire facility had been decked out with USA and Olympic banners, ribbons and other colorful decorations. Everywhere one looked was a sea of red, white and blue. There was track laid along one side of the pool for the moving television camera, as the events were going to be broadcast. Additional lighting had been installed for the cameras so the place was especially bright which added to the festival-like ambience. On the other side of the pool a long strip of carpet was laid. This was where the athletes would walk as they paraded out to their lanes at the start of each final race. Only athletes, coaches and officials were allowed on the pool deck, but everywhere else people were milling about – athletes, friends, coaches and parents. Everywhere the atmosphere was electric with excitement and anticipation.

In the locker rooms and in the pool I was rubbing shoulders with the best swimmers in the world and I was exuberant. It was such an honor just to be there as a competitor. I would look around me and see people like Tracy Caulkins (the Michael Phelps of her day), and Jeanne Childs – both childhood heroes of mine – and upcoming multiple Olympian Dara Torres practicing in the same lane with me or changing next to me in the locker room. I was awestruck in their presence but at the same time thought, "Hey – I'm here too. I'm *somebody* too."

When it came my day to race I was extremely nervous, but I kept thinking about Steve in Hawaii: "Don't be afraid, Christi. *Don't be afraid!*" I was to swim the two-hundred meter breaststroke, which was the only event in which I had qualified. There were five heats of eight athletes who were competing, forty swimmers total who had qualified to race in the event. In those days the format for the Trials was that the preliminary heats would swim in the morning and then the best eight would swim that same evening, in the Finals. Of the top eight that swam at night, two would make the Olympic Team.

I felt great in the morning warm-up and knew I was going to have a good swim. I could just feel it. "Don't be afraid," I kept telling myself, "Don't be afraid." I swam in heat number two of five and won the heat easily, breaking my best time by almost two seconds and now standing in first place. My coaches and I were ecstatic, but knew that the next three heats were coming up and those had the fastest swimmers. We watched the results nervously as the other heats swam. Slowly I was being bumped down in the standings, second, third, fourth. . . Then the last heat swam and. . . wow! I couldn't believe it at first. My coach Steve jumped and cheered, clenching his fist, "Yeah!!" I had made it into the Finals, in spot number eight. I was beyond happy – I was in shock!

After the prelims I remember how proud I felt as we ate lunch in a nearby restaurant. I had recently signed a National Letter of Intent to attend the University of Michigan on a full swimming scholarship. My soon-to-be new coach, Pete Lindsay, just happened to be in the same restaurant having lunch and I was thrilled when he came over to congratulate me and shake my hand. I felt like a new person somehow – suddenly no longer just that nice kid from Wisconsin. Suddenly I was an Olympic Trials Finalist, and I truly was a member of the swimming elite.

That evening we arrived at the pool early so I could warm up and have plenty of time to prepare, both mentally and physically. The atmosphere in the building was intensely energetic – you could feel the electricity in the air. I was very nervous but also excited at the same time. *"Don't be afraid. . ."* I repeated over and over, trying to quell the butterflies in my stomach. The stands were filled to capacity and everywhere one looked were decorations, flowers and banners, uniformed officials, athletes and coaches. Behind the starting blocks were the two platforms, the big boxes that the first and second place swimmers would stand on when they received their awards and were officially named to the Olympic Team.

My mom was in the stands and I sought her out. I was wearing the new set of team warm-ups that my coach had given me that afternoon, as a gift for working so hard all year and making the Finals. I felt so special! I waved at Mom and she stood up and waved back, a big smile on her face. Soon the competition would begin, and I started to get ready.

At competitions of that level and importance there is always a secondary pool in which to practice and warm up, either before or after an event or on an off day. Swimmers spend a lot of time stretching, "shaking out" their arms and legs and warming up in the pool. It's important to stay loose and relaxed, and this was always a challenge for me because I was naturally tense. I had to work very hard and play mind games with myself in order to keep the anxiety at bay and stay loose. As I swam in the warm-up pool I thought about taking my race out "long and strong," and bringing it home with everything I had left. I visualized every part of the race, from my perfect, fast start where I would cut neatly through the water and then have a strong glide before my breakout, to my powerful kick and smooth, undulating stroke, to my crisp, perfect turns and strong finishing leg. I pictured myself being fearless and calm before the huge crowd, drawing strength and power from their collective energy. My goal was not to make the Team – I knew I was too far off time-wise for that. My goal was to make my best time and to not place last in the heat. I wanted to place seventh or better.

Finally it was time to go to the Ready Room. The Ready Room is where the athletes all gather for the final ten minutes or so before the race, to make sure everyone is present and ready to start on time. I exited the warm-up pool, toweled off and adjusted my skin-tight red suit. I felt good as I slipped into my new, red and white warm-up suit, our team colors. All the athletes would be wearing their warm-ups, to look sharp for the parade down the side of the pool. I took a deep breath and entered the glass-walled room located at the far side of the competition pool. Inside the atmosphere was relaxed, but one could feel the nervous tension. My whole body tingled as I walked through the door. There in the chairs were the other swimmers, some of them heroes of mine from when I was young, some of them the up and coming stars of the day: Tracy Caulkins, the most decorated US female swimmer ever, Jeanne Childs, Susan Rapp, Kim Rodenbaugh. . . The others took a brief glance at me but then went back to their own thoughts and preparations. Some of the athletes chatted quietly, trying to dispel their nerves. I took an empty chair and sat down, my towel around my shoulders. I felt good and loose. Calm, but consciously working to control the butterflies in my gut. "You can do it!" I said to myself. "Don't be afraid!"

After what seemed an eternity an official came to get us, to lead us along the side of the pool to the starting area. The music started to play over the PA system. It was the theme song from the hit movie "Chariots of Fire," a song I will never forget. We walked in a line the entire length of the competition pool in the order of our lane assignments, so I was last because I was in lane eight. Slowly we marched down the carpeted walkway as the crowd cheered and the music boomed. I felt light and loose, tingling all over with an excited nervousness. We arrived at our designated lanes and started to undress. The crowd quieted and then cheered for each athlete as she was introduced and her various accomplishments listed. It took a long time to introduce Tracy, who had more American and World records than any swimmer, ever. When they got to me I was thrilled just that the announcer pronounced my name correctly! As I stepped forward to wave to the cheering crowd the announcer gave my short introduction, "And finally, in lane number eight, making her first appearance in a National Final, from the Badger Dolphin Swim Team, Christi Vedejs!" The crowd cheered and I even heard my coaches screaming for me. I bent down to my knees to splash water on myself as the others did the same. Then to my feet and some final stretching and shaking out of arms and legs as we waited for the Starter to call us to the blocks.

"Swimmers up," he said.

The crowd fell silent as we stepped up on the cool, wet starting platforms. It was so quiet I could hear my heart pounding.

"Swimmers. . . Take your mark."

"Beeep!!" went the starting horn.

We all exploded off the blocks and I remember hearing the crowd roar before I even hit the water. I had a great start and felt good in my first few strokes, which gave me confidence. As we raced down the pool I could see the other swimmers out of the corner of my eye. I stroked long and strong, just like our plan. The noise from the crowd was deafening as my head came up for every breath. I made a perfect turn and took a slight glance to see where the other swimmers were. The best were slightly ahead as I expected, but I was right next to the swimmer in lane seven. I had to beat her! I didn't want to finish last! The third length was my time to pick up the pace and I did, though I was starting to feel the beginnings of fatigue. My last turn was also good and I pushed off, pulling strong underwater and taking advantage of the long glide to rest my legs for a split second. I broke out for the home stretch and could hear the crowd roaring. My arms and legs were burning as I gasped for air, giving it everything I had and trying harder than I had ever tried. "Come on," I told myself, "Don't die! Just a little more to go! You can do it!" I stroked to the wall and touched, every cell in my body screaming with pain.

"Alright Christi!!" I heard my coaches bellowing above the thunderous crowd. "Way to go!!"

I turned and looked at the scoreboard and smiled. I had made my best time and there was a "7" next to my name. I hadn't finished last! My heart was racing as I shook my neighbor's hand and watched the swimmers in the middle lanes hugging and congratulating each other. Two of them had made the Olympic Team, but in my mind I had also "made it." I had just competed with the best in the world in the U.S. Olympic Trials Finals. I was overjoyed and filled with what can only be described as true, pure love. It was the best feeling, the greatest high. I was in ecstasy.

Shortly after the race I was cooling down in the diving well after having been congratulated by my coaches. My mom was smiling broadly in the crowd and pumped her fist when our eyes met. "Yaaaaaaay, Christi!" she shouted. I put my head down and pushed off from the wall, beaming. I was so happy.

~~~

Two weeks later I was relaxing in the sun in a lounge chair at our neighborhood swim club, on the far side of the pool. Suddenly a tall, familiar figure emerged from the men's changing room and strode purposefully around it and toward me. It was my dad, just back from his sabbatical in Germany. He had missed the Trials and had come to the pool to hug and congratulate me. I was disappointed that he hadn't been at the meet but thrilled that he had come to see me at the pool. He told me that his graduate students had plastered his office door with newspaper articles about me. That made me laugh but inside I was deeply, joyfully proud. As always I needed my dad's approval and validation, and it made me indescribably happy that he came to see me.

A month after the Olympic Trials I was in Florida to compete at the US Long Course National Championships. I hadn't wanted to go but my coach, Steve, had urged me to compete, and you don't argue with the coach.

"The Olympians won't be there," he had said. "You have a good chance to place well, maybe even in the top three."

That didn't change my opinion or make me want to go. I was still *so tired* from such a long season, physically but especially mentally. Also I was feeling a "letdown" after the extreme high of my experience at the Olympic Trials. I was exhausted and depressed, but I didn't tell anyone. My thoughts were all over the map about swimming. On the one hand, I had just reached an incredible goal and had had the most amazing experience yet of my life. On the other, I was so completely burnt out. I was looking at four years of school and intense competition at the University of Michigan on a full scholarship. There was pressure in that, as I knew a lot was expected of me. But I was so, so tired. How would I ever be able to do it, I worried? I knew I needed a longer break but wasn't going to get one. "Don't be afraid, Christi," I heard Steve from Hawaii's voice in my head. But I *was* afraid although I never told anybody. I honestly, truly didn't think I could start another season. *I was so tired.*

Michigan

I had a hole in my Self. It was shortly after the National Championships at the end of August in 1984, and I was getting ready to head off to school in Ann Arbor. My mom bought me a large, navy blue, cedar-lined trunk for my clothes and precious belongings, and I packed it tightly and carefully, making the most of the space. We loaded her small car, a brown Plymouth Horizon, with the heavy trunk, a few suitcases and miscellaneous odds and ends for my dormitory room. My ten-speed bike was strapped on a rack attached to the car's rear hatch. The little Horizon was packed to the hilt and sagged a bit at the back end. We stooped as we climbed inside, coffee mugs in hand, with Mom in the driver's seat. She would drive the first leg, through Chicago, and I would drive the second. The trip would take about seven hours.

We were both silent as Mom backed carefully out of the driveway of my childhood home, mired in our own thoughts. My mom was taking her only daughter to college, and thinking whatever moms think as they take their children to begin their journeys to true adulthood. Meanwhile her only daughter was stuck in the restless quagmire of her own anxious thoughts, quiet and brooding, gazing at the house and beautiful gardens as we slowly pulled away.

I remember feeling nervous, those familiar feelings of fear and self-doubt creeping in. What would my roommate be like? Would she like me? Would the team like me? What about the other "kids" in the dorm? I had that same sense of "weirdness," of heading off to a new place and worrying – again – about being an outsider. In one respect I was looking forward to the adventure of it, and to all the new experiences I would encounter. I was also glad to be leaving home, to be getting away from my mom and our still sometimes strained relationship. But as usual I was fearful of what lay ahead.

Partly I feared beginning a new phase of my life, going away to a new school, a new coach, new team, and new people. But I was also worried about what was going on inside my head. I had had only two weeks off from training after Nationals, the meet following the Olympic Trials that I had not wanted to attend, and I was still so tired, both physically and mentally. I had performed adequately at the meet but not great. It was a very "so-so" experience after the Trials and I felt very "so-so" afterwards. I decided that I was not going to drink for a while, maybe even a long while, and that I was going to make a new start when I got to Ann Arbor. I went for long jogs and bike rides to keep myself "steady" and "in check," and planned to continue those before my new team started up with training, which I thought would be during the second week of school. I made a plan to stay sober, to concentrate on my schoolwork and to try to get my head back into swimming.

Inside my head raced restless, confusing thoughts. There were those same old nagging, creeping, sucking feelings of emptiness and longing that came from deep within me, along with a profound sense of sadness – the "hole" in my Self, as I called it. I chalked it up to being tired and burnt out from a relentless year of training with few breaks, and to the letdown that I was feeling after the summer competitions. At least that's what I told myself at the time. And I think part of it was true – certainly the overall tiredness and burnout. It scared me because I didn't know if my burnout would go away or get better, and I didn't know how to "fix" it. In retrospect I believe I was entangled in the "down" phase of my bipolar disorder. Simply put, I was depressed, and I was very apprehensive about heading off to school in this psychological condition.

But the "hole" – those awful feelings of emptiness and longing, that intense *need*, that *hunger* that I felt so deeply. These were not new emotions. I had had them for a long time. These were feelings that I had violently tried to suppress by smothering them with swimming and/or alcohol because they were so uncomfortable. But now, as I sat in the car pondering my new life, I knew that I had to face them and figure out from where they came. I knew that somehow, some way, I had to get to the bottom of this "emptiness problem," as I called it, in order to stay sober and – if it was at all possible – to be happy. But I was terrified of these emotions and I think I feared discovery as much as I feared leaving them buried. Left alone, I knew I would continue to occasionally feel them, when they would surreptitiously emerge during a period of sobriety, a break from training when I wouldn't be beating on myself, or when I let my guard down. But discovery. . . what? What awaited me at the end of this long, dark hallway called *emptiness*? Was there illumination and freedom at the end? What if there was nothing, no hope? Darkness, despair, loneliness and longing. Scary emotions, I mused introspectively as we drove, I with my knees up and my bare feet on the dash as my mom silently pushed our little car along the long, flat freeway toward Ann Arbor. Scary.

I can't say that I was in the best of spirits when we arrived, but I did a good job – I thought – of faking it and hiding my lingering depression. My mom and I lugged all my belongings up many flights of stairs to the third floor of the dorm, where I would live during my first year at the University of Michigan. As usual, Mom was outgoing and smiled at everyone we passed, as other parents helped their "grown-up" children move into their rooms. I forced myself to smile and be outgoing too. A sea of cars lined the outside of the building, their trunks and doors open with a steady stream of people going in and out, carting boxes, suitcases, rolled up carpets, lamps, chairs, linens, wooden posts and piles of lumber to build bunk beds, and so forth. There was a certain order to the chaos, but all the activity made me nervous.

I was so uncomfortable socially – the thought of running into new people and having to greet them, and maybe even converse with them, was frightening.

The other things I worried about were the comments about my appearance and the misidentification that I knew I would endure at first (before everyone knew me) that I was a male. I dreaded the inevitable "er. . . you're in the wrong bathroom." Or, "Excuse me, but the men's room is downstairs on the men's floor." The worst comments, the ones I hated the most, would go something like this: "Are you supposed to be in here? What are you?" or "You should be down in the men's room. Oh – I'm sorry. You're a woman. . . aren't you?"

I survived my first trip to the bathroom, which also had shower stalls, without incident and I was relieved. Mom and I moved my relatively few belongings into my room and met my roommate, Sue Ellen, who was sitting on a bed talking with a large young man, probably a football player, who sat on the other bed, mine. From that moment I knew we were going to have problems. Sue Ellen was an incoming freshman diver on the UM team and was a friendly, clearly social, outgoing type of person. I knew she would make lots of friends and that they would probably visit our room often. Since I was the quiet, shy type who needed my own space, and especially needed quiet so I could sleep, I moved into my new room with a sense of trepidation. How on Earth is this going to work, I thought grimly?

Eventually we were finished unpacking and my side of the room was more or less "set up." The football player had left and my bed was now tightly sheeted and blanketed. The closet was full, my nice clothes neatly hanging and the empty suitcases standing next to a few pairs of shoes on the floor. My clothes were stacked in an orderly fashion in the "new" dresser. Boxes were flattened and gone, piled in the back of the Horizon awaiting recycling. A new typewriter, a gift from my dad and stepmom, stood on the floor next to the desk. On my desk were a dictionary and a few other small items. I had planned to purchase school supplies when I bought my books after I registered for classes, so I had only several pens and a couple of yellow legal pads for making lists. Overall my side of the room was tidy and sparse, organized with a militaristic neatness.

Sue Ellen's side looked like what I imagined must have been her bedroom at home, only more crowded because she had only half a room. She had the same bed, desk and dresser as I but the look was like night and day. Everywhere were *things*: hair care products and accessories, makeup and a large, oval mirror on the wall, dishes and various cooking utensils, a popcorn maker, a small boom box with a pile of cassette tapes, and a wooden rack of pegs attached to the wall on which hung at least twenty swim suits. There were many pairs of shoes on the floor near the closet, colorful, comfortable pillows on the bed and a couple of stuffed animals, framed photos on her desk, which was neat but cluttered, and a myriad of scattered homey items. Even a wicker chair with a padded footstool sat in the corner by the crowded closet. Sue Ellen was from Grand Rapids, less than a two-hour drive away, so as time went on her side of the room acquired even more items of significant importance to her. Mine remained relatively spare, although my desk did fill up and become home to books, folders and notebooks.

Sue Ellen and I were polar opposites in our personalities. She was outgoing and personable, like my mom, and wanted to get to know everyone on the floor immediately. She always fixed her hair and makeup before leaving the room, and even looked good in sweats or night clothes, which were "cute" and feminine-looking. I was shy and quiet, and it took me much longer to make acquaintances and friends. I rebelled against wearing makeup and almost never did, except when going on dates, or occasionally, to parties. My short, straight, fine, chlorine-bleached swimmer's hair could only be styled one way – flat. I wore "gender neutral" clothes as always since my first and foremost concern was comfort. I was a swimmer after all, and really didn't care too much about how I looked. This didn't help with the bathroom situation. As usual I was muscular and fit, and very masculine looking. My short hair and boyish clothes didn't do me any favors as far as my gender identity was concerned. Of course I felt like a woman inside but I still was often called "sir," "dyke," "fag," "lesbo" and other names when out and about in town or on campus, which hurt me very much. I realize it sounds implausible at that age, but this even occurred in my own dorm, on my own floor, in our bathroom on occasion throughout the year, although those remarks were always of the "excuse me but you're in the wrong bathroom" variety.

Sue Ellen and I tried to get along but we had problems from the start. She was often on the phone, which drove me crazy because I was generally studying whenever I was in the room. She listened to music when she studied, which I couldn't understand at all, being one who needed quiet in order to concentrate. I also needed quiet to sleep, and this was difficult in the dorm with so much activity going on at all hours of day or night. Also, Sue Ellen often had visitors or phone calls late at night, and this disrupted what little sleep I managed to get. Of course she was one of those people who could sleep any time, anywhere in any conditions, and that bothered me too. She was a diver and they also had morning practice, so fortunately she liked to get to bed early on most nights. But the late night disruptions were a real problem for me, and so I got almost no sleep when I lived in the dorm. Sue Ellen liked to look good before heading out, be it for classes or for morning practice. I could never understand why someone would mess with her hair before diving into a pool, but that was how she was. She also had a penchant for covering her body with baby powder, so our room always had a slight tinge of that sickly sweet odor and everything was covered with a thin film of talc dust.

But living in the dorm, painful as it was in certain respects, wasn't all bad. I did meet interesting and fun people and made some good friends. As usual I gravitated toward those who drank, and we had great parties and plenty of raucous, good times. When I first arrived in Ann Arbor I had been very serious about my vow to not drink. However that vow was soon broken, and I began to drink again after only three weeks of sobriety, two of which were while I was still in Madison.

My fears about having friends and being accepted were alleviated quickly once I met the other swimmers and we began to hang out together. We were not officially "training" yet, but a group of us were lifting weights, running, biking and swimming some on our own. I generally avoided the pool as I was still struggling with burnout and was mentally not yet ready to face water. But I needed to blow off my excess energy in some way since the manic side of my bipolar disorder was beginning to feel uncomfortable. So I went on long, introspective bike rides by myself out in the country. I loved feeling the wind as I raced through the beautiful landscape, along green fields of alfalfa and golden fields of corn, soybeans and hay, through woodsy areas and up and down steep hills. It was so exciting for me to explore the area, and a great way to relieve my "nuclear energy," as I called it, and the stress of being in a new place with so many new people.

One benefit of being on a swim team is that one has instant friends. When I first arrived on campus some of the older members of the team, some of whom I had partied with on my recruiting trip, came to greet me. We would eat together in the dorm as we got to know each other and, of course, there were parties to go to. My drinking behavior hadn't changed. Why would it have? There was nothing that had happened in that short interim period of sobriety that would have caused my drinking patterns to be any different. It is often said, "if nothing changes, then nothing will change." Once I broke my vow to not drink it was off to the races again. So nothing had changed and I still drank myself into happy drunkenness with my new friends. I suffered from terrible hangovers in the mornings and, most often, from guilt and remorse. I knew I was doing damage to my body, my precious fit body, and therefore I was doing damage to my self-image and self-respect. For this I punished myself by running stadium steps or going for hard bike rides. I would be desperate to pound out the poison streaming through my veins, the shame I felt in my heart, and the loathing I felt for myself in general. Why, oh why, I would think, does this always happen? Why can't I control myself? *Why do I not want to?!*

During my freshman year I was eager to "prove myself" in my schoolwork. I don't know why I felt it necessary to take on such a heavy academic load, but I signed up for seventeen credit hours my first semester at UM. All of the courses were considered "challenging," but the one that tormented me the most was Calculus. I had been a good student in math in high school and Calculus was the next logical step, plus it was a requirement for all kinds of majors and I hadn't yet chosen one. I felt that I should take it "just in case I need it" and get it out of the way. Big mistake. Not only was my instructor foreign and spoke English poorly, but Calculus just never made any sense to me. I studied it religiously every night for three to four hours, tucked away in a small, private cubicle in the Graduate Library (there was absolutely no hope of studying in my dorm room). For the first exam I studied three days straight and really felt prepared. When the exam landed on my desk I looked at the first problem and was completely baffled. I was very nervous for this exam and figured I was just tense, and that the tension would ease as I got into the "math headspace." I looked at the second problem. Then the third, fourth, fifth. . . Nothing was clicking – it was like trying to read ancient hieroglyphs. I became so flustered that my hands started to shake. The time was half up and I had yet to make a single scratch on the paper. Desperately I tried to solve an equation. "I can do this!" I told myself. *"Come on, just let go and do this!"* I moved on to the next equation and thought I got it right. Then my mind opened and I started madly working on the equations and scribbling on the paper as I anxiously watched the clock. Finally the time was up. I had solved – I thought – under half of the equations. I assumed that I had failed the exam and was devastated. It turned out that because the average was so low I got a C, but that still felt like a failure to me. My first exam at the University of Michigan and I got a C?! What was this?? I almost never scored below an A minus on anything! I was crushed, and even cried about it later at our team meeting as my teammates nodded their heads in solemn sympathy. From then on in Calculus I always scored C's on exams, regardless of how much I studied. For the final exam I didn't study at all – in fact I went out drinking the night before – and I still got a C, and ended up with a C in the course. That was the lowest grade I had ever received in my entire scholastic career and it bothered me for a long time. Could I ever learn to accept anything less than excellence? That course really kicked me down a notch when it came to my ego about my schoolwork.

But I still studied long and diligently for all my other classes, read countless books, wrote well-researched, studious papers and scored well on exams. I also did well in swim practice. Our coach, Pete Lindsay, was what I considered a "progressive" coach. His workouts were tough, but he did believe in recovery days and he was willing to talk about problems, be they swimming-related or otherwise.

Pete liked to play seventies rock, funk and soul music over the PA system during warm-up or other long, boring sets. He had a life-size poster of Tina Turner in his office and was always making wisecracks and joking around. I liked him. He told us that he was always available to talk if we needed anything. Sometimes I would go to his office to discuss an emotional problem and he would say (like Steve in Hawaii) "Don't be afraid." Regarding my depression, about which I tried to talk with him, he would usually respond with something like, "Are you getting 'the weepies' again? No 'weepies' allowed! Be tough!" I never spoke with him about my drinking, although I wanted to. I was too ashamed, and also afraid that by admitting how serious the problem was that I might lose my scholarship. I know now that this was an irrational fear but then, at the raw age of eighteen, I was very concerned about it.

In addition to our water and dry land training Pete also had us attend team meetings and other functions that were supposed to help foster a healthy attitude and cohesiveness. However this was not successful because the team my freshman year did not have a healthy attitude or cohesiveness. I liked my teammates well enough, but I would estimate that half the team just "wasn't into it," and didn't seem to care about training hard or winning. I was disappointed, and this didn't help my own attitude toward swimming or toward the team. I was still struggling with burnout and trying to get "back in the groove" of hard training, and to get excited about competition. Fortunately there was a handful of women on the team with whom I became very good friends, including the Assistant Coach, Sue. These women helped me to slowly, ever so slowly pull myself out of the "dumps" and get my head back in the place it needed to be in order to train and compete.

Sue was a former UM swimmer and NCAA champion, and quickly became my good friend and mentor. She was stylish and *cool*, with a fun and outgoing personality. Sue was always running, biking, lifting weights or doing some sort of exercise, thereby staying lean and fit. She became my idol of sorts as I respected her swimming accomplishments very much and just liked the way she was in general. I could always talk with Sue about my fears, anxieties and problems and she helped me a great deal, especially when it came to talking about my depression. Sue did know about my drinking and I believe she knew how serious it was. However she never said that I should quit or get help – I think, as such a close friend, that she knew she didn't have to say it. She knew that *I knew*, and I believe she knew that I was worried about my drinking problem as well.

During my freshman year all the self-imposed rules meant to control my drinking went out the window. I was constantly breaking them so I stopped making them. The only steadfast rule that I had was that I would quit drinking one month before our Big Ten Championship meet, and not drink between that and the NCAAs, the National Championship meet. Otherwise the field was wide open and I played it like a champ. It didn't matter if I was happy or sad, whether I had morning practice the next day or not, or an early class, an exam – anything. If there was an opportunity to drink I would take it. One point that I would like to note, however, is that I hadn't yet started to drink alone. As much as my drinking had increased, I was still drinking "socially" (albeit to drunken excess). This didn't mean that I denied the severity of my problem, however. I knew I was not a "social drinker" – I knew I was an alcoholic drinker. But despite that and my worries, I continued to drink and to drink more often as time went on. I had to "relieve the stress," after all, and plus it was fun, most of the time.

My friends on the team knew that I was a hard-core partier. I remember once we were being lectured about drinking during one of our team meetings. Pete was disgusted, he said, about the behavior of "certain members of the team." Apparently he had heard rumors that a few of the swimmers had been out partying and had gotten into some sort of trouble. He also said that he could smell the alcohol some mornings during practice. I was terrified that he was talking about me, and that I was about to be singled out in front of the team and punished. But then he said something to the effect of this: "I'm embarrassed to hear about this and you should be too. Our team needs to set a better example and live up to the high standards of the University of Michigan. What would people think, say, if they saw Christi staggering home some night from a bar? This is absolutely unacceptable. . ." I was mortified. Of course everyone knew that if *anyone* was going to be seen some night staggering home from a bar it would be me. The situation in the meeting that day was far too serious for anyone to stifle even a small giggle, but I'm sure my teammates, especially my friends, were cringing inside, as I was.

I dated several young men my freshman year. They were all drinkers and we had fun drinking together, but I would break off the relationships whenever they started to become serious. I was still convinced that any type of serious relationship would be detrimental to my swimming and swimming was always my first priority. I was no longer a virgin; I had lost my virginity the summer after my eighteenth birthday. It had been no big deal. Tim and I were good friends talking about sex one afternoon (while drinking, of course) and I mentioned that I wanted to lose my virginity to a friend, someone I trusted, and not just in a drunken spree some night with someone I barely knew. In a brainstorm I said, "Hey. . . do you wanna do it?" His eyes lit up as he said, "Sure, let's go!" My memory is that it was fun but no bombs went off. I was too drunk to have an orgasm but we had a good time anyway, laughing and joking as we held each other close, enjoying the warm sensation of skin against skin.

My swimming my freshman year was average in my opinion even though I won most every race I swam in my specialty events, the one-hundred and two-hundred yard breaststroke, and competed at the NCAA meet. My times didn't drop much, if any, and overall I felt that the season was rather lackluster. What sticks out in my memory the most is my struggle with depression and burnout, my escalating drinking, and the chest injury I wrote about earlier, *sternal costochondritis*, which was caused by overtraining. I also remember that there was a lot of discussion about weight, and that we often had our body fat measured. I never had a problem with my weight. I ate like a horse and was still very lean. But other members of the team were often singled out because they were overweight. The issue of weight seemed to always be in the forefront, whether it was discussed at team meetings, at meals in the dorm, or during those regular body fat percentage tests that we had every month.

This "fixation" bothered me because while there was much discussion about weight and eating control, nobody ever talked about eating disorders. Yet I was worried that I was developing one. I wasn't sure what it was exactly, but I knew that it wasn't healthy mentally to be always thinking and obsessing about food. I never told anyone about my concerns – who would believe me? Most people were jealous that I could eat whatever I wanted, in disgusting quantities, and still remain so thin. I still wasn't getting my period. Nobody ever asked if I was bulimic (I wasn't) or if I was developing any abnormal attitudes about food. Just like with my alcoholism, my excessive eating seemed to be looked upon as a badge of honor, something to be proud of: Christi can eat like a pig and still be thin. Christi can drink like a drunk and still be a great swimmer. These were the messages that I continued to receive.

Again I felt like I was living a double life. Outside appearances vs. inside realities. On the outside I was a very successful, high-functioning student and athlete with lots of friends and a positive, go-for-it attitude. But *also* on the outside, by this point in time, was evidence of the serious problems lurking below. My problems with depression and mania I mostly hid and kept to myself, except that I did talk about them some with my coach and my mom. Both essentially told me to "get over it" and that I needed to "be tough." But other things, like my obsession with eating and food and my excessive drinking, were very much out in the open. And *everyone overlooked them.* Nobody ever said to me, "Christi, do you think maybe you should try to control your drinking?" I grant that there was a partying mentality on the team and that others drank as well, but I was certainly one of the worst, if not *the* worst.

One incident I remember well is being at a party one night and being talked into calling Pete, our coach, to tell him about a grade I had received on an exam. In my drunken state I stupidly did this, much to my teammates' delight. The next morning we were sitting in the stands before practice and I said, "Hey, Pete, guess what! I got an A on my history exam!" To which he replied, "I know. You told me that when you called me last night, *or were you so drunk that you don't remember?!*" He said this angrily, and loudly enough that both the men's and women's teams *and* the diving coach, heard it. But he never said a word about it again, nor did anyone else except for a few of my teammates, who only expressed how bad they felt that I had been embarrassed like that in front of everyone.

I want to make it clear that I don't blame anyone but myself for my drinking problem. Nobody forced me to jump into River B, and nobody forced me to stay there. What I regret, and what hurts, is the denial that was certainly part of the equation when I asked for, and should have received, help. First, there was the denial in the school counselors' offices when I asked for help at my high schools in Madison and Honolulu. Both are excellent schools, and even in the Dark Ages of the 1980s those counselors should have been equipped to handle the problem of alcoholism. Next there was my disclosure to my mother about it when I was a junior and living in Hawaii. She cared, and she tried her best to talk me out of drinking, but ultimately nothing came of it. Why? Was she in denial about the severity of the problem, or was there truly nothing that she could do? My excessive drinking in both high school and college was apparent to everyone, as my nickname, "Christi Crash," indicates. Nobody ever expressed concern that my drinking was over the top, except for a friend or two in college and my friend Sue, our Assistant Coach. Even that dreadful night when I called Coach Pete (in what must have been a blackout) didn't result in any repercussions.

So as time went on my alcohol use continued to ramp up. The summer after my freshman year I went back home to Madison to train with my club team, the Badger Dolphins. We had crazy parties as usual and there were plenty of opportunities to drink. The first half of the season I was forced to take off due to my chest injury, and the second half I trained but I didn't take it very seriously. Again I tried in vain to control my drinking. By then I was certain I couldn't "just quit" and I was starting to think that maybe I never could quit. Alcohol was so wrapped up with everything I did and felt, with how I handled stress and painful emotions, with my ability to be social, with my ability to sleep (or pass out) some nights. It had become an integral part of my existence and I couldn't fathom living without it. But I knew it was damaging to my mind and my body and this worried me greatly. I often thought to myself, "what if I didn't drink at all? What if I was loose and relaxed and knew how to handle stress? Would I be that much better of a swimmer? Would I have placed higher at the Olympic Trials? Could I ever be good enough to win Nationals? What if I actually *could* have a social life without alcohol? *What if, what if?*"

I tried again to control the time periods when I would go without drinking and I generally made it to two or three weeks at a stretch. But then it just became too uncomfortable to *live*. My stress and anxiety levels were always high and I continued to have such an awful time with insomnia. I was much more edgy and tense during those short periods of sobriety. Even my training couldn't alleviate the feelings of constant tension, of being "too tightly wound." My dad used to say to me, "Why can't you just 'be'? Why do you make everything so difficult for yourself?" I didn't know how to "just be" – how to be comfortable in my own skin, how to relax. And I still felt that awful emptiness inside, that "hole." Even though I was surrounded by teammates and friends I felt lonely, and I could never get past the feeling that I was "weird."

Alcohol relieved all these feelings, at least temporarily, and this was the main reason why I kept going back to it. I hadn't yet learned how to deal with emotions; I simply hadn't given myself a chance while burying myself under my training, my schoolwork and my drinking. Swimming provided external "liquid relief" by enabling me to pound away my sense of fear and inadequacy. Alcohol gave liquid relief that accomplished the same thing, albeit internally. Both formed a protective cocoon around my inner self, keeping feelings in and the pain of situations and circumstances out. Both enabled me to avoid dealing with issues and to grow emotionally, thus blurring my sense of "Self." I was a glorious model of success on the outside but a ticking time bomb on the inside. Nobody knew how serious my problems were except me. It was a very lonely, and scary place to be.

At the beginning of my sophomore year at UM my teammates and I arrived on campus and discovered that we had no coach. Pete had resigned during the summer and the athletic department still had not found a replacement. We worried about who would take the reigns, and how we would fare in the Big Ten with such a small team. A number of the women on the team had quit, and we had a handful of new freshman that we didn't know. I wondered if it was going to be a really crappy year. How could we possibly have a good season, what with this largely untested skeleton crew and God-Knows-Who as a coach? Obviously nobody who was any good wanted to take the job, or it would have been filled by now. The only saving grace, I thought, was that we had an excellent diving team, the best in the country. Even if our swim program was horrible, at least we wouldn't place last in the Big Ten meet because our divers were that good.

But then, on the first day of classes, a new coach was officially named to lead the swim program. Jim Richardson had been the Women's Assistant Coach at the University of Iowa, and I already knew him because he had recruited me heavily when I was in high school to swim on their team.

Jim was charismatic, energetic, always smiling and had a positive outlook about everything. His southern roots left him with a comforting accent that we loved to mimic. He had a wife and a young, growing family that he was clearly devoted to. As we got to know him we realized that Jim was also devoted to building an excellent team and to developing UM women's athletics in general. He was a dynamo, a very driven man filled with high hopes, high expectations and an abundance of confidence.

From the moment I saw Jim I knew it was going to be a very different year. Secretly I was thrilled that we had a small team, and therefore the opportunity to build it. I loved that sort of challenge. We had eleven swimmers – ridiculous! We added several more later but honestly we were weak by the numbers, which Jim was always analyzing.

"By the numbers, ladies," he would announce most seriously, "we should get our fannies whipped. But we're gonna dig deeper! (then there would follow a long, inspirational speech) We're gonna *show 'em what it is*, aren't we ladies?! Let's hear it for the team!"

I liked Jim immediately, and as time went on I grew to love him personally and respect his coaching immensely.

Jim inspired confidence. He was bursting at the seams with energy nearly all the time. He was always on the move, going from the pool to a meeting, to home, to another meeting, to the pool and so on. Jim's workouts were unbelievably hard, but he was always "right there" with us, running up and down the deck and cheering us on. He gave tremendous motivational speeches, the likes of which I have not heard elsewhere. Jim loved to challenge us to do a grueling three hour workout on a Saturday morning and then "show 'em what we're made of" in the duel meet afterwards. It was painful and intimidating and I often dreaded it. But his methods worked, rewarding us with confidence and toughness as well as making us better swimmers. Jim coaxed us beyond our imagined limits, and our "half-squad" team worked like nobody's business. We became close as a unit and committed to each other and our goals. By the sheer force of our collective will and our determination to win we beat teams we shouldn't have, and ended up a respectable fifth at the Big Ten Championships. It was a wonderful year of growth for the team, as we built a solid foundation for the program: a winning mentality and high expectations for the new athletes coming in.

For me personally it was a frustrating year. I had worked harder than I ever had before (which even I hadn't thought possible) but my swimming had reached a plateau. Sure, I still won my races and was Big Ten Champion, but my times hadn't improved and overall I felt that I should have performed much better. I knew that I had needed more of a taper and more rest for the Big Ten Championships. But I also knew that I wouldn't give myself a chance to truly rest. I just couldn't. My problem had never been the lack of motivation to work. I loved challenging workouts and felt great about myself when I could clobber myself into next week. That had become a large part of my self-esteem, in addition to being the only way I knew how to control my bipolar disorder. My problem was being unable to *stop*. I couldn't do anything in moderation, so when it was time to taper, to reduce our workload and start to rest, I struggled. I always worried about the timing of my taper, that it wouldn't be "just right," and that I would begin to get out of shape before the big competition arrived. It was a ridiculous notion in light of how hard I worked during the season, but I felt it anyway.

As for my bipolar disorder, which baffled me, I worried that when my workload decreased I would either become very depressed or very manic. I knew this problem well since I had been dealing with it for years, and in fact I did have a significant episode during the Big Ten Championship meet that same year.

It was a period of high stress and tension, and I remember at the time thinking I was just overly worried about my performance at the meet. Certainly that was a large factor, but in hindsight I now recognize that I had experienced a bad manic episode. I was in my hotel room, alone and literally starting to "wig out." I was so edgy and uncomfortable that I wanted to crawl out of my skin, run screaming down the hall and blast through the glass window at the end. I remember pacing back and forth in the room, desperate to "escape," crying and wringing my hands – totally out of control. A teammate, a good friend of mine, came in and saw this and thought I was having a nervous breakdown because of the meet.

"God, take it easy," she said. "It's just a fucking swim meet! It doesn't matter!"

I didn't tell her that it was much more than that. I never told anybody. I was just as embarrassed, ashamed and frightened of my depression and mania as I was about my alcoholism. I knew there was something major wrong with me but I couldn't explain it, not to myself and certainly not to others. First, I didn't think anyone would understand, and second, one just didn't talk about these things. There was such a stigma associated with alcoholism and even more so, I believed, with mental illness. I simply didn't know what to think about myself – I felt like an imposter. I was the best swimmer on the team and one of the best in the country. I was a team leader and, some people told me, a role model. I was a great student. But inside I felt out of control and, therefore, weak. I abhorred weakness. It – the fear of being *weak* – was something that I had been battling my whole life, from my earliest years hiding and crying in my deep-water sanctuary to my latest hard months of training. I was a fighter, had always been a fighter, and was proud of my tough, killer work ethic. But *weak?!* I couldn't live with that notion and I hated myself for thinking it. I was super-successful Christi on the outside and a scared, timid little girl on the inside. Outside appearances vs. inside realities. *"Don't be afraid!"* I kept hearing Steve say. Yeah, right. I was always afraid, deep down, of myself, and I just couldn't shake that feeling of "weirdness." I felt like a freak.

~~~

After the NCAA meet was over when we were taking a break from training I had another bout of serious depression and deep soul-searching. This followed weeks of reckless, desperate, out-of-control drinking and I had had enough. I was desperate to "escape" from myself and was having suicidal thoughts. It was time to try, again, to get some outside help. I walked into Jim's office one afternoon and sat down in front of his desk. Without preamble (I was so nervous I thought I would explode) I just blurted out, "Jim, I have a serious drinking problem and I need help." I started to cry. Jim told me not to worry, that he would get me help, and he did.

The next day I had an appointment with a counselor in the athletic department. He was a nice man in his mid-thirties with a gentle voice and a kind, quiet demeanor. I liked him but also felt a bit disappointed. I had such a difficult time communicating, I had hoped that my counselor would be a woman. But I thought it fair enough to give this guy a chance so I met with him for a handful of regularly scheduled sessions.

We talked a lot about my drinking and tried to discuss other issues as well. I don't recall that we had much success. I just couldn't open up about my deepest fears. I was still confused about my sexuality and gender identity, as I again found myself occasionally attracted to women. I didn't want to talk about this issue, and certainly not with a man, who I didn't think could possibly understand it. I was also worried about my depression, anxiety and manic episodes. I had a hard time talking about these too because I feared – seriously feared – that I might be "crazy." Our family did have some history of mental illness, after all. What if I also had those deadly genes? Would that be a "weakness?" I thought yes, of course! No way was I prepared to talk about *that*. Then there was my drinking, which is why I was there in the first place. This I could talk about.

Our discussions about drinking seemed very sophomoric to me. He asked me all kinds of questions about my drinking behavior and I answered them matter-of-factly. I told him about how I started, when I was fourteen, at the State Party. I told him about all the bingeing, the passing out and the blackouts (I had blackouts frequently now), how my drinking had progressed, how often I drank every week, with whom I drank, when, where and how. We talked about why I drank. It was all very thorough and in line with what I expected from a counselor. At one point in our conversations I remember being told that "it's not unusual for a person of your age to party to excess in college." That's right, I thought, it isn't unusual at all. But when I told him I couldn't stop and I didn't know how to live without alcohol he had only two solutions to offer. The first one was prayer.

"Have you tried praying?" he asked.

I sat staring at him incredulously. Praying?! This guy is out of his mind, I thought. At that time in my life I had no spiritual context in which to even place this concept. Praying! How absurd! But what finally ended our relationship was when I heard these words, again:

"You need to stop drinking. You need to *just stop*."

"Idiot," I fumed, standing up, "if I could 'just stop' I wouldn't have this problem!" I stormed from his office without a backward glance.

That was my last attempt to get professional help until I was thirty-two. I told Jim that it wasn't working out with the counselor and that I had stopped going to the appointments, but I didn't tell him specifically why. He was disappointed and expressed sincere concern. He asked what else he could do to help. I said I didn't know, but I would think about it. I was just too confused, too angry and too ashamed to go any further at that time.

This is one of my deepest regrets, that I had an opportunity to get more help from a person whom I respected and trusted, but because the first try didn't pan out I had thrown in the towel and given up. It was not like me to give up – on anything. But alcohol was slowly consuming me, eating its way through such important parts of my Self: my tenacity, my integrity, my toughness. I was afraid to look for more help after "giving up" and I was discouraged. I was also afraid because I couldn't see a solution to my alcohol problem. If the pros didn't have an answer, what could I do? That I couldn't manage the problem myself disgusted me, as it always had. So there was nothing to do but smash those emotions down and try to regain my self-respect. I went back to Madison for the summer and trained like a mad woman. I can do better, I thought! *I must do better!*

~~~

The summer passed and I both trained and competed well. I did my share of drinking too, though I did try – again – to impose limits, with varying degrees of success. Sometimes I managed to make it a week or two without consuming any alcohol but most of the time I drank on a regular basis: when opportunities arose during the week, like if I had a date or a party to attend, and on the weekends, if we weren't out of town for a competition.

~~~

THE DEEP END

At the end of August I returned to Ann Arbor to begin my junior year. One evening shortly before classes started a good friend and I were out drinking and my ankle buckled on a curb as we staggered back to our rented house near the pool. Our other housemate wasn't home yet so my pal, who was quite a bit smaller than I, helped hoist my injured body up the rickety stairs to our front porch by herself. She held the railing with one hand and my arm, which was clutched tightly around her shoulders, with the other. Hopping up the stairs on one foot was all the more difficult because we were both very drunk and were laughing hysterically. When we finally got to the living room and she plopped me on the couch we were shocked to see that my ankle had swollen to the size of a grapefruit. Even with my ankle packed in ice and me anesthetized with alcohol I was in terrible pain. But I managed to survive the night and the next morning she helped me hobble to the training room.

It turned out that I had a severe sprain on both sides of my ankle. The damaged joint had turned an ominous shade of blue, green and yellow overnight. They put me in a cast, which I was to wear for five weeks. I had a horrendous hangover and must have stunk to the moon like alcohol, but nobody mentioned it either in the training room or in the doctor's office.

I crutched my way across the parking lot and into the Matt Mann Pool building to give Jim the bad news. He was sitting at his desk working as I entered his office. The look he gave me when he glanced up was one of calm resignation. If he knew I was hungover (or smelled the alcohol) he didn't say so. All he said was, "Don't worry, you'll be alright. It's early and there's plenty of time to train. We'll work on your upper body strength while your ankle heals, OK? But let me know if there's anything I can do to help."

I somehow made my way back to our house, where, thankfully no one was home. I located the cassette tape (this was before the days of CDs and MP3 players), put in my favorite album and turned our stereo, a big boom box, up loud: *Quadrophenia*, by The Who. I propped up my casted leg and eased back into the couch as the music started, singing along with the first song. *"Can you see the real me, can you? Can you?!"*

Had I been a superstitious person I might have looked at my torn ankle and immobilized, casted leg as omens of bad things to come. But I had no such premonitions and just thought of it as a very stupid event and piece of bad luck. The weeks passed and I crutched my way to classes, which was difficult, and spent hours in the training room lifting weights and riding the stationary bike. Eventually – against the trainer's orders – I started riding my real bike and took long, hard rides outside the city, still wearing my cast. The rest of the team was training in the pool and I needed to do something to stay fit and keep myself on an even keel mood-wise. This I managed to do, and I was greatly relieved when the cast finally came off and I could get back in the pool. I was horrified to see my shriveled leg with its still yellowish-green hue. The flesh seemed to hang on the bone like limp, rotting meat. But I did the rehab exercises faithfully and between these and the work in the pool, my leg healed quickly and regained its former strength.

Love, Reign O'er Me

I was in love. This was not like my first love, which was swimming, and I suppose in all truthfulness my second love was alcohol. This new love, profound as true loves are, was unique. It was different from the pure, innocent infatuation I felt for Steve in Hawaii. Like with Steve, this was also a true, honest and genuine emotion. But this love existed on its own distinct metaphysical plane. It was deeper than any love for another human being I had yet allowed myself to feel. Like swimming, it was all-consuming. It was sensual and gentle, sexual and passionate. It was romantic, beautiful, exciting, lustful and erotic. It was so rich in depth, emotion and feeling that it overwhelmed my senses and made me tingle in every way, both physically and mentally. I was on fire. I had found it. *This was the real thing.*

    I first noticed him striding along the pool deck one afternoon in early autumn. He was tall and fit, lean and strong, with the long graceful muscles of a world-class swimmer, which he was. His wide shoulders rolled loosely back and forth and his narrow hips swayed from side to side as he walked, giving him a distinct swagger. He held his head high and slightly back, which gave him a cocky, sure-of-himself air, like that of a well-groomed lawyer or statesman. He had short, curly brown hair, light brown skin and deep lines in his face when he smiled, which was often. He had a chipped front tooth and large, beautiful brown eyes. Something about his eyes reminded me of a poster I had seen once, a closeup of the famous Argentine writer Jorge Luis Borges. His eyes were large, expressive, deep and penetrating. "Borges eyes" I called them, from then on.

I studied this enigma as I sat in the stands by the pool, waiting for practice to begin. My head slowly followed him as he walked along the deck and rounded the edge of the pool where we sat. He strode directly in front of me and turned into the men's team coaches' office. I was transfixed. "Who on earth is *that?*" I thought. He was the men's Assistant Coach, and I fell for him instantly.

I can't say that it was exactly love at first sight. I was far too reserved for that, too timid. But there was something new here, something captivating about this tremendously handsome man. I thought about him the rest of that afternoon and evening as I grinded my way through the workout, then walked back to our small rented house, still mired in thought as I made dinner. I tried to study that night but couldn't. My mind was too flustered and cluttered, recalling the image I had seen that day. To me he was beyond gorgeous. I just had to get to know him.

And I did. He was friendly and outgoing and we connected immediately. He was charming and personable with an open, easygoing manner that made him very approachable. Everyone liked him. I was enamored and obsessed and couldn't get him out of my mind, not even for a moment. I thought about him while I swam, as I walked to class, as I sat in class trying to concentrate and as I tried to fall asleep at night. While locked away studying in my secluded Grad Library cubicle I would find myself staring wistfully out the window, my mind totally absorbed in some part of the day, some time when I had seen him, which was usually at the pool. I would find myself smiling and daydreaming about him, what it would be like to kiss him, how it would feel to make love with him. I wondered if I could find a reason to hug him, just to touch him somehow.

And so it went for several weeks. We spent time together before workouts at the pool and got to know each other better. We laughed and joked about all kinds of things and became friends. He had a wonderful Puerto Rican accent which I found tremendously appealing. Everything about him was appealing. I was *enthralled* in every way.

Then one night my roommate and I were in the process of getting drunk and we had the wild idea to go visit, just to say hello. She knew how much I was infatuated with him and we both thought this was a good plan. He was surprised when he opened the door of the small house a few blocks away from ours where he helped care for an elderly lady in exchange for rent. Mary was an interesting character, always bundled in a crocheted blanket on a rocking chair smoking long, thin cigarettes and drinking an occasional shot of whiskey. She was over ninety years old and fun-loving with a gleam in her eye and a keen, sharp mind. She told great stories.

So we were invited in and had more drinks. The three of us went to his bedroom and smoked pot while we drank, then laughed hysterically as we told stories and entertained each other. I don't remember how it happened or when, but at some point my housemate left. He and I were kissing on the bed. I remember massaging his back, neck and shoulders as we kissed passionately and deeply. Clothes started to come off as we continued to kiss and explore each others' bodies with our hands and mouths. I felt such a hunger, such a deep, physical longing to be close, to touch and be touched everywhere. We slid between the sheets and it was a magical experience. I couldn't believe I was there – with *him*. I was totally immersed, filled with love and joy and pleasure.

Thus began the next phase of our relationship. Every day I would see him at the pool and would become more enraptured. I would arrive early to practice just to be able to spend time with him. When nobody was there we would touch each other, rubbing each others' backs and shoulders, or running our fingers through each others' hair. He would take my hand and massage my arm, and tell me what a beautiful body I had. I would look into his big brown eyes and tell him how hot I was for him. We flirted continuously, and he smiled every time our eyes met.

We started going out on dates – dinners at small, dark, romantic restaurants with round tables, candles and checked tablecloths. We drank excellent red wine and ate delicious Italian food. Sometimes we would go to bars and listen to music; jazz or reggae or "home-grown" music. But most of the time we either went to his house or mine. We might drink and chat with my housemates for a little while, but we always ended up in my room. We made gentle, passionate love. It was so full of emotion and depth – it was like nothing I had ever experienced or imagined. It was nothing like the stumbling, fumbling, groping sexual experiences that I had had in high school or during my earlier years in college. This was so intimate, so special. I was opening myself up in a totally new way, allowing this man to penetrate deep into the very core of my Self, both physically and psychologically. I was truly and wholeheartedly in love.

I was telling F. things and showing him things about myself that I had never exposed to anyone else before. He was attentive and patient. He listened, and had much to offer by way of helping me address my fears and variety of confused emotions. He gave me books to read, books about spirituality, personal growth and hope. He taught me how to breathe and how to relax. In one of the exercise rooms at the pool we worked on breathing techniques, stretching and yoga – all meant to help me relax and find my "center." He believed in me and my swimming. He told me I had the "best turns in the world" and could be the best in the world, but I needed to learn to relax. He promised to help me, and he did.

I was exceedingly happy. My swimming did improve, both in practice and in meets. I found myself able to relax more and keep my focus on my "center," as he was teaching me. I started to think about a Higher Power, "God," if you will (though we didn't talk about God per se). Somehow I found enormous, new, positive energy bubbling from me that I was able to channel into my swimming and it was *good*. I trained like a wild woman, even sometimes making NCAA time standards in practice. My times at meets were respectable too. We continued to make love. Everything was good. Almost.

There was a problem with our relationship, and her name was Jacqueline. Jacqueline was tall and thin, had medium-length brown hair and wore classy, designer clothes. She was beautiful and elegant, and had a sophisticated, confident persona. She would often show up at the pool during our workouts, striding down the pool deck in her artsy coat and European beret to the coaches' office. I was appalled. I didn't hate her, but I hated that she was there, and that he allowed her to come to *my* place, to *my* space.

Jacqueline was his girlfriend, the beautiful, stylish woman that he dated outwardly, in public. I was his secret mistress. I was devastated when I learned about Jacqueline but also confused. In the beginning he told me he was in love with her and that it was very serious, and that he probably was going to marry her. Later we would be in one of our beds, I most likely drinking and on my way to being drunk, he high from smoking pot, making wonderful, gentle love to each other. I didn't believe what he told me about Jacqueline. I couldn't. How could it be possible, I thought, for us to have such deep feelings for each other and yet, for either of us, to make but a sideways glance at anyone else, let alone profess to being in love with that person? It just didn't make sense. We were so connected, so entwined, so physically attracted to one another. We were like two magnets that locked tight in every nook and cranny. There was so much positive energy between us. How could there possibly be anyone else in this picture?

This was all the more confusing to me because he would tell me that he loved me. He gave me thoughtful gifts: books, flowers, little glass art forms, ceramic animals and various cute items for my desk. He wrote sweet letters that always ended with "I love you" and "kisses" in Spanish. Sometimes when we were making love he would tell me, "You are *the one*. You are *it*. You are so special and I love you." He would also tell me things like, "You will make a wonderful mother some day." I assumed he was talking about *our* children. Apparently I assumed incorrectly.

He continued to date Jacqueline openly while sleeping with me on the sly. One day he told me that her parents were coming, that they were coming to meet him and this was a very serious thing. I nodded in agreement as we lay entwined and naked in my bed. What could I say? My eyes filled with tears and sometimes so did his. He would lick my tears away and hold me close.

As my junior year went on and we became more serious certain things began to improve dramatically as other things began to fall apart. My swimming was going great, both in training and in competition. I was so energized and centered – it was like all the love and energy of the universe was pouring into and through me. I was riding a wave of joy and it was coming out in my swimming.

In other respects certain aspects of this "universe of power and joy" were starting to collide and self-destruct. My drinking had escalated dramatically. During the second semester of my junior year I drank more than half the nights of the week, all the while trying to train and keep it together academically. Early on I decided that this was just not possible; something had to give. I decided that I would simply not attend one of my four credit classes, American Politics, and just allow myself to fail it. This seemed like a rational idea at the time. I needed to carry the credits in order to be eligible to swim but nobody would know that I had failed the class until after the fact, until after NCAAs were over. By not attending I would free up a lot of the hours that I would have spent studying, reading, writing and attending class. I could use those hours in other ways, like doing coursework for my other classes – or seeing my secret lover.

I had never before thought of myself as a sexy person. I liked my masculine body and was proud of my high fitness level and lean, "body-builder" muscle tone. Sometimes I would feel "feminine" when I dressed up, wore makeup, earrings and made an attempt to look "pretty." But for the most part I saw myself as androgynous – I looked at myself as a nonsexual being. Sure, I flirted with men on occasion, but this was almost always when I was drinking. I was uncomfortable with my body as far as sexuality goes. This was made all the more confusing and difficult by the comments that I continued to receive that I was a man, gay, lesbian or "whatever you are."

He changed all of that. He told me I was beautiful, and sexy, and that he loved my hard, fit body. He would touch me sensually, everywhere, and I would touch him back. I was quite shy at first, but he slowly coaxed me out of my inhibitions and helped me start to form an identity of myself as a sexual being. His attentiveness gave me confidence in my sexual prowess, in my ability to flirt and "turn him on." Alcohol was often still in the picture as was marijuana. He was a smoker more than a drinker, and often had a joint with him or was high when he would surprise me with a visit. I would be studying in my room in our small house or sleeping, and then suddenly he would appear. In the early stages of our relationship I loved these surprise visits. I was so crazily in love with him, I would drop everything I was doing or sacrifice precious sleep to spend even short periods of time with him.

Alcohol was my ally and also my enemy. Initially it enabled my deep feelings of loneliness, shyness, fear and "weirdness" to come out, be exposed, and quickly be stifled. Because of that stifling and numbing of my innermost "weaknesses" alcohol helped me make connections with other people. With my secret lover, alcohol enabled me to open up enough to form the very, very deep connection that I felt, the intense love that I felt for him in every cell of my body. It allowed me to become "consumed," and this began to frighten me because I had never let anyone this close to my "center" before. But even before I began to feel angry and ashamed about being the "mistress," even when I still believed him when he said, "you are *it*," alcohol was destroying my identity at the very same time I thought it was helping to build it. As much as I felt I was becoming more confident about myself as a sexual being and more confident in myself in general, alcohol was insidiously working in the background, chiseling away at my integrity. I already felt guilty and ashamed for my heavy drinking and therefore physical self-destruction. Now I also felt guilty about being *weak*, about allowing myself to be so consumed by my love for this person that I could live with being his mistress, that I could live with being lied to, used, with being "cheated on."

My dignity took blow after blow, yet I allowed it, and therefore the circle continued: crave him, sleep with him, hate myself, need comfort. . . crave him, sleep with him, hate myself, need comfort. . . Throw in the alcohol factor and it became even more complicated: alcohol allowed me to become "open," it *enabled* me to make the deep connection, it *enabled* me to feel a sense of strength, power and awareness of myself as sexual. Alcohol *enabled* me to "crave him, sleep with him. . ." But at the same time it eroded my self-respect as I permitted that deep connection to consume me. My identity as an aware, strong, powerful woman was being destroyed. I even *knew* it was happening, but I accepted it anyway because I was so in love, or at least I thought I was. I began to hate myself and my lack of self-control when it came to F. And how to remedy this pain? The only way I knew how – beat the tar out of myself in swim practice and drink.

He and I were still "dating" and spending lots of time together in bed. He was still seeing Jacqueline, and this just burned me up. There was so much pain and I was merely beginning to get a taste of what was still to come. The painful part is obvious: watching the one you love with someone else, and knowing that he is loving someone else too. Then there was the fear of loss. We had spent so much time together working on my fears that related to my success in swimming and life in general. I felt connected to him in ways that were also very connected to my swimming success, and therefore to my identity. I had never allowed myself a serious boyfriend before because I worried that a relationship would interfere with my swimming. In this case, not only did I permit a serious and very intimate relationship, but I allowed it – wanted it, needed it – to become intrinsically intertwined with my swimming.

a *need*: his energy and positivity mixed with mine in order for me to get into the right headspace to perform. Without realizing it I had set myself up in a dangerous position. I had allowed my success in swimming, my happiness and my identity to become entangled in an intimate, sexual relationship with a man.

My drinking was still excessive. I no longer had any rules except that I would try not to drink within two weeks of the Big Ten Championships and not drink two weeks before the NCAA meet. When we went on dates we drank and I occasionally ended up at his house for the night, although I never slept. I started to miss morning practices, something I had *never* done in my training, no matter what condition I was in. Even though I was not attending the one class, my coursework in my other classes suffered also. I just didn't care. I was swimming well – amazingly, considering how much I was drinking – and most of the time I was filled with the joy of true love. Swimming and drinking were now my second (close second) priorities and all else was a distant third.

The Big Ten Championship meet came and I won my event, the two-hundred yard breaststroke, placed a close second in the one-hundred yard distance and made personal best times in both events. I also helped two of our relays to win and set conference records. For the first time ever, the University of Michigan Women's Swimming and Diving Team won the Big Ten Championships. It was an unparalleled year of intensely hard training for everyone, and an amazing team performance at the meet. We won by a substantial margin and we were the first team of the next twelve consecutive years to win the Big Ten title for Michigan.

I received wonderful love letters – at least that's how I took them – and "good luck" notes before the NCAA meet, the National Championships. I left for the meet still flying high on love, but it was starting to dwindle. Not the love, for I felt that as strongly as ever. But the relationship had been faltering because there was so much conflict about Jacqueline. He was still seeing her and professing his love to her while sleeping with me. I couldn't understand it, was having a harder and harder time living with it, and was feeling more angry, guilty and ashamed. This was on top of the guilt and shame I already felt because of my heavy drinking. I knew I was destroying myself but I couldn't stop. I broke my "two weeks" rule, and drank a week before we left for the NCAA meet.

I swam reasonably well at NCAAs and placed a respectable fifth in the nation. I also qualified for the US National Team for the first time and made the World University Games Team, to be held in Zagreb, Yugoslavia (at the time it was Yugoslavia, before civil war divided the country). I found out about making the USA team later so didn't know about it while at the meet. The only significant thing I remember about the NCAAs that year was warming up before the Finals for my event, the two-hundred yard breaststroke, and thinking, "I'm bored. I'm so very, very bored."

When we returned from the meet my life really began to fall apart. I was drinking nearly every night to dull the pain of a collapsing relationship. I was now undeniably angry and was trying to pull away, but found it extremely difficult. Even though there was so much pain and suffering for me, thinking about the loss of my only true love – it was very hard to let it go. I still loved him, after all, even though I felt cheap, used, betrayed and ashamed. I drank to stuff my conflicting emotions back down inside, and to numb the pain. I kept thinking he would dump her and come to me, but that wasn't happening. My friends were telling me to dump him, that he was treating me like shit, and that he was never going to ditch Jacqueline. Inside I knew that was true, but still I struggled to let go.

Meanwhile the semester had ended and I had officially failed the first class of my entire life. The grades in my other classes were poor too, by my standards. The Women's Athletic Director called me into her office one day. I was nervous and scared. Earlier that fall she and a panel of esteemed university women had awarded me the Marie Hartwig Scholarship, an honor bestowed upon one female student-athlete each year in recognition of academic and athletic excellence. As I stood anxiously before her, the Director informed me that I was two credits short, and that if I didn't take a class that summer I would be ineligible to swim my senior year. But that was all she said. She didn't comment on my weak grades, the failed class or ask if anything was wrong. I left her office with the name of a professor to visit, to inquire about doing an independent study course to get my needed credit hours.

Shortly after the semester ended I made a critical mistake. I kept thinking that my relationship with my secret lover was going to turn around and that he would "choose me." He told me that he would be leaving soon to go back to Puerto Rico and I couldn't quite believe it. I decided to stay in Ann Arbor to train for the World University Games rather than return to Madison to train with my club team as usual.

This was a major turning point in my life. I finally realized that the relationship was over, and I was drinking myself into oblivion to dull the pain. The training situation was terrible for me, the pool was crowded, and all of the workouts were geared toward the top male freestylers, which I was not. The workouts were so beyond my ability that half the time I couldn't even make the warm-up sets, so I was demoralized from the start of just about every practice. There was little emphasis on the specialty strokes, like mine, and since I was training with three others who were also going to the Games, all freestylers, I had a difficult time working on what I needed to do in order to prepare for my own event. In short, it was awful, and I had no confidence in my training at all. I was also feeling guilty and remorseful about my drinking, knowing I was sabotaging myself but unable to stop. I was so very, very angry and confused. I was now "alone" and really didn't have anyone to talk with about my conflicting emotions. I had been madly in love and thoroughly rejected. I received a letter that said, "We are friends, Christi, friends. That's all we have ever been: friends. But I still love you. . ." I felt so totally, utterly, completely used.

The other serious repercussion of the end of that relationship was how much I had tied it into my swimming and my overall happiness and satisfaction with the sport. Granted I had been struggling with burnout since after the Olympic Trials in 1984, three years earlier, but now that my muse, my mentor and my lover was gone I was having a tough time. What's the point of all of this? I thought to myself. Where is the happiness anymore? Where is the joy? I was finding no joy in the pool at all, only more frustration as my training suffered and my drinking continued.

But I tried to develop a positive, happy attitude for the World University Games. I was proud, after all, to have reached one of the major goals in my life: to make the United States National Team. As time went on the pain of loss did lessen, and anger took its place. I tried hard to impose limits on my drinking as it got closer to the Games, and I did swim fairly well on occasion in some practices. Deep down I felt depressed, but I really made an effort to hide it and to stuff it away where it couldn't surface. I had become quite good at that, and especially when I was training hard. So as usual I pounded on myself to bury my emotions and stifle my sadness and regrets.

For the most part it worked, and although I was not confident in my preparation, I managed to start building feelings of happiness and enthusiasm for the Games, which I had lost during the breakup. There was a lot of buildup and press coverage, so it wasn't difficult to get psyched for the trip itself, which would be about three weeks long. I had never been to Europe, and this particular trip (the World University Games) was supposedly one of the best trips for which to qualify. I just wasn't confident or satisfied with my training. Somehow I couldn't see how my swimming career was going to continue, but I had to press onward for just a little while longer, so that's what I set out to do.

I was extraordinarily happy when we boarded the plane for Washington, D.C. There we would meet up with the rest of Team USA and train for a few days before heading to Yugoslavia. I felt happy for several reasons. One, I was proud of myself for making the team. I wore my Team USA gear with my head held high and a sense of total gratification and pleasure. Second, I was happy to be leaving Ann Arbor and "leaving all my sadness behind." I intended to make a new start, and use this trip to catapult myself into a new, happier phase of life. And third, I was simply excited to be going to Europe for the first time in my life.

The Games proved to be everything I was told they would be and totally lived up to my expectations. The format was just like that of the Olympics: several weeks of competition in all of the Olympic sports, a beautiful new Athletes' Village, many new facilities and elaborate Opening Ceremonies in the gigantic new stadium. I met athletes from around the world and we traded pins, clothing and other items. I was especially thrilled to meet the other Team USA swimmers. We had the largest team of any country and the atmosphere was pure electricity and anticipation. I found the majority of the other swimmers to be relaxed and happy, and I absorbed this attitude and thrived in the casual-yet-serious atmosphere. Normally at a big meet I would be very anxious and tense, but here, for some reason, these feelings were nonexistent. I found it easy to make friends and connections, and met some wonderful people, in addition to meeting up with old friends, fellow swimmers, from my club team in Madison.

There were a few team rules, but overall they were pretty loose. We were allowed to move freely about the city, either walking or using Zagreb's public transportation by showing our Games credentials. We could go to any venue to watch the other sports and were free to explore the main public square with its many vendor booths, shops and small cafés that seemed to be everywhere along the narrow streets. The only firm rule that I remember was curfew. This was very strict. We had to be in the Village and in our dorm by ten o'clock at night or we would be sent back home. Period. Regarding drinking I don't recall any distinct rules, although we may have been told not to do it. I, of course, found the other drinkers on the team and we did drink occasionally during the Games. This was the closest I had ever consumed alcohol before a major competition. I even went out three nights before my event and drank beer with a new friend I had made on the team.

As for my swimming I was frustrated from the start. I had no speed in practice and just couldn't seem to get psyched up for practice or the competition. Oddly I wasn't nervous, and this in itself made me uncomfortable. My coaches thought I needed more rest, and so my pre-meet practices were easy and short, with just a small amount of pace work. I knew deep inside that I hadn't put in the work, that I wasn't prepared physically. Therefore I just couldn't get fired up mentally. The fact that I went out drinking three days prior to my event didn't do me any good either, as I knew that alcohol was detrimental to performance. So when the day finally arrived for me to compete I arrived at the pool with a sense of dread. I had made lots of friends on the team and knew that everyone was pulling for me and wanted me to do well. But the passion just wasn't there. I tried to get nervous, thinking my usual pre-competition frame of mind would help me, but I couldn't. How bizarre, I thought! Nervousness and anxiety – the bane of my life and what I had always struggled to keep under control – and the one time I actually needed it, I couldn't generate it. I swam my event and did poorly. It was a disappointment, but on a deeper level I had known that I was not going to swim well so it wasn't all that surprising.

I had a great time during the trip, and it was enriching from a cultural and a social standpoint. I made several very good friends on the team and was able to talk about my fears and struggles. One afternoon two older teammates and I were eating lunch at an outdoor café, discussing burnout. They had suffered the same negative feelings and struggle to get started again every season as I. I told them that I didn't think I could do it again, that I just didn't think I had it in me to train and compete for another season. They urged me not to quit, to somehow find it within myself to get through another year. They said that they knew a few people who had quit before their senior years and really regretted it. My older friends thought that if I quit without finishing my senior year I would regret it terribly and it would haunt me for the rest of my life. . . and they were so right.

The trip ended with a big, drunken party in the Athlete's Village and the drinking continued for a few of us on the flight all the way back to the States. Oddly, and despite my poor performance at the meet, I was happy and felt a deep sense of contentment. Somehow I had "arrived" somewhere, although I wasn't exactly sure where. The pain of my lost love was still there, deep inside me, but it was muted. I was relaxed and, like my dad always said, I could "just be." I didn't understand it, but I felt comfortable in my own skin, which was rare, and I actually felt good inside myself. I believe now that it was simply acceptance working for me. I was accepted and cared for by the team, and most importantly I accepted and cared for myself. It was a novel experience.

Had Enough

After the World University Games I returned to Ann Arbor and soon found myself lost in a sea of self-absorption. I had no motivation to train and didn't know what to do with myself. I went on long, introspective bike rides and jogs through the woods along the Huron River. I went out with friends, to bars and to parties. I went to the Art Fair and met a guy named Bob who played guitar and sang on the street. He was a nice man, with a short beard and reddish-brown hair, and we soon became friends. He wasn't athletic at all and was slightly overweight. We would meet at a park along the Huron. Bob would teach me the harmonies to songs – Jim Croce, Carole King, Simon & Garfunkel, The Eagles – and then play his guitar as we sang folk and country together and I drank beer.

Bob rarely drank. He might have half a beer or, on occasion, drink a whole can. I could never understand this – I just didn't get the point of drinking if the objective wasn't to get drunk. So I learned to drink alone, and I didn't mind it at all. I would buy a twelve pack of beer and slip the cans into my backpack, then ride my bike to the park in the evening, where Bob would be waiting for me after he finished work. Then we would sing as I let the beer do its magic, easing me into a relaxed state of happiness, and after a while, when I was drunk, Bob would offer to give me a ride home. Sometimes I would take it and sometimes not. I loved to ride my bike loaded, in the dark, along the curvy path that followed the river and into the dark and creepy Arboretum. I enjoyed the extra high that riding fast on the uneven and dangerous night path would give me. Always looking for more – that was my style.

As July wore into August I started to fall into a slump. Again there was the letdown after the high of being in Zagreb and I couldn't find a way to steady myself. I took the Amtrak to Madison and stayed with my mom for a few weeks, hoping this would elevate my mood. It was the same-old, same-old at home, and our relationship was still occasionally rocky and strained. Mom was just so exacting about everything, and I felt I could never do anything right. By then I was twenty-one and had been openly drinking at her house for a while. She also drank so this was not a problem, though I am certain she was not aware of the extent to which I did. We typically drank in the evenings, before, during and after dinner, and the alcohol eased tensions between us and helped to lubricate our discussions. We had deep, meaningful talks about my swimming, about school, my fears, my relationship with my ex-lover, my burnout and how I was going to get myself "up" for my senior year and my next season. I didn't tell her that I was becoming more and more depressed, and more distraught as the school year approached. I don't know why I couldn't tell her how serious it was. I suppose I felt that she would be disappointed, and I couldn't abide that.

I truly didn't know what to do. It was expected that I would complete my swimming career and graduate with the same success and honors in academics and athletics that I always had. But I honestly didn't think I could do it. I didn't *want* to do it. I was so, so incredibly tired, physically but also emotionally. It was just like after the Olympic Trials in '84, only worse: this time I had the exhaustion and scars of three more years behind me plus the damage from the only relationship that broke my heart. Or, more accurately, that crushed it and splattered the pieces as though they were fired from a cannon at a brick wall. I felt dead inside toward swimming. There just seemed to be no embers glowing at all, nothing left to puff into even a tiny flame.

In August my guitar-playing friend Bob drove his truck from Ann Arbor to Madison to help me move and secretly haul back a small motorcycle, a Honda 350, that my brother Mike had given me. I hoped that something new and fun to "play" with might help ease me out of the dumps. It was a secret because I thought my mom would be very upset if she knew that I was riding a motorcycle. She found out anyway because Bob accidentally spilled the beans and Mom was, indeed, very upset. But I gave her the "I'm a grown woman and can do what I want" speech (which never failed to ignite an argument) and we ended up taking the bike back to Michigan, much to her displeasure.

When I got the bike my brother told me that I would need to learn to fix it if I planned to ride it regularly because it was old and things were bound to go wrong with it. This turned out to be true and I spent more time pushing it than I did riding it. But I did learn to fix it, at least to fix some of the simple problems. I had always been good with my hands so fixing my road bike (which I had been doing for years) and learning to repair my "new" motorcycle didn't intimidate me. I had fun riding it when it worked and managed to not injure myself, but eventually I got tired of pushing it and getting my hands greasy. I parked the bike and tried to figure out what to do next.

I knew that alcohol was a depressant and I was having such a terrible time with depression, which had worsened during the month of August. I also knew that I was facing a huge dilemma and that I needed a clear mind in order to sort it all out. So I decided to attempt – again – to quit drinking. As usual I went for long runs and bike rides to try, with increasing desperation, to steady my mood. I was extremely edgy, tense and uncomfortable, with an abundance of restless, untamable energy. Sometimes I would pace back and forth in our living room, my thoughts spinning wildly. I had that same feeling of wanting to do something drastic, to run naked screaming through the streets, through the countryside, up steep hills and down rocky trails, full speed ahead like an out-of-control train zooming toward a sharp turn at the end of a steep grade. I thought about the freedom of soaring, of shooting off the tracks at the bottom, sailing over the edge and plunging, accelerating with my arms and legs braced in an X form as I pressed against the racing wind, like a skydiver.

At the same time I was feeling this crazy, manic energy I was mired in depression and inner turmoil. I couldn't sleep, couldn't eat and couldn't concentrate. I felt an overwhelming sense of sadness and despair, aloneness and despondency. I cried a lot, hidden in my room or walking by myself in the Arboretum or along the railroad tracks that went through Ann Arbor. What to do about the "swimming problem?" I just didn't want to swim anymore. I loved the feeling of being *free*, of being able to sit by the river and sing with Bob, of being able to sleep late if I wanted, to go for runs when I wanted, to walk in the woods and relax by the river, to read a good book or just stare at the reflecting water. I felt so stuck in the identity of myself as a "swimmer" and was desperate to get away from it and explore my many other interests. I rebelled when people would introduce me as "Christi the Swimmer." I would say, "yes, I swim, but I do a lot of other things too." My mind was a tangled mess of thoughts and emotions. My parents, family, coaches, teammates – everyone – expected me to swim and study my senior year and be great. I was Co-Captain of the team and a member of ADARA, the University's Senior Women's Honor Society. The thought of disappointing everybody made me physically sick. My head would throb and I experienced sharp, stabbing, clenching feelings in the pit of my gut, sort of like extreme hunger. I would feel nauseous as I sobbed, actually heaving and gagging on my own spit and tears. It was desperation mixed with deep heartache, and I couldn't see any way out.

One day in early September I was walking alone in the quiet woods of the Arboretum, listening intently and feeling the early morning coolness encircling me. Nothing was moving, not a single leaf on a single tree. Only bird and insect noises and the sound of my footsteps pierced the pressing silence. All else was still. I hadn't been drinking now for over two weeks and felt better physically, though I was low – very low – in depression, and exhausted from lack of sleep. I was calm and oddly at ease as I wandered down to the river and sat on a damp rock at the river's edge. I hugged my knees and stared at the gentle, moving water, every now and then tossing in a small twig or blade of grass and watching it swirl slowly away.

An idea came into my head. This was not the first time this thought had entered my consciousness – I had thought about it many, many times. But usually I quickly squashed it away like I did all painful thoughts. *I want to kill myself. That's my way out.* I turned the notion over and over in my mind and it became more real. I fought the urge to stifle it like I always had – *suicide is weakness* – and allowed myself to feel the idea, to experience it as a solid *thing*, and to slowly embrace it. I remember *wanting* to feel it, to carry it through in my head and explore it, truly explore it, as a real option. *I am going to kill myself. I am going to kill myself.* What would that be like? The tension in my neck and shoulders oozed out of me and seemed to drift away. My persistent headache slowly abated and I felt warm all over, as if a soft, soothing blanket was wrapped around me. There was an overwhelming sense of inner peace, like I had felt in Zagreb during the World University Games. I just wanted to sit there forever in that moment, in that feeling. I remember sitting for a long time and just free thinking, letting my mind wander and float, the idea evolving into more of a surrounding awareness than an actual solid thought. I am going to kill myself. Freedom. Freedom. . .

~~~

Later that afternoon I tidied my room and wrote a short letter to my mom. I left it on my pillow in an envelope, and I still have it today. That is when things became truly strange. I have no memory of what happened next, of how I spent the following five or six hours.

Suddenly it was night, and I was standing on the top level of a parking structure in Ann Arbor. I stood looking down the six stories at the sidewalk below as an all-encompassing sense of calm and peace washed over me. The decision to kill myself had evaporated all my fears and distress. I don't know exactly what I was thinking, I just remember being there with the firm conviction that I was going to dive headfirst to the pavement below, and hopefully not "fuck it up." I knew one thing, that I didn't want to somehow survive and end up crippled or paralyzed.

So there I was, aware, relaxed, fully in the moment and feeling something close to rapture when it happened. It was like what you might experience watching a movie and my memory of it is kind of like that: of being so engrossed in a film or book that you feel you're actually *there*, and it's almost, but not quite, *real*. That is when I heard a voice, a female voice. It was everywhere: all around me and under me, over and inside me, and it was firm, measured and calm. *"You don't have to do this,"* it said, *"just walk away."* She repeated several times, *"You don't have to do this. Just walk away. Just walk away. Just walk away. . ."*

I thought I was crazy, hearing voices. Maybe I was, maybe I am. But that voice – whatever it was – saved my life. I vaguely remember leaving, walking across the nearly empty top floor of the lot to the stairwell, and slowly making my way home. Then I went up to my room and slept. Finally I slept, like I rarely ever did. Blessed, deep, wonderful, peaceful, restful sleep.

The next morning I awoke with a sense of happiness and freedom that brings tears to my eyes when I think of it. It was overwhelming then and still is today. I was one hundred percent decided and at peace with myself. I was really going to do it, and I did. I went to the Administration Building and formally withdrew from all my classes. Just like that, in about five minutes of actual time, I had *quit*. I had quit school and therefore had quit swimming. The deed was done. I finally had the guts to do it and I felt empowered and elated. I had taken control of my life.

I walked back to our little house near the pool and sat down in the living room. Nobody was home so I just sat with myself and my feelings. It was an odd sensation, to just be there with myself and not feel the need to escape, to run. I thought about how I was going to tell Jim, my coach, and how I was going to tell my parents. My heart started beating faster as I began to get nervous. I had to get this done. I got up and headed toward the pool.

I wrote earlier about how I anxiously walked into Jim's office and gave him the news. He said he would call a team meeting the next day and we agreed that I would tell the team myself. He also said that he would help me, that we would figure out a plan, and that he didn't want me to just "drop out of the picture" without some sort of structure to follow. I agreed halfheartedly. I didn't know what my future held and was leery of making commitments, but I went along with the idea anyway because I didn't know what else to say.

I exhaled a huge breath of relief as I left Jim's office and strode quickly from the building. *I was free!* I was so happy. It's hard to put into words the elation and pure joy I felt at that moment. One of my housemates, a good friend, passed me on the way as I headed home and she to the pool. We had talked about my dilemma and desire to quit many times during the past months so she was not surprised and must have known by the look on my face.

"Did you do it?" she asked.

"Yup. It's a done deal! I am a free woman!" She gave me a high five and we both laughed.

"Way to go," she said, smiling, "Way to go!"

The next thing I had to do was tell my parents. This I dreaded more than anything. I went back to the house and sat down, and started thinking about how I would tell them. I decided to call my mom first. She would be at work, so I knew this would throw off her whole day, but I couldn't wait. I just had to get this huge news off my chest.

She answered her office phone on the first ring.

"Good afternoon," she said in her usual upbeat, sing-song voice.

"Hi, it's me." I just blurted it out, "I'm calling to give you some news. I've decided to quit school and swimming. I already dropped all my classes and I already told Jim. It's a done deal."

There was a long pause.

"OK," she said, slowly. "OK. I need to think about this. Oh my God, Christi! Are you sure?"

"Yes, I'm sure."

"Oh my God. OK. Let's talk tonight, OK? I have a big deadline to meet today and I have to concentrate. But we'll talk later when I get home. I'll call you."

"OK, that works. And Mom, don't worry. It'll be fine. Everything will be fine."

Another big sigh of relief.

Next I called my dad at his office, and was surprised to also reach him on the first ring.

"Hi Dad," I said, my heart pounding, "I have to tell you something." I started to cry and hated myself for it. I always started to cry when I had to tell my dad something important and it made me feel vulnerable and weak.

"I've decided to quit swimming and school. I just can't do it any more," I sobbed.

There was a long silence and then he finally said, "OK, I think I could see that coming. But don't drop out of school. You have to stay in school."

"It's too late," I said, trying so hard not to cry, "I already dropped all of my classes."

Another interminable silence. "OK, Christi. I need some time to let this all soak in. Let's talk later tonight."

I hung up the phone, relieved for having told both parents the news, but also dreading having to talk with them again in the evening. Had I really done the right thing?

By far the most painful thing I had to do after I decided to quit was to tell the team. The next day Jim called a meeting of all of the swimmers and divers. Of course the news had already spread and most everyone knew, and I knew that, but I was still as nervous as I had ever been. I walked into the room where everyone sat waiting for me and sat down. Jim said that I had an announcement to make.

"I know that most of you know this already," I said, "but I need to tell you that I've decided to quit swimming and school." Then I started to cry, the tears streaming down my face. My heart was pounding wildly. "This is the hardest decision I've ever had to make, and part of that is that I really feel that I'm letting you all down, and I'm sorry." I paused, trying to catch my breath. The room was dead silent. "I'm so sorry, but I just can't do this anymore. The love is gone – there's just nothing left."

Now I was really crying and everyone was looking at me. I remember feeling so deeply sad, so lonely. I told them that I didn't know what I was going to do next, and that I was scared, but that I knew I had made the right decision. I had collected myself by the time I finished talking. Then Mary, one of the best divers in the world and our other Co-Captain, said, "Christi, you know you'll always be a member of this team, whether you're in the pool, in the stands or wherever you are. We'll always love you." That started the tears all over again and I nearly choked as I thanked her, and then thanked everyone for being such great teammates and giving me so much joy over the past three years.

Finally, mercifully, I was done. Jim said a few kind words about me and I left the room with a heavy heart, and headed back to our house. I passed my other roommate, a dear friend, on the way back home.

"Oh my God," she said, "Are you all right?" I was still crying and must have looked terrible.

"Yeah," I said, "I guess so. That was tough. I'm glad you didn't have to see it."

The team meeting was done, the talks with my parents were over and I was free. I felt so light, happy and loose, and proud of myself. My joy during the next few days was incredible. I felt like a new woman: strong, confident, and immensely happy, happy to the core of my soul. I was still not drinking and had decided that I wouldn't drink for a while, that this was a good time to "start over with my new life," and be sober and healthy.

I let myself enjoy a few days of my new freedom but certain realities were starting to creep in. I had decisions to make and serious matters to attend to. The biggest thing was my financial situation. Because I had quit swimming, I had lost my scholarship. Therefore I had no money – no money for rent, food, incidentals or anything else. I had a modest amount of cash in my savings account but knew it wouldn't go far. I also had a credit card with a small line of credit but I decided to save that for emergency back-up. After about a week my housemates informed me that I would either have to pay rent or move out. They simply couldn't afford to have me live there unless I was paying rent, and I understood that.

I had no job, no college degree and no work history since I had always been a student-athlete. The only job I had ever had was as a lifeguard and swim instructor at our summer club in Madison. For the first time in my life I started scanning the classifieds, looking for work. Meanwhile I also had to find a place to live and, I reasoned, a mode of transportation other than my bicycle in order to get to work, wherever that might be. Again I sifted through the classifieds of various publications until I found the perfect solution: a large van fitted out like a camper, with a bed, curtains, "mini-kitchen and plenty of storage." It also "needed work," said the ad. Perfect, I thought! I could get the van fixed, park it behind the house where I no longer lived and take showers at the pool.

I purchased the van for two hundred dollars. It was huge – a full-size Econoline – and white with "some rust." The inside was nice and fairly clean, and I loved it. I took it for a test drive and it shuddered and bucked every time

I pressed the brake pedal. "It just started doing that," the guy I bought it from claimed, sheepishly. It also emitted huge clouds of blue smoke, which he also said was a "fairly recent issue." I bought it anyway because of the camper aspect, figuring I would get it fixed and live in it while I worked and saved money. Then I would rent an apartment in town. I was excited about the idea of living in the van. What an adventure, I thought! I could go anywhere I pleased and take my "home" with me. I lovingly named my "new" van Betsy. I bought a small porta-potty and I was all set.

It cost more to fix Betsy than I expected and took a sizeable chunk from my savings account. I also found that it wasn't as easy to find places to park and sleep as I thought it would be. I ended up parking her most nights behind my "old house" by the pool, but that wasn't an ideal situation because I was using paying tenants' parking spaces. I was told that I had to go elsewhere.

Meanwhile I had found a job working as a waitress in a nice, upscale restaurant in Ann Arbor. I worked the lunch shift, which took about four hours every day, and expected to make good tips. But I was a terrible waitress. Everything about the job was difficult for me, from greeting and smiling at the customers, to putting in the orders correctly, to getting the drinks right, to managing the bills, to making sure the water glasses were filled, to remembering to put bread out. I was so overcome with nerves that my hands shook and I could barely pour water to refill glasses. Between the five or six tables I had to service at the same time there seemed to be eight million different things going on all at once. I was no good at that kind of multitasking and the job was overwhelming. I did so poorly on my first day that my very first tip was a penny. I was demoralized but the manager assured me that I would do fine once I "got the hang of it." I never totally got the hang of it and, although my waitressing skills did improve, I hated the job. After three weeks I couldn't take it anymore and quit.

My mother was appalled that I was living in a van and worried about my safety. I had to continually assure her that I was doing fine and not to worry.

THE DEEP END

But after I left my job at the restaurant I looked at my savings account and knew I was not doing fine. I had to find another job, and find it soon, if I was going to afford gas for Betsy and food for myself. The whole experience was very eye-opening, and also disheartening. I was still enjoying being "free" from swimming and school, but I was also becoming concerned about what I was going to do. The economic realities of life were starting to set in. Winter was coming. I was jobless and nearly broke, sleeping in a junk van in strange places and taking showers in the dingy locker room at the pool. It was uncomfortable to go there and I started to feel like an outsider. I also felt a bit ashamed about my living situation, just because it was so odd, so I would sneak into the pool and take showers when I knew no one would be there.

After a month my mom convinced me to move back home to Madison. The plan was that I would live in her house, get a job and pay a small amount of rent. She really thought that I just needed some serious time off from swimming and that I would be going back the following year, to swim and finish school. I wasn't so sure about that but I went along anyway because I didn't know what else to do. So we called my time off a "year of rest and recovery" and I started my life over again in Madison.

With Betsy parked in the street in front of Mom's house I moved back into my old bedroom. It was strange "going back," but also comforting. I was relieved to have a place to stay and was feeling pretty good both physically and mentally. I still wasn't drinking. It was now over a month and a half that I had been sober and I felt very good about that. I had no desire to drink and even watching my mom with her daily gin and tonics didn't bother me. I felt that maybe I finally had my drinking problem under control, and if I could just stay sober for a while my life would get better. So I decided that I would stay sober for at least the rest of the year and see how things went. From there I might try drinking again, in a controlled way, but I wanted to give myself a substantial period of sobriety first to "get a handle on things."

I signed up for a temporary job agency and started working odd jobs around Madison. Some of the jobs were easy and fun and I enjoyed them. Others, like working in the high-volume bagel factory, were pure hell. For that job I had to stand at the "assembly line" all day and work as fast as my hands could go, flipping the hot bagels over as they passed me on a quickly moving conveyor belt. I struggled to keep up and continually flipped bagels onto the floor as I tried in vain to stay in time with the belt. The job was hot, sweaty and physically demanding, and the whole place smelled like yeast. The fumes made me nauseous and by the end of the day I thought I would pass out from that and the heat. Needless to say I didn't last long in that job – one day was all I could handle.

The next job I landed went much better. I worked outside at a landscape company, doing all sorts of things from moving trees and shrubs, to wrapping root balls in burlap and securing them with long nails. I loaded and unloaded trucks and helped with a variety of physical tasks around the "tree farm." Because I was one of the more "favored" employees I had the opportunity to learn to drive a semi-truck and other heavy equipment, like big earthmovers with tires as tall as I, and smaller landscaping vehicles, like bobcats. The work was physically hard but I enjoyed it, since I still needed a lot of daily exercise in order to "feel right" and keep my mood steady. I continued to run every day, jogging in the dark early morning hours before the job started at seven-thirty. This helped me stay fit and lean, which was still such a large part of my identity and self-esteem.

At the end of November the tree farm closed for the winter and I again had to find a job. After the New Year, which I proudly passed sober, I worked at a fast food pizza joint for minimum wage, which at that time was $3.35 per hour. Meanwhile I had met a man, a nice fellow named Russ who had also worked as a temp at the landscape company. He was a musician who was actively working in a country band, playing in bars and clubs in the outskirts of Madison. We started playing guitars and singing together, and eventually (to make a long story short) I bought an electric bass, a beautiful blonde

Fender fretless, and an amplifier. The idea was that I would learn to play it and become the bass player in his band.

We became friends and as time passed the relationship evolved into a more serious affair and we started casually "dating." I was leery of any seriousness in a relationship because I was still recovering from my heartbreak and really didn't want to get too involved with another man. I considered Russ more of a good friend than a boyfriend. I had also started drinking again, but in a much more controlled way. I would buy a six-pack of beer and Russ and I would split it, and that would be it. Three beers and we would call it quits. I was very proud of myself for this and felt I had solved my alcohol problem – that I now could have "just a couple" of beers and that would be enough. Again I thought that maybe I could drink like a "normal" person as long as I "kept tight control over myself."

That idea didn't last long. Soon three beers turned into four. That's OK, I thought. Four beers still isn't very much. I drank that way for maybe two weeks: just four beers, every other night. I have to keep this under control, I kept telling myself. Then four became six. At that point, just like I had many, many times in the past, I gave up lying to myself that I was able to drink like a normal person. But I still kept trying to impose limits. I would buy a six-pack every other day and that would be my "allowance." I had worked hard, I reasoned. Didn't I deserve some sort of reward? Some days I would also have a glass or two of wine that I would "sneak" from my mom's gallon jug of Gallo that was usually on the floor in the kitchen. And every now and then I would augment my six-pack with a big slug of gin from her bottle under the sink. She won't notice a little bit missing, I thought. I also again kept a bottle of some horribly sweet liqueur hidden in the bookcase in my room. That was only for "emergencies," when I had run out and needed a little more or if I was going out and needed something extra to quell my anxiety. I tried not to drink every day, and if I drank on consecutive days I would make sure I took a day or two off. I had a calendar where I noted this, drawing a small X in a circle in the corner of each page on the days when I drank, and a plain circle on the days when I didn't.

I was keenly aware that my alcohol use was escalating again, and again tried hard to control it. One time my mom and I were eating dinner and she commented that I was drinking an "awful lot." She asked me if I was drinking every day. I replied that I was trying to limit my drinking to every other day, to which she replied that that was still "too much." I said, "What's the big deal? You drink every day. Besides, I'm trying to control my drinking. I promise to keep it to every other day, and not more than six beers." I omitted the secret glasses of wine, the stolen gulps of gin and the hidden bottle in my room. I felt deceitful about those omissions but I reasoned that it was "just a little more" than I promised, plus I didn't want her to worry.

During this same time period, just after the New Year, I was learning to play the bass and was slowly becoming more proficient with the instrument. One day Russ told me he thought I was ready to play in the band, and that I would be the bass player at the next gig, which was that weekend. I was petrified. Not only did I feel that I wasn't ready – after all I was just barely learning to play – but playing in the band meant standing up in front of a crowd. I was still very shy and had terrible social phobia (unless I was drinking, of course). The thought of playing in front of a large group of people was frightening and set my heart thumping. But somehow he talked me into doing it. "It'll be easy," he said. "All of the songs are basically the same. You'll do fine."

It was a nightmare. Nobody had told me in advance what any of the songs were so I had nothing to practice. I knew the basics of playing but was still a total newbie, and I had never played bass with anyone before except Russ. I went into the bar terrified that I would screw it up. Of course I had to calm myself by drinking, so I had several beers before the show began. The drummer started the first song and I missed the first note. In fact I missed the first line of the song because I had no idea what I was doing. I totally blanked out, as if I had never played before. It was just like the first calculus exam I had taken at

UM – my mind went dead. So there was no bass guitar at all in the first song. On the second song the lead singer/guitar player started calling out the chords for me with every change. I still missed them, coming in late for every one, and it was terribly embarrassing because you could hear his voice calling the chords over the PA system so everyone in the bar could hear this as well. I struggled through the next song and saw that everyone in the band was getting frustrated and mad. The crowd was silent and staring too. Finally Russ put his guitar down and took my bass from me, and played bass the rest of the night. I slunk off the stage and ambled toward the bar, my head down and my body quaking inside. I was mortified and so embarrassed I just wanted to die right there. A heavily made-up, attractive lady at the bar put her cigarette down and her arm around my shoulders. "Oh you poor thing," she said, exhaling smoke in my face, "Why did they do that to you? Let me buy you a drink."

The following week I went to the lead singer's house and asked him to teach me all the songs. We made a tape of the tracks so I had something with which to practice. I went home and practiced like a mad woman, playing five to six hours a day, until my hands hurt so much I could barely move my fingers. I was determined to become a good bass player and that's exactly what I did. I was always good at setting goals and reaching them, and I had that crazy work ethic from my years of being a competitive swimmer. This has been a constant throughout my life – my ability to set goals and succeed in most everything I do because of my work ethic, my positive "can do" attitude and my tenacity. The main thing I have *not* been able to do, the only big goal I have never been able to reach, is that of controlling my drinking. Even with my tremendous will power and confidence in my ability to succeed in nearly all aspects of my life I have not been able to do this one, seemingly simple, thing. It is, and always has been, a very humbling part of my life.

I felt lost inside. Even though I was playing regularly in the band (I had improved tremendously) and was dating Russ I felt lonely and "out of sorts." Other than Russ I had no friends in Madison. Everyone I used to hang out with was off to college somewhere or had already graduated and had a job. I discovered that the working world was the pits. All the jobs I had were low-paying and I generally made around four dollars an hour. I realized that I couldn't get a better job without my college degree, and that I needed to prepare myself to go back to school.

I knew my parents couldn't afford to send me back to Michigan as an out-of-state student, so I had to consider my options. One, I could transfer to the University of Wisconsin and finish my degree there. The other option was to start training again and see if there was any way I could get my swimming scholarship back at Michigan. I had started to miss swimming and had fond memories of the friends and camaraderie I had had on the team. As difficult as the swimming life was, and as dramatic and painful as it had been to quit, it was the only lifestyle I knew. I was very uncomfortable in "the real world" and didn't know what to do with myself. It was just weird to me, and nothing "felt right." Swimming had been such a huge part of my identity. Without it I didn't know who I was anymore and nothing was filling the void I felt inside. I enjoyed playing the bass and being in the band, and my relationship with Russ was pleasant, but I was confused. It bothered me, and I spent a lot of time thinking and talking with my mom about my self-esteem and self-identity. I still felt a "hole" inside, and a pain in my heart that I couldn't pinpoint. I started to get depressed again and this worried me a lot. To numb my feelings I drank, and that bothered me too because I knew so well that drinking was not the solution. I decided to start training again and just see what would happen. I told myself that I didn't have to make any decisions. I would just give it a try and see if I could generate any desire.

So later during my "year of rest and recovery" I did start training again with my club team, the Badger Dolphins. I was swimming only once per day and this suited me just fine. I continued to go for long bike rides and runs to stay fit, and started to lift weights again. I was woefully out of shape for swimming at the elite level, but because my general level of fitness was so high I began to swim better in practice relatively quickly, although it hurt a lot. By summertime I was swimming quite well and actually enjoying it. I loved to train hard and my friends were back on the team, having returned from their respective schools to train in Madison for the summer. The workouts and friendships seemed to fill the "void" that I had been feeling so strongly. My depression went away and was soon replaced by a steady, more or less happy, state of being.

My mom had always assumed that I would be returning to academia so our relationship didn't change too much when I announced that I was going to start training again and try to return to Michigan. What did change was that I no longer had to work those horrible, low-paying jobs. She said that she would support me financially as long as I was training and planning to go back to school. On my dad's side of the family things seemed to improve a lot as well. I had felt very uncomfortable in the past six months or so, that I was the "black sheep" of the family since I was a "college dropout." But when I informed my dad, my stepmom Pat and my grandmother that I had decided to train again and return to school everything improved. Perhaps this was only my perception, perhaps not, but I remember then feeling much more accepted and "approved" by my dad's side of my family.

I didn't tell either of my parents – or anyone else except my therapists many years later – about my suicide attempt, that fateful night on top of the parking structure the day before I quit swimming. At the time I was too ashamed and too embarrassed. It still seemed like an incredible weakness to me, to commit suicide, and I tried not to think about it. But every now and then it crept back into my mind and I was confused. Was that really me? It seemed so strange and foreign, that dreadful night when I "almost did it," and so far removed from my current psychological state of mind. It scared me to think that I could have allowed myself to become that desperate. Was I really that weak inside? And what about The Voice? What was that all about?

I noted that I had been relatively happy while I was staying at my mom's house and playing in the band, and that my mood had been pretty stable even though I was drinking. I wasn't having the erratic mood swings that had plagued me for so long, and I wasn't having those awful nightmares. I thought that it was all related to stress, the stress of my former lifestyle as a swimmer and a student. I also realized that in order to go back I had to find some way, some new way, to deal with that stress. Certainly I couldn't allow myself to become so damaged inside that I drove myself to the brink of suicide again. I had to find another way. But what? Again I felt very lonely and somehow fragile. The swimming "machine" was now grinding away as usual. I was doing well and had achieved my goal: Jim had offered my scholarship back, to finish my senior year at Michigan. But nothing was different. We were working extremely hard in the pool and cranking out the workouts every day. There were the usual parties and social events to go to. I looked forward to going back to Ann Arbor but was also concerned. I had been training well but hadn't competed at all during the summer. I just hadn't wanted to. So I had no way to gauge my progress or see if I could handle the pressure of competition again. I knew there would be high expectations of me and deep down I worried. How was I going to get through this? I had yet to generate that strong feeling of desire that had served me so well in the past. What if I couldn't get it back? Could I perform reasonably well without it?

I said goodbye to Russ and my family and left for Ann Arbor. Trepidations aside, I was ready to leave Madison and to be "going away to school" again. Waiting for me was a beautiful new swimming facility, the Don Canham Natatorium, which had just opened. Many of my old teammates and friends were still there too, plus some new faces. I rented a small apartment and prepared for the next chapter.

I remember my last swim practice very clearly. We were doing a set called a "T-30," a horrible workout that I detested. I had been training with the team for about a month when it came time for the dreaded time trial. It worked like this: after a long warm-up we were paired off. One swimmer would do the T-30 while the other wrote her "splits," the times for each one-hundred yards, on a clipboard. Later these splits and the total distance swum would be fed into a computer program that would calculate optimal training times for all sorts of distances at all sorts of intervals. The idea was that you swim as hard as you can, maintaining as fast a pace as possible without dying, for thirty minutes. The information gathered from this torturous swim would be used to create optimal plans for the next segment of training, perhaps a month or so, before the T-30 was done again and the process repeated.

I hated the T-30 more than any other workout. For one, it was boring. I was already having a problem with boredom in practice and swimming a straight, hard, thirty minutes seemed the apex of boring sets. At least if it could be broken up into two-hundreds or one-hundreds that might make it more interesting. I liked Jack's workouts in Madison a lot better than Jim's. Jack was always inventing creative new sets, ones that would accomplish the same objective as something like a T-30 but wouldn't be so mind-numbing. Jim's workouts were predictable and dull. One could count on every Monday being generally the same, every Tuesday we would do "this" or something like it, every Wednesday it would be "that," and so forth. I needed more mental stimulation, especially with my attitude toward swimming being so tenuous already.

I was having a tough time getting enthusiastic to train and compete. One problem was that I was no longer the best breaststroker on the team. In my absence two of my teammates had really stepped up their game and were now routinely beating me in practice. It bothered me that I was being beaten because of my competitive nature. But oddly I also didn't really care. I was struggling to find motivation. I felt such despondency after that T-30 that one of my teammates, a fellow breaststroker who was beating me, actually came up to me and said, "Hang in there. It'll get better." She told me later that she knew I was going to quit after that, and she was correct.

The love was gone, and this time I was even more sure of it. There was no wish to kill myself, no feelings of being "stuck," confused or desperate. I wasn't even depressed – I just felt a little down – probably more disappointed in myself than anything else. The day after the T-30 I told Jim I just couldn't do it anymore. I was sorry, but that was it. There wasn't a drop of mental gas left. Since the season had already started and the money allocated, I was allowed to keep my scholarship. So rather than swim with the team I worked on deck as a Student Assistant Coach. It was a good arrangement, although it took some getting used to, both for the team and for me.

As my senior year passed I did fairly well in my classes and enjoyed my coaching "job" with the team. I continued to run and bike and I swam quite a bit on my own as well. This was both to keep fit, which I deemed as a necessary part of my "self," and also to keep my moods under control. As had been the case for years, I found that if I didn't exercise enough I would be either climbing the walls with untamed energy or heading toward depression, or sometimes both. The mood issue was complicated as I could never predict what was going to happen. I might feel perfectly fine one morning and then a few hours later I would be absolutely going out of my mind, having a manic episode. Or my mood would slide quickly down the slippery track into "the black hole of hell" as I called it.

Either way, the extremes were unbearable, and I didn't understand why I had this problem while no one else seemed to. Was this a result of my excessive, overzealous training? Was it in part due to stress and anxiety? I wondered if so many years of such an extreme lifestyle, of not getting my period and excessive eating had ruined my body's natural ability to regulate itself. Maybe I had managed to screw up my hormones and body chemistry to such an extent that I had too much testosterone coursing through my veins? Perhaps that would explain the aggressive energy and the erratic, sometimes rapidly changing highs and lows. I tried to think of other people on the team who might have mood problems but I could only think of one, a diver, and I was certainly not like *him* (I just thought he was off his rocker, or on drugs, or both). So I struggled internally with more questions about myself and didn't feel like I had anyone to talk to about these issues. I was surrounded by teammates, friends and coaches and yet I still felt terribly alone. My solution to this quandary was, of course, the same as always – drink, and forget.

Maggs and Jacques

The first time I saw her was on a sunny, blustery day in the middle of February. I was returning to my apartment and she and a somewhat nerdy looking guy were unloading their small car, which was parked in front of our six-unit apartment building. Ah, I thought, my new neighbors. The unit next to mine on the second floor had been for rent for a short time and apparently these two, or at least one of them, were moving in.

The woman was small, slender and wore a long, leopard-spotted fake fur coat with a thick, dark fur collar. She wore elbow-length, tight black gloves. Her hair was long, straight and a beautiful light, sun-bleached blonde, and she looked as though she had just returned from a tropical vacation. She held a thin cigarette, from which she took frequent deep drags in one hand and a jewelry box in the other. There was a lightness to her step and a certain jauntiness about her as she walked, with her head high and her back straight. She had grace and poise and elegance. Except for the fact that she was moving into our modest building my immediate thought was "movie star," or perhaps a former professional dancer, or something similar.

She came confidently toward me with her hand outstretched and a big smile on her face. "My name is Maggs, short for Maggie," she said. "Do you live upstairs?" I introduced myself and said that yes, I was her neighbor-to-be. We chatted for a few minutes while her "friend" went back and forth, carrying boxes and other items into the building and up the stairs. The gentleman with whom she was living was a quiet man named Keith, and the two couldn't have been more different. Maggs was gregarious, energetic and outgoing, and was constantly laughing and smiling. Keith was quiet and shy and hardly said a word. Maggs was petite, very thin and smoked like a chimney. Keith was a somewhat large man, of average build and slightly overweight, and didn't smoke at all. He wore beige trousers with short-sleeved, checkered shirts (with pens in the chest pockets) and no jackets. He had a light beard and wore thick, oval-shaped glasses. Maggs had a ruddy, time-worn face and deep lines when she smiled. I could see that she was a drinker and obviously a person who liked to have fun. We hit it off immediately.

One afternoon several days later Maggs knocked on my door, happy and smiling in her tight-fitting jeans and colorful sweater.

"Would you like to come over for dinner tonight?" she said. I thought for a moment.

"Sure," I said, "I'd love to."

I don't remember what we ate, but I remember the drinks beforehand, the nice red wine during dinner, and the many beers consumed later. We talked and laughed and exchanged stories as we got to know each other. There were many differences in our lives but we also had a lot in common. Most importantly we understood one another. During our first dinner date I confided many personal secrets to Maggs, and she to me. We talked and drank into the wee hours, long after Keith went to bed. We *clicked*, and I was thrilled. I had found a person who seemed to truly understand me: my swimming, my alcoholism, my mood problems, my fears, my confusion about my sexuality and other serious issues. We accepted each other from the start and quickly became good friends.

Several weeks after I met Maggs I met another interesting person. It was March 14, 1989. I remember the date because March 14 is my mother's birthday. In fact her birthday was the reason why two of my good friends and

I were at Rick's in Ann Arbor, drinking beer and eating nachos at happy hour and slowly getting loaded. It was a reason to celebrate, of course (not that we needed a reason).

A tall, good-looking guy stood near the stage. My friend, who had been paying attention to the music more than I, said, "Hey Christi, why don't you go over to the sound man and tell him to change the music. He's cute. Go tell him to put on some reggae."

So I got up and sauntered over to him. He was kind of cute, with big, deep-set blue eyes, a friendly smile and nice, straight white teeth. A big man with strong, wide shoulders and a broad back, he wore jeans, a T-shirt and a French-style black leather cap. A leather pouch and tool belt hung loosely around his waist. He said he would change the music, no problem, and I went back to our table.

"Oh, he *is* cute," I reported, "Seems like a nice guy, too."

I poured more beer from the pitcher as we all turned to look at him, standing near the sound console.

"Why don't you go talk to him?" my friend said.

"Maybe I will," I replied, "after a couple more beers."

I was still – as always – very shy without alcohol to help bolster my courage.

A short while later I got up my nerve and walked over to the sound booth.

"So. . ." I stammered, "do you really know what all these buttons do?" I asked, feeling like an idiot.

"No," he replied, smiling, "haven't got a clue."

I looked at the equipment with its glowing colored lights and LCD screens. I made another dumb remark about how complicated everything looked and then finally remembered to introduce myself. He introduced himself as Jacques, though his real name was John, and told me that he was hired by the bar to run the sound equipment for the various bands that came to play. I thought about Maggs and how outgoing she was and tried to be like her. Somehow I managed to get through the conversation, which I don't quite recall. But I thought he was a classy guy, that he was easy to talk to and I liked his personality. Eventually he said he had to get back to work but could he have my phone number and call me sometime. Sure, I said as I wrote it down for him. I wandered back to our table where my friends were smiling in anticipation of hearing all about my adventure. I told them about it, including the part about giving him my phone number. They were impressed. "He won't call, though." I said. "I just bet he doesn't call."

The next morning my phone rang and it was Jacques.

"What a surprise," I said, "I wasn't expecting to hear from you." I immediately felt like a moron for saying it.

"Oh," he laughed, "I guess it is kind of quick. I was wondering if you would like to go out sometime?"

"Sure," I replied, "I would love to."

"How about tonight?"

Yikes, I thought! But I said yes and we agreed to go to The Bird of Paradise, a jazz club in Ann Arbor. He would pick me up at seven.

Even though I had sworn off serious relationships with men and had no intention of entering into another one, I was nervous before the date. Friendships are always good, I thought, and anyway I liked this cute sound guy. So I dressed up, did the best I could with my hair and even wore makeup. I thought I looked about as good as I could and was pleased with my appearance. When I opened the door for him that evening he looked at me with surprise. "What?" I said, "Do I look funny?" When I met him my hair had been a mess and I was wearing sweaty, dirty workout clothes. At first I thought he was disappointed and didn't like the made-up me. "No!" he said, surprised at my remark and eyeing me up and down. "You look great!"

And so started our first date and the rest, as is said, is history. We went to

"The Bird," drank beer and ate pretzels. The band played gentle jazz music in the background while we got to know each other. We discovered that we had many things in common as we talked excitedly about all kinds of subjects. The attraction was immediate. Jacques was a UM graduate and very smart. In addition to being a sound engineer he was an accomplished musician and had played trumpet and saxophone for the popular local Ska band, SLK. There was nothing we couldn't talk about. He was interested in many of the same things as I, was fluent in politics and current events and was very well read. *And* he was good looking. He was tall, big and fit in a "working man" sort of way rather than in an athletic way. He had thinning brown hair which was hidden under the stylish black leather cap, a cute smile and those big, gorgeous blue eyes. He was confident, strong, and had the air and mannerisms of a man who was used to being in charge. I remember going home after the date and thinking, wow, what a great guy! He was obviously very interested in me, and I liked him a lot too. But I feared serious relationships, opening my heart again, and exposing myself to so much potential pain and heartache.

But Jacques was persistent. He either called me every day or would show up at my apartment unannounced. He got along well with everyone, it seemed, and my friends liked him, especially Maggs, whom he got to know well because she was almost always home when he stopped by. I would be walking back from the pool, after the afternoon workout, and there they would be, Maggs sitting in the sun on a blanket drinking beer and smoking and Jacques next to her, chatting and laughing. Sometimes I would be annoyed by this but most of the time I enjoyed his company and was flattered by the attention.

As time went on Maggs would tell me, "He really loves you, Chris. You should keep this guy!"

And I did have strong feelings for him, but deep down I was so very afraid. Of course I drank to smother those feelings, but they came out anyway. I told Jacques about this, about how hesitant I was to get involved in a serious relationship because of what had happened the year before. He was patient and understanding, and would often say, "That's OK. I can wait."

~~~

By the end of the summer our relationship had definitely progressed to "serious," though I still had doubts, reservations and inhibitions. These were not about Jacques' professed love for me – he was obviously in love and said so often. My doubts were about my own ability to open up my heart and soul and to truly love someone so completely again. Sexually I was inhibited and shy, and naturally tended to avoid sexual relations unless I was drinking. But I tried. In August Jacques went with me to Madison to meet my family. Everyone liked him as I knew they would, and it was a fun and memorable trip. After the trip we returned to Michigan and officially moved in together, in Jacques' apartment in the small, dumpy town of Whitmore Lake, just outside of Ann Arbor.

Jacques and I had our share of conflicts and our relationship – though usually pretty good – was not a bowl of cherries. For one thing, we were very different in temperament. Jacques was calm and laid back most of the time and tended to take things in stride. He was generally in a good mood and happy, though he did have an angry side that emerged now and then and would come boiling to the surface. This usually happened when he felt wronged by another person or was frustrated to the extreme, or somehow injured himself, like by bumping his head or accidentally smashing a thumb with a hammer. Then he would be enraged and would slam around the apartment, taking out his anger on inanimate objects. He would become like the cliché – the fuming, snorting bull in a china shop. I hated these "childish tantrums," as I called them, and truly feared his anger. Sometimes I would chastise him or make a remark, and this would erupt into a fight. Many years later, after I got sober, I learned that the best way to deal with these situations was to avoid them, so I would leave the house and go for a walk while the pot reduced to a simmer. Fortunately it took a lot to unleash that whirlwind of fury and rage, and Jacques was never physically violent or abusive towards me. Most of the time he was patient and even-keeled and, except for a few annoying habits, was pleasant to live with.

Of the two of us I have to admit that I was the more difficult roommate. Maggs used to say to me, "Wow, Chris, you can watch your moods change like the weather." She was right about that. I continued to have a terrible time with severe mood swings. I tried to control them in the usual way: with hard exercise and/or drinking, but this didn't always work. Sometimes I would start getting "too manic" and Jacques would tell me to go for a run or a bike ride. This I would do with mixed results. Sometimes blowing off lots of steam that way would calm me, other times it would crank me up even more. Regardless, when evening came I would drink. I didn't need a reason, but being "too manic" was often the case, and I used alcohol as a sedative, to help calm me and quell the "nuclear energy" that seemed to always be steaming and bubbling inside me.

Of course alcohol is a depressant, and I also had my share of major depressions. It's difficult to sort out whether these were due to my bipolar disorder, to my drinking or to both. Regardless, they were often severe and would sometimes last for weeks, and occasionally, months. On some of my worst days, Jacques might come home to find me curled in a ball on the floor sobbing uncontrollably, my mind swirling in its darkest corners, feeling deep despair and hopelessness. I would tell him that my life was worthless, that I was a failure and that I was so miserable I wished I was dead. He would pick me up off the floor and hug me while I cried, and reassure me that all would be OK.

I don't think Jacques *truly* understood these depressions. I don't think anyone really can who hasn't experienced them. But he tried – he was sweet and patient and would try to get me to talk about my feelings. If I was willing to talk at all, the conversation usually would come around to swimming or to the man who broke my heart. I still wasn't over him and it took a long, long time to finally come to terms with that episode in my life and to find peace with it. As for swimming, I struggled with the fact that I had quit before I was "done," before I swam my senior year and another Olympic Trials. I agonized over whether I had made the right decision, and often felt that I had not. *If only I had been stronger*, I would think to myself in despair. *If only I could have toughed it out for one more season. Maybe I could have turned my attitude around and had a successful year.* If only I had done this. . . If only I hadn't done that. . . I tortured myself with "if onlys" and "what ifs."

I was still in touch with my good friend Sue, who had been our Assistant Coach, and she would remind me of the state I was in when I made the decision to quit. She would remind me of my desperation, of my feelings of being "stuck," and of the fact that I had made the best choice I could at the time, given the awful situation I was in psychologically. She would tell me to remember all the good things that came from that decision, and how I had felt empowered, happy and free.

My mom would say the same thing whenever we would talk about it. Sometimes she would become impatient with me and tell me that I needed to "accept it and let go," and move on. "Stop being a victim," she would chastise me. "You're allowing yourself to be sucked onto the shit pile again." The "shit pile" was drama, negativity and negative thoughts. Her statement that I was being a "victim" meant that I was blaming life for *happening to me*, rather than accepting that I made my own decisions and therefore determined the outcome of my life to a large degree. "Being the victim" means living in the negative world of feeling self-pity and lack of control over one's destiny. When she told me to "stop being the victim" that meant I needed to stop feeling sorry for myself for what happened in the past and take control of my life in the present: to *empower myself* by looking forward, with hope, positivity and action, rather than to *victimize myself* by looking backward with remorse and self-pity. She was right of course, but often those words didn't help me when

I was mired in a deep depression. I *did* often feel like a victim – not of life's circumstances, but a victim of what was going on inside my own head that I could *not* control, but tried *so hard* to control. It seemed that nobody, except perhaps Sue, truly understood these depressions. I couldn't just "snap out of it" or "put a happy face on and get over it." Without the necessary medication I was left to my own devices, and as usual I tried to pound the darkness out of myself with extreme exercise and extreme drinking. Certainly the drinking didn't help. I'm not sure that the exercise did either, when it got that bad. It seemed that the serious, major depressions just had to slowly go away on their own. Sometimes the days seemed interminably long and "waiting to get better" hopeless. This was when most of the awful thoughts would creep in – desperate thoughts – suicidal thoughts.

But my life with Jacques wasn't always wrought with depression and unhappiness. I vacillated between these and a more comfortable state, which was somewhere between "normal" and "hypomanic." Webster defines hypomania as "a mild mania especially when part of bipolar disorder." Mania is defined as "excitement manifested by mental and physical hyperactivity, disorganization of behavior, and elevation of mood; specifically the manic phase of bipolar disorder. Excessive or unreasonable enthusiasm. . ." I tended to exist in the "hypomanic" state for a good part of the time, and I rather enjoyed it. I generally would feel decent, happy and super productive. It was a good place to be, and I tried to maintain the feeling. But occasionally I would climb even higher, into the bizarre and frightening world of mania. This was almost as hellish as being in deep depression. My mind would be spinning so fast I couldn't concentrate. I would pace back and forth like a caged lion, so full of energy and internal discomfort that I would want to do drastic, crazy things, as I've described before. And again, my solution to being in this state was to run, run, run as hard as I could, or bike, or swim – just beat myself into complete exhaustion to make the spinning and "craziness" subside. Sometimes this would work, sometimes not. Again I used alcohol to self-medicate. I would drink myself into a gentle state of calm and peace and, eventually, an alcohol-induced sleep.

Jacques endured my mood swings with patience and understanding, at least as much understanding as one could hope for. He also tolerated my drinking. Jacques wasn't much of a drinker; he drank like a "normal" person, usually satisfied with a glass or two of wine or a few beers. He enjoyed smoking pot more than drinking, and this was often an issue of contention between us. Even though I was drinking heavily, probably five or six nights of the week, I had issues with his smoking and said so. I knew it was hypocritical, but I was against smoking pot even though I had done plenty of it myself (though I did not like the effects of the drug, which made me jittery and paranoid). I told Jacques that I couldn't live with a "drug addict" and that I thought he was addicted to pot because he smoked several times every day. To prove that he wasn't a drug addict he actually quit smoking for eight months, much to my surprise and happiness. After that period of "sobriety" he did start smoking again, but much less than before and only on occasion. I think he wanted to prove to me and to himself that he was not addicted, would not become addicted, and could control his marijuana use.

In 1991 Jacques and I started a band, a ska band called the "Goon Skwad." For the uninitiated, "ska" is a style of music similar to reggae but usually much faster in tempo. "Reggae on steroids, as I liked to call it, or "punk-reggae." It first gained popularity in England and Europe in the 1970s and started to become more mainstream in the United States as well, with bands like the English Beat, Madness, The Specials and Bad Manners leading the way. Jacques' previous band, the by then defunct SLK, had been very popular regionally and had even opened for some "big-time" acts like The Clash, Peter Tosh and Stevie Ray Vaughn before breaking up in 1985.

The Goon Skwad played ska cover tunes and a handful of original songs, mostly in bars in and around Ann Arbor, Ypsilanti, East Lansing and Kalamazoo. College bars, with rowdy college kids in college towns. We had a drummer, bass player (me), lead guitarist, keyboard player, lead singer/guitarist and a three piece horn section consisting of Jacques on trumpet or saxophone, a trombone player and another saxophone player. I had an absolute blast playing in the band and worked diligently, practicing for hours every day, honing my technique and learning the songs. I also played bass in an all-women's band, the rock cover band called "Y Not." That too was initially a lot of fun, although we only played one gig before we broke up. This happened primarily because the drummer and I didn't get along and I got tired of clashing with her, so I quit the band.

But the Goon Skwad adventure lasted for a couple of years and we had a good time with it, playing regular gigs, making a little bit of money and, in my case, drinking. I never drank when I practiced by myself. I knew I needed to concentrate and work hard in order to become a good player. But during practice with the band or when we played gigs I always drank. I was just too nervous and shy to play with the group or in front of crowds unless I was drinking. Eventually, as is almost always the case with bands, we had conflicts among the players and broke up. Jacques and I tried to get a new group together but we could never quite find the right mix of people to make it work again, so after a time we gave up trying. But it was fun while it lasted.

I continued to drink heavily during my early relationship with Jacques. I spent a lot of time with Maggs and the two of us had uproariously good times going to bars, often gay bars, hanging out with Jacques when he was working, or just hanging out together, usually at Maggs' house. I often rode my bike or rollerbladed the twelve miles from Whitmore Lake to her house in Ann Arbor if Jacques was working nearby. Then I could get drunk with her and catch a ride home with him, stowing my bike or skating gear in the van with the sound equipment. But, like all practicing alcoholics who have cars, I did my share of driving while under the influence. I say "all practicing alcoholics" because I, personally, don't know of any exceptions, though I will submit that there might be a car-owning, drinking alcoholic somewhere who hasn't driven while under the influence. At any rate, I did drive while drinking and while drunk, and I have also driven while in blackout states. I am not proud of this, but those are the facts.

We lived "in the boonies of a small town," and my life required that I drive: to school, to see my friends, to work, or to attend events. And so I did, and was fortunate that I never got a drunk driving ticket. I was pulled over many times on suspicion of drunk driving or for other reasons. On one occasion I had a cooler full of beer on the passenger seat. I was coming home from a long, hot, work day and night in Detroit. There were empty bottles on the floor, a freshly opened bottle between my legs and a donut in one hand as I steered with the other. It was four o'clock in the morning. I was going eighty-five miles per hour in a sixty-five zone, and had literally just slammed four beers in the space of about fifty miles. I didn't want to drive drunk, of course, so I had a rule that when driving home from work I wouldn't start drinking until I was one hour from home (another self-imposed rule that I sometimes broke). As I was being pulled over I hastily capped the full bottle of beer and stuffed it back into the cooler. I tried to cover the empties on the floor with trash and the donut bag but the endeavor was fruitless. When the officer came to the window and asked how much I had had to drink I honestly told him I had had four beers. I neglected to mention that they were all consumed in the last half hour. Because I was so close to home, had a clean driving record and passed the breath test he let me off with a warning. I exhaled a big sigh of relief as I drove away and the officer pulled out behind me. I was starting to feel the effects of the beers I had drunk so quickly, and was grateful to make it home unscathed.

I had similar incidents where I was pulled over, either drunk or drinking (this was obvious), but was "let go" for whatever reason. Usually it was my clean driving record and/or the fact that I was close to home, plus being an attractive female might have contributed. I don't believe the law would be so generous nowadays as there has really been a nationwide crackdown on drunk driving. Looking back I have mixed feelings about not having ever been "busted." On the one hand I'm grateful that I avoided all the legal headaches and expenses (and possible jail time) from a drunk driving ticket(s). I'm also deeply grateful that I never injured myself or anyone else. On the other hand, had I "gotten in trouble" earlier it might have forced me to quit drinking at a much younger age, and my life might have turned out differently. But that is all speculation. Again, more "what ifs."

Two years after I met Jacques I finally completed the remaining twelve credit hours I needed to earn my Bachelor's Degree from the University of Michigan. I was proud to have the degree under my belt but the event was also somewhat anticlimactic, as my swimming friends had already graduated and I had only been a part-time student. I did not attend the graduation ceremonies, but I did receive nice gifts from my dad, Pat and my mom, and a few cards from various members of the family. My grandmother, my dad's mom, was unmoved. "Well congratulations," she said without emotion when I gave her the news, "I didn't think you would do it." Later I cried. Did all of my successes and accomplishments mean nothing to her? Although we were not close, I did love and respect her and her opinion always meant a lot to me. Again I felt that nagging sense of not being "good enough." I wanted her to be proud of me and was confused by the belittling remark. I realized that only I knew what I had been through, what it had taken to get that degree. Even so my sensitive nature got the better of me and I allowed this singular episode to overshadow the positive responses I received regarding my graduation. As time went on the hurt lessened, but my grandmother's reaction bothered me for a long time afterwards, and it took some effort to eventually forgive her for her flippant statement, that without her knowledge caused me such pain and sadness.

During the time period when I was first living with and getting to know Jacques Maggs met a fellow named Greg. Greg was the epitome of "nerd." He was shy and quiet, dressed in jeans and wrinkly T-shirts and always looked like he just got out of bed. He had messy black, wavy hair and slightly squinty dark brown eyes that gave him a perpetually "sleepy" look. He loved books and reading and was extremely smart and – once he came out of his shell – quite witty. Maggs was in love. They moved into a house with another roommate in Ann Arbor and threw amazing parties. The four of us became good friends and we traded having dinners at each others' houses, going canoeing, hiking and camping. Greg was a pot smoker so he and Jacques would enjoy their drug of choice while Maggs and I drank. We had tremendous fun.

Jacques had a large boat, a twenty-three foot Mako ocean fishing boat. We would take it on fishing adventures in Lake Michigan and, when it was running well (it always needed some sort of repair) on camping trips with Maggs and Greg to the remote wilderness of North Manitou Island. We had great fun hiking and exploring the island's many beautiful natural features, its old farmsteads and the historic, dilapidated logging village located near the small campground. Most people visited the rustic island to backpack, eating freeze-dried food and the occasional fresh fish they might catch in the inland lake. Because we had the boat we came in high style and comfort, hauling large coolers filled with delectable vittles and, of course, beer and liquor, to our rustic campsite.

We had many adventures on the island, starting with our first trip. Monster waves and a small craft advisory were in effect but we decided to make the twelve-mile crossing to the island anyway, knowing the Mako could handle the rough seas. It was harder for us, however, as we clung to the rails for dear life while the boat pitched about, drenching us with icy water (we all ended up suffering from mild hypothermia). When we finally made it to shore we were greeted by masses of biting stable flies that had hatched in hordes during the past few days. I remember Maggs running, screaming hysterically, back and forth along the trail to our campsite, her spindly long legs prancing wildly and her skinny arms waving as she was chased by a cloud of the insidious, blood-thirsty insects.

On another trip we battled an infestation of raccoons that found our campsite and its well-stocked coolers too alluring to resist. The cooking fumes from our thick steaks and greasy fried potatoes must have invited every raccoon on the island. They stalked us at night as we sat by the fire, moving about in the underbrush and getting into screeching battles as they jockeyed for position, surrounding our campsite and moving ever closer. Their masked faces and glowing eyes poked menacingly through the tall grass. They were so desperate for food they were brazen and bold, both at night and during the day. One afternoon a raccoon slunk right up to the fire pit as Maggs was cooking, plucked a pot by its handle and carried it off while Maggs just sat there, immobile and staring in slack-jawed wonderment. The raccoons were fearless in their desperation. We were all concerned about the possibility of rabies so we tried to avoid direct confrontation with them if possible, though Jacques and Greg often engaged them with large sticks, but to no effect.

During one of our most memorable trips to the island our faithful Mako beached during a storm. We had spent the day inland on a long hiking trip, completely unaware of the blackness that was slowly engulfing the island. As we exited the sheltered forest at the end of the hike, we were nearly blown over by the howling wind. We all looked at each other and immediately started running downhill, along the path through the old apple orchard toward the beach and the unsheltered spot where our boat was anchored offshore. Sure enough, it had dragged its anchors and was being slammed on the rocks by the incoming breaking waves. Except for Maggs who was too small and thin, we all waded in and tried to wrestle the boat back into deeper water on every incoming wave, hoping to save its keel and propeller from damage. Meanwhile Maggs had brought the park rangers who saw our plight and came to help. But try as we might the waves were just too powerful and the situation was very dangerous, with the big boat bouncing on the waves and rocks, nearly crushing us as we tried to turn it around. Long story short, we ended up winching it to a tree and hauling it partly up on shore, hoping to prevent further damage from the heavy wave action.

Once the storm blew past and the lake calmed we spent the next three days digging, eventually building our own miniature "marina," floating the boat on shore in a shallow harbor. This was so we could remove the propeller to prevent damage to the drive shaft, and also to make it easier to haul it back into deeper water. The rangers radioed a salvage crew from the mainland to come rescue our stranded boat. With every man and woman on hand helping, we and the crew were able to haul it off the beach. It was a big and expensive job, but we were successful and the boat sustained only minor damage to the bottom of the hull.

I have many fond memories of our trips to the island, but some frightening and sad ones as well. One of my scary experiences occurred when I had drunk so much rum that, while passed out in our tent in a drunken sleep, I actually stopped breathing for a short while. I woke up heaving and gasping for air, knowing that I was in serious trouble. Jacques spent the rest of the night watching me once I passed out again, to make sure I "made it through the night" as he said. I was so hungover the next morning I felt like a freight train had rumbled through my head. Everything was shaking and quaking inside and even my brain seemed to be quivering in my skull. It had been another epic night of drunkenness followed by morning remorse. I swore I would never drink again, but by evening I had cracked my first beer of the night and started the process all over again, although I tried to keep the drinking somewhat under control (i.e., no hard liquor that night).

We missed our annual trip in 1992 because Greg was in the hospital, being treated for acute myelogenous leukemia. It was an awful ordeal for him and for Maggs, as he endured many indignities and suffered terrible side effects from the chemotherapy. Already more than a year had passed since his diagnosis.

He had lost much weight and was fighting for his life. Eventually the leukemia was pushed into remission and he was released from the hospital, though he was too weak to do anything that year except stay home and slowly recover.

Jacques and I continued along in our sometimes rocky relationship, working our respective jobs and trying to make a decent living. He was busy being a sound engineer and I often joined him on gigs, helping to move heavy equipment and set up/tear down shows. By this time I had also become quite successful in my own business, as the owner of a marine fabrication company. I designed and built canvas covers for boats of many sizes and styles, created steel framework and a variety of custom canvas and plastic "glass" enclosures for large boats. I did all the steel work myself, as well as the patterning, construction and installation of the huge and heavy canvas goods. The work kept me strong and in great shape, which I both enjoyed and sometimes hated. The jobs were difficult and nitpicky. Customers were demanding and it was stressful maneuvering on the expensive boats, trying not to damage anything while building heavy, often hard-to-handle products. Weather conditions made it all the more challenging. It was often windy, which made patterning the large, three-dimensional objects very difficult. I had a crate full of clamps of all shapes and sizes that I used for this arduous task. I often worked in the rain as well, stepping carefully on the slippery fiberglass as I inched my way around windshields and consoles. Once I even worked during a blizzard, on a huge yacht moored at the mouth of Lake Erie. I was making great money and had promised the job would be done by a specified date. Blizzards aside, I tried to stick to my word, so I toiled even as my hands froze and I almost fell off the boat many times during the dangerous final installation. By day's end this sort of effort always called for a big reward – alcohol, and lots of it.

I bought a small bus which I converted into a mobile "shop" to use in addition to my large work space at home. This I drove to marinas and private residences throughout southeast Michigan, particularly along the Detroit River between Toledo and Lake St. Clair where the big boats and "big money" were. The work was hard, physical, strenuous and dangerous. For the most part I really enjoyed it, as I loved the challenge of designing and building the fancy enclosures and miscellaneous items for the large, extravagant yachts. Sailboats were particularly challenging, with their many lines and winches that needed to be accommodated in unique and carefully crafted designs. I also repaired and constructed new upholstery and did much interior work on these boats. This didn't interest me as much and it was still very physically demanding, but I did it anyway because it paid well.

Sometimes I worked on boats that were so large I needed to hire a few extra guys to help me. Occasionally this turned out well but for the most part my "help" ended up costing me more time and money than it was worth. Expensive stainless steel fittings frequently went overboard, the distinct "plunk" sound ringing in my ears as I calculated the dollars lost. No matter how many times I instructed my helpers not to leave items on the gunwales they always did. I would turn around to see a two or three hundred-dollar drill or riveter resting precariously on the edge of the boat. Every now and then something would fall in, something expensive enough that I would have to go diving for it. I would put on my snorkeling gear and a weight belt and sink slowly to the dark, murky bottom, feeling around in the muck until I found the expensive item. It gave me the willies, imagining dead bodies and all sorts of creepy-crawlies slithering around in the black sludge. Needless to say this was one of the least enjoyable aspects of the job.

I found some of my helpers, big strong guys that they were, to be wimpy. It was always hot, the hours were long and the work very physical. My "strong guys" had no stamina, and after eight hours or so they were whipped and ready to call it a day. For me, the hours at the "away from home" jobs were long by necessity because it cost a lot of time and gas money to drive the bus back and forth. I would take it to a marina and live in it for several days, sleeping in the bunk I had built into the workspace where I had my industrial sewing machine, shelves, tools and supplies. The bunk was in front, under a long plywood work table, and was quite comfortable. My friends called it the "coffin" because it was small and dark, and if you sat upright you would knock your head on the underside of the table. I used the marina's facilities to shower and sometimes eat if the marina had a restaurant. Other times I prepared my own food using the camp stove and other cooking utensils I kept on the bus. If there were no shower facilities I would take a "camp shower" at the end of the day, using gallon jugs of water and strong soap to wash off all the sweat and grime from the day's efforts.

In addition to the great pay I enjoyed my job for several reasons. For one, I spent much time outside and on or near the water, which I loved. I also loved being my own boss, and having the freedom to do what I wanted, when I wanted, and how I wanted it done. Being a perfectionist required me to do most or all the work myself because I couldn't find many people who met my expectations. I had an excellent reputation for first-rate product and honest dealings, which I tried hard to maintain.

Another thing I loved about my occupation was that I spent most of the time alone. I was either working on the boats when the owners weren't there, or at home in my large basement (and eventually pole building) shop, or I was on-site working in my bus. I was always a "lone-wolf" type and, with the exception of my swimming years, was never one to have a lot of friends. Being my own boss also meant that I could drink on the job whenever I wanted, although I did have "rules." I tried not to drink during the day, or when owners were present. If I was shaking badly in the morning or had a hangover I might drink one beer to steady my hands but that was the limit.

Generally my days went like this: I would wake up early, around seven o'clock, have coffee and get started on the boat right away. This was to avoid the thermal winds that always kicked up near the big lakes as the sun rose, sometimes making the work impossible. I would pattern first, stepping carefully on the dew-covered decks, enjoying the morning stillness. Then, after several hours had passed and the winds started, I would spend much of the day sewing in my air-conditioned bus. Depending on the job I might go back and forth to the boat many times, fitting and refitting as I constructed whatever it was I was making. My normal "quitting time" was six o'clock, but I never actually "quit" then. It just meant that I was officially working "after hours" and therefore could drink. By then I was hot, sweaty and tired and nothing tasted better than a cold beer. I planned my days so I always had something to either start making or to finish into the late hours, so I could sit at my sewing table while I drank beer, listened to music and slowly got loaded. I worked past eleven o'clock on those long jobs, trying to get as much done as possible while at the marina. How I managed to go full steam from seven in the morning until close to midnight and still do high quality work I don't know. It must have been my young age and manic energy – and the large amounts of beer and wine – that kept me going.

Marriage and Codependence

Sometime early in 1993 Jacques proposed that we get married. It was one of those strange proposals that nobody envisions. It wasn't special or romantic, in fact it occurred during a fight. We were in the midst of a heated argument when Jacques essentially told me he wanted to marry me and that I either had to say yes or move out. I don't remember how the argument ended, but I do remember saying yes. We started making plans for our wedding.

We decided, with my dad's and stepmom Pat's generous financial support, to have our wedding on North Manitou Island, our favorite place to go camping and one of our most special places, period. The Mako would be docked in the public marina in Leland waiting to take us, Maggs and Greg to the island afterwards for a week-long "camping trip honeymoon."

We had an amazing wedding. My dad and Pat rented the ferry that services North Manitou, which is still a wilderness island, and all sixty-plus of our beautiful, formally-dressed guests climbed aboard for the several hour voyage. When we arrived we found a lovely spot in front of the historic "Monte Carlo House." The wedding was informal and ad hoc, and couldn't have been more perfect. It was a spectacular warm, breezy, sunny Michigan day, not a cloud in the sky and – most importantly – no bugs. The late June foliage grew in various shades of green and gold and the wildflowers bloomed in full glory, purple, pink, yellow and white. The scene was idyllic, with wild, prickly rose vines engulfed in white flowers flanking and climbing around the door of the old house, the tall, green grass surrounding it and the old apple orchard in the background. We had found a Baptist preacher to perform the service. Our good friend, the accomplished musician Neil Woodward, provided fiddle and mandolin tunes as the guests walked and assembled in front of the house. My cousin Ingrid played *Ashokan Farewell* on the violin when the wedding party proceeded around the house in a somewhat traditional manner to begin the service. The actual ceremony was short and sweet, romantic and beautiful. It ended with another moving performance by Ingrid, who sang Bellini's *Vaga Luna*, accompanied by Neil. Everyone clapped and it was official – the woman who said she would never marry had gotten hitched. We were both ecstatically happy.

After the ceremony we headed back to Leland for the post-wedding dinner at The Cove, an excellent restaurant close to the Lake Michigan shore and overlooking "the falls" of a river flowing into the lake. I drank outrageous quantities of wine and liquor, and as usual, got drunk. By this time my tolerance was so high and my ability to hide my drunkenness so well practiced that few were aware, at least not until later, that I was extremely drunk. After dinner we returned to our suite to open our gifts in front of many of the guests and I remember being very inebriated. I'm sure that people noticed – how could they not? I only hope that I didn't make a fool of myself because my recollections of that part of the evening are still quite fuzzy.

Jacques and I had always had a somewhat tenuous relationship and we still had fights after our marriage. Like most people, we both carried baggage from the past into the relationship, and raw emotions from that sometimes surfaced and caused conflict. We were tireless workaholics, in our jobs and around the house. We both felt that we contributed greatly to our common good. Our fights were almost always about money – we would argue about whether or not I was contributing enough to our overall financial situation. Jacques would claim that I needed to make more money. I would insist that he needed to spend less. He would always tell me that we were "just barely getting by and going deeper in debt" and then he would go out and buy some piece of equipment that cost anywhere from a few hundred dollars to a few thousand. This situation became even more serious when Jacques decided to start getting into video production in addition to audio production. Now we needed cameras, tripods, better computers, monitors, expensive video editing software and an assortment of related pricey items. As usual, Jacques believed in buying the best quality, so we rarely bought cheap or used gear. This was a good thing in the long run, because it enabled excellent production value, however it did take a lot out of our bank account (or credit cards, as was often the case).

So we had fights about money. Not often, but often enough that it was a significant source of stress in our relationship. Mostly I tolerated his spending sprees and kept my mouth shut, though inside I seethed with anger. We also started fighting about my drinking. Jacques would claim, and I would always agree, that I was drinking too much, and that it was costly as well. I would promise that I would try to control it, and I truly did want to, but as usual I could not. My moodiness was often a problem as well, and Jacques had to deal with either my depressions or my hyperactivity. Sometimes he would accuse me of taking too much time for myself, (i.e., too much exercise and drinking), rather than working to make money. I would insist that I needed my daily exercise like I needed food (to keep my head on straight), and that I needed to drink because I was addicted. It was hard to argue either point because each was true. We sometimes talked about my quitting drinking altogether but these were usually casual conversations. Both of us knew how many times I had tried – and failed – to quit. Talking about quitting seemed a pointless exercise so we rarely did.

Shortly after our wedding, at the end of August in 1993, Greg's leukemia got the best of him and he died in a bed at Detroit Mercy Hospital. He had undergone a bone marrow transplant that failed, and so spent the last month of his life in a sterile, quarantined room, mostly alone. Greg slowly dwindled away physically until Maggs inevitably had to make the difficult decision to take him off the medical equipment that was keeping him alive. Jacques and I drove Maggs to the hospital the morning she got the call that Greg's systems were failing and the end was near. The windshield wipers barely kept up with the deluge of rain as we drove. When Greg actually died Maggs came out of the room and asked if we wanted to go in to say our last goodbyes. Jacques said no. He had already had one dear friend die of cancer and this time he wanted to remember his friend as he had been in health. I said no too, although have always regretted it. Even though Greg had been reduced to a shell, and Maggs said it was "an ugly scene in there," to this day I feel bad that I didn't go in and hold his hand one last time. I loved Greg. There was, and will always be, a special place in my heart for him.

Greg's death hit me hard. I had never before had anyone so close to me die, and I couldn't handle it. At the "wake" at their house the following day all his friends and relatives gathered and I drank until I couldn't see straight. I also drank before and (secretly) during the memorial service, which was held at Gallup Park along the Huron River. I simply had no way to cope with this new pain, as I had never experienced it before. Whenever pain surfaced I buried it in my usual way – by mentally forcing myself to stifle it, by pounding myself with exercise, or by drinking. The pain of Greg's dying went so deep that I had to employ all three of my techniques, and it took a toll. I was physically and emotionally exhausted, and either drunk or hungover much of the time. It was an awful way to live. I knew I was destroying myself and yet I couldn't stop. I became very depressed and this gave me even more reason to drink and feel sorry for myself. In my darkest moments of despair I contemplated suicide, and then hated myself for thinking it. After all, I thought, poor Greg wanted to live so badly and here I was thinking about killing myself. Again I punished myself with self-loathing and disgust.

Much later, in 2008 when I went into treatment and had quit drinking for the last time, I was asked why I thought Jacques had put up with me for so many years, what with my heavy drinking, our alcohol-laced fights, my oversensitivity to criticism and my moodiness. I would reply that it was a two-way street, that I put up with a lot from him too – his excessive spending, his angry, childish rages and his controlling nature. But we endured each others' flaws, I would say, because we loved each other. All of that was true, but during treatment I also learned a new term and began to understand our relationship in a new way – "codependency."

Codependency is defined as "of or pertaining to a relationship in which one person is physically or psychologically addicted, as to alcohol or gambling, and the other person is psychologically dependent on the first in an unhealthy way."

A codependent relationship may also involve people who are not addicted to a substance. Regardless of substance addiction, codependency often occurs when one of the persons involved is preoccupied with controlling the other's feelings and behavior, and the other person allows these actions (which can be physically or emotionally abusive) to interfere with his or her own personal growth, relationships and contentment. Sometimes both individuals engage in controlling behavior, in an attempt to manipulate the other. The result is that neither person feels healthy, balanced and whole, and the relationship is destructive to one or both participants.

Some believe a distorted and damaged sense of Self is at the root of codependency. Healthy people with high self-esteem understand that they cannot control others' feelings, ideas and behaviors, and they make decisions that are best for themselves, affording the same right and responsibility to others. Unhealthy people – people who suffer from damaged self-esteem due to past experiences – often make poor or unhealthy choices, for example they either engage in controlling behavior or they allow themselves to be controlled and/or abused.

Jacques and I both had unusual upbringings and challenging family circumstances that may have resulted in a distorted or damaged sense of Self. Certainly I believe that this was the case with me. I have already described the trauma and sadness I felt after my parents' divorce. I have also written about the stressful environment in which I lived, with my mom's difficult job, her coping as a single parent and the constant strain and worry over finances. My mom's drinking was also a factor. She had a fiery side to her personality that was fueled by alcohol, and sometimes she released her anxiety by yelling and being unnecessarily or unfairly verbally abusive towards me. This was hard on me, and made me furious. The unfairness of being yelled at for sometimes very minor reasons created a rage toward her that I buried and carried with me for a long, long time.

I likewise had my own personal stresses and strains, with the excessive pressure of swimming at such a high level and my desire to perform well in school. Despite my many successes both athletically and academically I suffered from damaged self-esteem. This was due in part to my drinking and my inability to control it, but also in large part to my perception that I was never "good enough," and could never "be enough" to satisfy my parents' expectations. I was always very sensitive to criticism and would often agonize for days over even a small remark or comment that I felt was negative or critical. As confident and poised as I appeared on the outside, inside I was a fearful person. I was afraid of failure, of my confusion about my sexuality, of intimacy, of pain, of loss. These feelings all contributed to a low sense of self-worth and esteem, which I learned to hide well.

Jacques lived with two alcoholic parents who were not physically demonstrative or affectionate and a sister who was always getting into trouble. During his boyhood Jacques' family was the picture of chaos and drama, with Jacques always being the "good boy" and the "calm one" who tried to control and "fix" the chaotic situations and relations within the family. Eventually his sister, Daryl, became an alcoholic and drug addict, and the drama in their lives escalated. Fighting and screaming at each other was the norm in his family.

Jacques' father, usually neatly dressed in jacket and tie, was polite and sedate. He was a professor of Russian Literature and, as such, a well-educated and cerebral man. He was also quite witty and funny in a quiet, wry sort of way. Jacques' mother was fanatical about horses and kept a dozen or more on their large property in the country. Because she raced thoroughbreds she was constantly busy with the horses, training or caring for them, transporting them to races, feeding, cleaning out stalls and so forth. They also had five big dogs that lived in the house so, even though it was neat and clean when we visited, the place always had a slight yet distinct aroma of horse and dog.

The family obviously had money but I still frequently heard about financial difficulties. Between their several rental properties and the horses, plus my soon-to-be mother-in-law's used car business and other enterprises, their financial situation was complicated and stressful. In addition they supported their drug-addicted daughter, who was constantly getting into serious trouble due to her addictions. The family supplied her with cars which often became wrecked or were "stolen," a house in which to live, money for daily necessities (that she used for drugs, although they were in denial about this) and legal assistance when she was arrested and needed to be bailed out of jail or required a lawyer. Thus the family lived in constant chaos and drama which seemed to emanate from everyone except Jacques' father, who appeared to tolerate it all with a subdued patience and resignation, just as he also subconsciously, or perhaps consciously, enabled it.

I'll never forget the first Thanksgiving I spent at their house, the same year I met Jacques and just a few months after we moved in together. We arrived at the house to find Daryl (whom I had met only once before) and her mother yelling at each other in the kitchen. Jacques, his father, and I went to the den for drinks and polite conversation as though nothing out of the ordinary was happening.

Next I remember hearing Jacques' mother shout, "John! You *RUINED* the turkey!!" Jacques' dad took this loud admonishment in stride as we moved to the kitchen where an argument ensued about the turkey's doneness. "It's cooked 'til Hell won't have it," Jacques' mother muttered under her breath as she carved the meat. Then, with me standing aside watching in wonderment, the four of them attacked the buffet-style dinner in a frenzy, heaping food on their plates as though they hadn't eaten for days. I slowly served myself and joined them at the table, where everyone was eagerly waiting to begin the meal.

The conversation was light and cheerful, as if the fight between Daryl and her mother had never occurred, or was such the norm that nobody gave it a second thought after the storm had passed. Everyone ate hungrily and noisily, talking and joking with good humor. Soon, one by one, they all returned to the buffet for seconds as I worked on my first plate.

With their second servings quickly finished they commenced to slam about in the kitchen, putting dishes in the dishwasher, hand-washing the family silver, putting away the food and arguing about this or that. I had never seen anything like it. I sat alone, dumbstruck and staring at my as yet unfinished first plate of food, while the entire family was engaged in a loud, noisy, clanking battle. I poured myself another glass of wine and felt depressed. Eventually Jacques' dad returned to sit with me at the table and we conversed lightly while the rest of the family bounced off of each other in the kitchen.

And this is how I characterized their family dynamic – constantly colliding and bouncing off one another. Jacques was always trying to assert himself by advising his parents to change their ways. He insisted that their lifestyle was draining them monetarily and would eventually result in financial ruin. For example he opposed their keeping so many horses, as it is very expensive to feed and care for them. He was also angry about all the money that "went down the drain" in the "swirling black hole of Daryl's drug addiction." Despite everything that had happened, all the arrests, the "stolen" cars, the bad marriages, this disaster and that disaster, the failed attempts at treatment and so on, Jacques' parents were still in denial about the severity of Daryl's drug use. "Oh, she's been clean for several weeks now. I've never seen her better," his mother would say, each and every time Daryl tried to quit, episode after episode, literally hundreds of times. "Daryl's the best she's ever been." After a while Jacques and I began to joke about it because she said it so frequently.

So that was the situation in which Jacques grew up. He had a strong-willed, busy mother who was involved in multiple, stressful and expensive enterprises. He had a relatively subdued father who spent much of his free time supporting these activities in various ways and self-medicating with alcohol, plus a drug-addicted sister who was the focal point of the family's energy, time and resources. Jacques tried to assert his influence over various decisions that were made but his efforts were in vain. His parents did what they wanted, spent money with abandon and situations remained chaotic despite Jacques' every effort to change them.

In some respects our relationship was similar and we both contributed our share of past baggage. Both of us were strong-willed and liked to be in control, so we often clashed in that regard. Though we didn't argue often, when we did the arguments became very heated and usually ended up with me crying and storming out of the house. I wasn't used to such loud arguments while growing up at our house. Certainly we had disagreements and, as I have written before, my relationship with my mother was difficult at various stages of our lives. Granted we occasionally raised our voices and yelled at each other, but this was not the norm in my family. Many times I stifled my anger for fear of repercussions, and if I felt that a situation was unfair or unjust I often repressed those feelings.

By contrast Jacques was used to expressing anger overtly and without reservation. It scared me, and was, in a way, controlling on his part. This is one aspect of the relationship that I now consider codepend ent: one person needing to argue and thereby pushing the other into a heated argument in order to "win" by making the other person (me) cry or run out of the house. This didn't always happen, and Jacques was mostly calm, like his father. But every now and then I believe he needed the arguments to assert his feelings of self-worth and his need to dominate and control. I was the one nearby, and because of my own self-esteem problems I allowed it, so I was the unlucky recipient of his wrath and the second half of the codependent equation.

My personality was another factor in our attraction to each other and in a certain way to our codependency. I am a lot like Jacques' mother and my own mother, always needing to be busy and boldly taking on new and "different" enterprises, learning through experience and often the school of hard knocks. For example I taught myself the marine canvas business, which, even though it eventually became quite successful, was initially a very difficult and expensive venture. I basically learned everything about the trade by doing it, making mistakes, reading books, attending conferences and so forth. When I bought my bus Jacques informed me that I "had better learn to fix that old piece of shit because I'm not going to be your bus mechanic." He himself owned a full-size, thirty-five foot long converted school bus and had his share of mechanical and other work to do. So I did teach myself to fix my bus, with my ace mechanic brother's help. I replaced master cylinders and brake lines, calipers, rotors, rebuilt the carburetor, replaced spark plugs, distributors and bad electrical wiring, put on a new starter motor and once even tore most of the engine apart in order to replace a bad distributor coil. That job I did on the road, stranded overnight in a storage lot in over one hundred-degree heat. It was such a complicated operation that I just assumed I had made some sort of critical mistake along the way. But to my astonishment the darn thing actually started when I turned the key, and only needed a slight distributor adjustment to correct the timing. After that incident I always carried tools and many spare parts when on the road in the bus because I never knew if a brake line was ready to pop or some other disaster was about to happen.

I was also very handy and adept with construction work and helped build a big pole building on our property, which I paid for myself, in order to have a larger workspace. This was before my body became so damaged and while I was still able to do hard physical labor, like installing roofing plywood and shingles, working with drywall, doing both rough construction and finishing work, installing insulation in high and dangerous places and so on. I really was a dynamo physically, and rather than hire people to help us, Jacques and I believed in doing everything ourselves. So we did all the interior and exterior work on our old house, which was always in some need of repair, and all the yardwork and landscaping around it.

I believe Jacques' and my personalities had a lot to do with our codependency. We both were multi-talented, hard-working and self-motivated. Sometimes we would almost get competitive about it (or at least I would). When I was younger I always felt that I had something to prove. First it was in swimming and academics. Later I turned my attention to my occupation and to my work at home. Because I came from a stressful environment growing up I believe I inadvertently created difficult situations for myself that caused stress and anxiety, perhaps out of a subconscious need to live in a familiar, challenging environment. I think Jacques was drawn to those personality traits – my stress and anxiety – because there was always so much stress in his own household that he had tried in vain to change or control. On my end I was always looking to please my parents, or my coaches, or to live up to someone else's expectations. Being married to a man like Jacques satisfied that need, because he also had high expectations. And as much as I liked to be in charge, there was also a certain part of me that was so used to being controlled (e.g. by the rigors of swimming, and by my coaches and parents), that I needed that in my life too, and I found it in Jacques.

My drinking and associated behavior were certainly large factors in our codependency. By the time I was in my late-twenties I was drinking very heavily and nearly every night. I was also engaging in reckless and dangerous behavior, which I wrote about earlier (drunken windsurfing in blizzards, extreme rollerblading, etc.). Jacques was generally against this and occasionally we would argue about what I was planning to do, but he "allowed" my reckless behavior because he knew he couldn't stop it. I know he wanted to curb it because he had tried, but failed. My drinking and my exercise – crazy as they might be – were sacred to me, and nobody was allowed to touch them. It did create a certain amount of tension in our house, as Jacques would comment on the sanity of what I planned to do and sometimes make critical or negative remarks about my mental state. But I took these as they came and had my fun anyway, and I do believe Jacques got a certain amount of amusement from my behavior. But being pragmatic like his father, he knew there was nothing he could do to change it short of divorcing me, and he never threatened to do that.

As for my drinking, I believe Jacques learned a lot about denial from his side of the family. Even though he saw it daily, even though he picked me up or helped me stagger from parties nearly passed out from alcohol, even though he found me many times still in bed at noon or later with horrific hangovers (he would come into the dark room with coffee and ask "is there life?"). He sometimes found me passed out on the floor at home, yet he would still make remarks now and then that indicated his denial. For example, one time we were talking about how serious my drinking had been (this was at the "end," just after I went into treatment in 2008). He said something to the effect that he "didn't realize it had gotten so bad." Well of course it had gotten bad! Alcoholism is a progressive disease. Drinking or not, *it doesn't get better. It only gets worse.* I reminded him of recent episodes – of driving home drunk from friends' houses, of the late mornings and terrible hangovers, of the arguments about how much I was consuming. But to give him credit, I did do most of my serious drinking alone, after he had gone to bed, which was usually around ten or eleven o'clock most nights. I often couldn't wait for him to go to bed so I could drink in peace. So he didn't see the worst of it and probably wasn't aware that I often stayed up until three or four o'clock in the morning drinking.

After I had been in treatment for a while I was in a "confession mode" one day and began telling Jacques about the many things I had done while drinking. One thing that surprised him was my secret "stash" of alcohol. It's very common for active alcoholics to stash liquor around the house (or car, or workplace) to make sure something is always available in a pinch. Usually this is a good indicator that the disease has progressed to the point where it is no longer merely (merely!) a psychological addiction but is now a physiological *NEED*. The body physically *needs* the drug or it starts going into withdrawal, which is very serious medically and can be life-threatening.

In my case my secret "stash" was in my closet, easily accessible behind a stack of shoeboxes but not visible by a casual glance. The stash was often stocked with expensive booze that I would normally not buy for myself. Jacques was not much of a drinker, but he did enjoy a good – very good – margarita on occasion and so would buy excellent liquor to make his delicious concoctions: El Patrón tequila, or some similar brand, and Grand Marnier. He also occasionally received gifts from clients: Wild Turkey whiskey, Dewar's scotch, expensive bottles of port. Sometimes I would make myself a "starter drink" with these but most of the time I would hit them late at night, after my own daily ration had run out (I always bought my alcohol daily, to ensure that I didn't buy "too much"). I would pour myself a glass from his special collection, or sometimes two or three. Then in the morning I would check the level in the bottle to see if it had gone down enough for him to notice. Usually it had. I knew Jacques would be angry if he found out that I was drinking "his" booze (and how much of it) so I would immediately go out and buy a replacement bottle. Then I would refill the violated bottle and put the new one in my closet. It provided a certain sense of relief to know it was there. The bottle was like an old friend waiting for me, waiting to help me in time of need. Sometimes when these pirated bottles ran out I would buy something for my closet myself, just to maintain that sense of hidden comfort and security. Usually this would be a pint or a fifth of Jim Beam, my favorite, less expensive brand of whiskey. As mentioned earlier, I never told Jacques about my stash until well after I had quit. I didn't want him to worry, and I didn't want to hear the lecture about how much I was drinking.

It was no secret that I drank too much, at least not in our household, which is why Jacques' "sometimes denial" was confusing to me. One time when I was in my early thirties he had me sign a piece of paper that said, "I, Christi Vedejs, hereby promise to allow Jacques M. to do anything in his power to keep me from, or stop me, from drinking alcohol." This included chaining me to the basement wall and other similar delightful tactics, as he would claim with a grin. I still have that paper; it's hidden at the bottom of my jewelry box. It is interesting that he was aware of my heavy drinking early in our relationship – we met in a bar, after all, as I was getting drunk – and he acknowledged it often, yet he also said that he "hadn't realized how bad it was."

My explanation is twofold: one, denial is a very powerful thing. Jacques truly didn't want to believe that I was "that bad" so his brain twisted the reality into something much more palatable to him. Two, he was an enabler and a codependent. He enabled me to drink by purchasing alcohol for us both (even though he knew most of it would be consumed by me) and by turning a blind eye when I would drink excessively. Granted sometimes he would vehemently suggest that I quit, or "cut back," but there was no strong resolve to these demands, no threats to leave me or to "punish" me in any way.

The codependent part seemed complicated when I first began analyzing it. But once I got to the root of it, it seemed quite simple. Somewhere deep in his sub-consciousness Jacques needed me to be the heavy drinker. Why? *Because in this condition he was in control.* And even though he couldn't truly dictate my behavior he was, in effect, "in control," because he was "the strong one who didn't drink, who worked regular hours, who didn't make (alcohol-related) mistakes, who picked me up when I had 'fallen' or was 'needy,' who handled problems and who made sure that everything got done." He was embracing the same role as "caretaker" that he had played while growing up in his family. This isn't to say that I wasn't also capable – I was a very high-functioning alcoholic, after all, and a very strong-willed and *mostly* strong person, both physically and mentally. But alcohol had eroded a lot of my inner fortitude and self-respect. In Jacques' mind I'm sure he saw me differently than how I saw myself, and I know this because of the things he said. For example one time we were talking (actually fighting) about the possibility of divorce and he said, "Oh, well you'll find another man to take care of you." I heard that statement on more than one occasion and it never failed to infuriate me. It denigrated me, belittled my many accomplishments and contributions to our household, and I felt it was a deep attack on my character. It implied that I was weak and unable to take care of myself. Of course this kind of statement affected my self-esteem negatively, and I used my available tools to combat it – exercise and drink. So the drinking behavior continued, the enabling continued, the denigrating and controlling remarks continued, my self-esteem suffered and I drank. The negative, codependent cycle repeated over and over again.

    I feel it necessary – for the sake of our current happiness and harmony as a couple – to point out that Jacques disagrees with my perception of his role in our relationship as I have described it. His response to the question of why he stayed with me through all those years is not that he was a "codependent enabler," as I characterized him, but that he loved me and was loyal and faithful to me and the vows we made at our wedding (i.e., "For better or worse, in sickness and in health."). I believe that this is true, knowing Jacques as I know him, and perhaps what I wrote is harsh. But I stand by what I wrote, though I respect Jacques' opinion of it. As I have said before, I have never blamed anyone for my drinking other than myself. Saying that Jacques was a codependent and an enabler means that his actions *contributed* to the situation, it does not mean that he had control over my drinking or caused it in any way. Clearly he did not. The act of drinking or not drinking rests squarely on my shoulders and I know that.

Another point I would like to emphasize is that after I quit drinking in 2008 the pattern of our lives changed dramatically. It is common for relationships or marriages to fall apart when one partner quits abusing a substance or stops engaging in negative, self-destructive behavior. The circumstances become different, the former user (in recovery) starts to feel empowered and his/her feelings of self-worth and esteem begin to improve as the dynamics of the relationship evolve. Sometimes the other partner doesn't like, or can't adapt, to those changes. Once I got sober it took a certain period of time for us both to "get used to it" and to re-learn how to relate to one another in a more equal way.

In our case Jacques' dad was dying of cancer at the same time that I was in treatment and my mother was in intensive care at a hospital, suffering from liver failure due to *her* alcoholism. Jacques took a very active role in helping each of us get through this extremely difficult time period: what we thought was the end of my mother's life, his father's imminent death with all the horrors that that entailed, as well as the "beginning," so to speak, of my new sober life, which also had a learning curve. It was an acutely intense and stressful time in our lives, and it says a lot about us and the strength of our friendship and marriage that we were able to get through it.

Jacques would work a full day, then go to "the farm" to help his mother and father, then come home and ask me how my day at UMATS had gone and how my mother was doing. Sitting in our small living room we would share our experiences and talk about the events of the day. This sharing helped us form a new and deeper bond, and allowed us to learn from each other and grow together in a very positive way. It took a solid half-year or perhaps even more, after his father had passed and my mother had recovered, but we did re-learn how to relate to one another and respect each other. It wasn't always easy, and we did still have the occasional argument, but the difference in our relationship was truly amazing. We had rebuilt a foundation of love, trust, respect and empowerment for each other that has continued to grow and improve to this day.

The Beginning of The End

I wish I could end my story with the last paragraph of the previous chapter, but I feel it essential to backtrack and explain some important things that happened. The last ten years of my "drinking life" held some events that were so pivotal to my life that they need to be explained in order for my story, such as it is so far, to be complete.

In 1996 my brother Mike moved to Michigan to join me in my business and add another dimension to it: marine mechanical service. We thought it a great idea, since I had so many customers and many of them told me there weren't enough good mechanics working on-location on boats. Mike is a Master Mechanic and was looking for a change of scenery, and we were both intrigued about the possibilities that this new enterprise could provide. So he came to Michigan and lived with us while we started working to grow our fledgling business.

One thing I learned from this experience – much later, of course – is that in this day and age, generally speaking there are few "open markets." In other words, if nobody is doing something there is probably a good reason for it. We bought a trailer and some extra equipment to augment Mike's already large collection of tools, and we set to work. His good reputation spread quickly and there was plenty of work, but we soon found out why very few people perform on-location mechanical repairs and service. Frankly, it's a

The Beginning of The End

pain in the ass. First of all, by the nature of their design, working on boats is physically difficult, and requires one to twist and contort one's body in all sorts of ways to reach hard-to-fix problems. Mike was good at this but it took a heavy physical toll. Second, since every situation and every boat is different, it is nearly impossible to have all the replacement parts necessary for the job in stock, so one is constantly going back and forth to the parts store or waiting for a special-order part to arrive. This eats up time with hours that are not billable, so much time is wasted. Third, some jobs – like hoisting out an engine – are simply too large to do on-site and require lifts and other heavy equipment that can only be used on land.

It didn't take much time to realize that this type of business wasn't viable in the long run. We decided to rent a building closer to home, work on smaller boats that could be trailered to it and fixed either on the property or inside the building, sheltered from the weather. We also decided to expand the business to include cars and just about anything that had an engine, to diversify and ensure a steady inflow of cash.

The nice thing about our building was that it was large, had a decent reception area that we built and finished ourselves, plus an extra "side" room for office work, which was mostly my job. The shop area itself was wide and deep, with two big bays, each with its own garage door. In between the bays was the reception/office area, a restroom and another fairly large area where I set up my huge worktables and sewing space.

It was an excellent working situation but renting the building had downsides, and these were mostly financial. First, the overhead – rent, insurance, taxes, utilities, advertising – was substantial and we had to make a fair amount of money just to turn the key in the lock every day. Second, we had to make a number of additional purchases of tools and heavy equipment in order to do the mechanical work. This we financed using my personal credit – my credit cards – which we also used when we were short on cash. The start-up costs for this type of business were very high even with what

Mike and I already owned, and even though we obtained a good deal on rent for the building. We were both surprised at how much it cost just to get the business started.

We worked extremely hard and really put our noses to the grindstone. I kept up my marine fabrication work, both on-location along the Detroit River and Lake St. Clair and in our shop closer to home. Sometimes Mike would help me on the larger jobs but mostly he was busy in our new shop, working on whatever came in.

Sometime during the summer of Mike's and my first year in business together I met a woman named Clara. She was a client who owned a big pontoon boat. I made a fancy cover for it and Mike performed engine work on one of her cars. Clara had a solid job, was a moderate drinker and a very social person. We soon became friends. She was also a lesbian and was clearly attracted to me. I knew this because she said so, not in so many words, but in offhand remarks and comments about my body and my personality. I was also attracted to her, though I didn't say so and was, once again, apprehensive and confused by my feelings.

At that time Jacques' and my relationship was quite strained, both from my heavy drinking and our financial difficulties. Even though my brother was an ex-drinker (a successfully recovering alcoholic) and a respectful, courteous housemate, it still put some stress on our marriage having him living with us because our house was so small. We were together almost all the time and there wasn't much privacy. Also I knew that Mike disapproved of my drinking and that made me uncomfortable. Every now and then, when talking about some problem or another that I was having, Mike would tell me, "All your problems will go away if you quit drinking." I found that difficult to believe. "All" of my problems? The financial stresses of our new business put pressure on all of us as well. So to escape the discomfort at home I spent a lot of time away, either working at marinas or spending time with my new best friend, Clara.

Clara was going through a difficult breakup and was in the process of moving so there was substantial stress in her life as well. We talked about our various problems while drinking beer on her boat or barbecuing on the porch at her house. I confided many things to her, including the difficulties I was having in my marriage, my problems with mood swings, my difficulty with intimacy ever since my big heartbreak, and my confusion about my sexuality. It was refreshing to talk with her about that because I felt I had finally found someone who could truly relate. She herself had experienced plenty of confusion in her life about being gay and had also endured verbal abuse from others about her perceived sexual orientation.

We spent a lot of time discussing deep subjects but we also enjoyed "light" fun, like roller blading, playing hockey or golf, going boating, biking and going to bars. Clara was much more social than I and had more friends, so there were often parties or other events to attend as well. These were always with other members of the gay and lesbian community, and I enjoyed the people and the good times we had. Naturally I drank a lot to overcome my shyness, but I was drinking a lot anyway in those days so it didn't alarm me.

I became very confused. I was feeling more and more attracted to Clara and there was a large part of me that ached for closeness and intimacy. I would characterize this as more of an emotional need than a physical one, at first. I just wanted to be held close and loved by someone, to be comforted and told that I was beautiful and special, like I had been with my first love, F. Somehow I suspected that this need, this yearning, could be filled if I would just allow it – try it – with her. But I was scared. As always, I was afraid that I might actually be bisexual or a lesbian. Hell, I had heard it so many times throughout my life: "dyke," "lesbo," "fag," "freak," "weirdo"... Maybe there was some truth to it? And how many times had I been attracted to women? It confused me that I had experienced such an intense, pure, deep, romantic involvement with a man who thoroughly broke my heart, and yet I was again attracted to a woman. And then there was Jacques who, despite our problems at the time, I still loved and cared for. It was all very trying and I again felt like I couldn't talk with anyone about it. Certainly not to Jacques. I also didn't feel that I could confide in my mom, because I knew she would disapprove that I was strongly considering (yes, I did strongly consider it first) having an affair with a woman. I don't think it was the fact it was a woman that would have bothered Mom, it was the idea of having an affair at all. I knew she would be very upset if I was unfaithful to Jacques.

So I kept my thoughts a secret from everyone, even Maggs, because I worried that if I told her how I was feeling it might get back to Jacques. Clara made it clear that she wanted a physical relationship with me but she didn't pressure me in any way, she just constantly flirted, and I flirted back. "What's the harm?" I thought. And besides, it was fun and exciting to have someone want me. I hadn't felt "wanted" in a long time and I enjoyed it.

As much as I tried to fight it, however, eventually the inevitable happened and our relationship changed from flirtatious friends to passionate lovers. The attraction was so strong, and all the flirting, teasing and anticipation finally broke the thin strand of restraint that had held us back from one another. For me it was like every wall, every self-protective piece of fortress that I had built around my inner core came crashing down all at once. The sheer passion, depth of emotion and physicality of our "first time" was beyond my wildest imagination. Honestly it was the best sex I had ever had, and it was like a drug. I hungered for the closeness, the intimacy, the searing, uninhibited, totally fulfilling physical and emotional aspect of it. Between that and the alcohol – which was always present – I was experiencing such amazing, complete pleasure. There was no longer a "hole" inside, like I have described so often. With Clara every physical and emotional need that I had seemed to be fulfilled.

I was in a real psychological and practical jam. I was still very confused about this relationship, and – despite the pleasure, which I yearned for and craved – I tormented myself with worries and concerns. I knew what I was doing was wrong. I was being unfaithful to my husband and, as *right* as my relationship with Clara often felt, there was a part of me that truly didn't want it. *I did not want to be gay.* Period. Between that possibility and my infidelity I felt ashamed, and terribly, terribly guilty.

From a practical standpoint I feared what would happen if either Mike or Jacques found out. Mike is pretty open-minded, but I still thought he would be disgusted and I knew without a doubt that he would condemn my infidelity. Would that affect our business? Would he leave? I didn't think so but I wasn't sure about that. And Jacques, well. . . of course he would throw me out of the house for having an affair, and he would have every right to. It would probably be the end of our marriage, we would get divorced, our meager assets divided. . . leaving me heavily in debt. And then what? I played the scenario through in my mind. What if we *did* get divorced? We talked about it often enough, during our ever-increasing fights and arguments. I mulled it over. *Maybe that's what we should do anyway. Maybe all along the problem with our relationship was that I was gay, and that's why I felt so empty inside, and that's why we argued so much, and that's why we were almost never intimate anymore, because I wasn't internally happy.* It didn't occur to me that it might be my drinking that had something to do with my internal happiness, or lack thereof.

As time passed I became more confused, and more enmeshed in my complex relationship with Clara. Of course she wanted me to divorce Jacques, and she often said so. Then, out of the blue, she quit her job (without another job lined up first) and overnight had terrible financial problems. Since I felt sorry for her, and somehow partly responsible, I hired her to work with me on canvas jobs, even though she wasn't good at it and we really couldn't afford it. I had encouraged her to quit because she was so unhappy at her workplace, but I didn't know she was going to do it without securing another job first. Consequently after a few months she was in dire financial straits and couldn't pay any of her bills. She began to be hounded by bill collectors, which did nothing for her self-esteem and only added to her resentment toward everyone, including me.

Our relationship had already been problematic. After all, I was conflicted because I was married, and she wanted to be with me all the time, and I felt so guilty. Now things really began to suffer for the added financial strain. We started having serious, vicious arguments and fights. Looking back I don't even remember what they were about, only that there was much drama: yelling, crying, door-slamming, throwing things and so forth. Clara often talked about suicide and one time even locked herself in the bathroom, leaving a suicide note on the door for me to find. I called 911 and a police officer came, but by that time the situation had calmed and for some reason I said that everything was okay, so the officer left. Clara was also drinking heavily, so between the two of us we had plenty of alcohol fueling our conflicts, turning what should have been small arguments into screaming battles. We made many night-time threats to each other that this was "the end" and that it was "over," but the next day we would be filled with remorse and regret, and would somehow make up. We were both depressed and angry.

The relationship was a classic model of unhealthy codependency: two participants who abused a substance, were neurotically needy and suffered from damaged self-esteem. We were both controlling and tried to change the other's behavior to suit our own expectations and wants. Naturally this didn't work and we became resentful toward each other, which only added to the codependency. It made us more angry and "hurt," hence more needy, hence more controlling, and finally more verbally abusive toward each other when we didn't get what we wanted. We would make up and have "peace" for a while, and then the cycle would begin all over again. We were both drinking heavily. Clara seemed to like to fight and argue, but I did not. In fact I hated it, and I started to want out of the relationship.

At about that time Mike and Jacques found out about it. I remember coming home one night to a stone-faced Jacques who told me that he knew

I was having an affair and that we needed to talk. He was very angry and hurt, as was to be expected. We talked about what was happening and why, and what to do next. I cried a lot as I tried to explain what the relationship was like, my confusion about it and also that I wanted out of it. We discussed my drinking and how it had contributed to my having the affair, and that I needed to quit using alcohol. We talked about our future as a couple and our marriage, and decided to separate for a period of time while I figured out what I wanted and "got my shit together." I agreed to quit drinking and start seeing a therapist. Just as I predicted, Jacques told me I had to move out, and he gave me three days to pack up and go.

It was a sad day when I loaded my bus with most of my possessions and pulled out of the driveway of our home. I left behind my precious pet bird, who was tame like a human child and whom I adored. I left my husband and my brother, who continued to live at the house. I moved to our shop and set up my bedroom in the side office, which smelled slightly of solvents and gasoline. Mike would arrive at eight in the morning to work and leave around six o'clock. It was lonely at the shop when he wasn't there. I would eat at fast-food restaurants or at Clara's house. We were still trying to sort out our relationship and keep it going but it just wasn't working anymore. I was now sober, seeing a therapist and had started going to Alcoholics Anonymous meetings in a serious effort to quit drinking. Clara and I continued to have horrific fights. I was living in the shop and every now and then, late at night, she would show up drunk, in a state of fury, and demand to talk to me. I wouldn't let her in and this would only add to her rage. I even called the police several times to get her to go away. The relationship was slowly ending, and – despite the negativity and drama – it was still difficult for both of us to let go.

I was extremely depressed, and the solitude and strangeness of living at the shop didn't help matters. As time passed and my period of sobriety lengthened I began to see things more clearly, without the haze of alcohol distorting my vision. My therapist recommended that I see a psychiatrist so I did, and was put on antidepressant medication. She also helped me sort out my confusion about my relationships with both Jacques and Clara, and to see how unhealthy each relationship was. We talked in depth about the destructiveness of my alcoholism, what it was doing to my self-esteem, how it was negatively affecting my job performance, our financial situation (it was expensive to drink as much as I did every day), how it affected my decision-making and reckless behavior, and finally how it affected everyone around me. Therapy was another financial hardship but it proved to be an invaluable part of my recovery.

After several months of sobriety many aspects of my life improved. My relationship with Clara had completely ended and that was a huge load off my back. I felt such freedom and peace without the constant arguments and fights, and the strain of guilt and remorse that I had been feeling for so long. Because the relationship had turned so ugly at the end I had no problem quitting it and was happy to move on.

Throughout my time away from home I had been talking with Jacques on a regular basis, and we were slowly working out our problems. He was pleased that I was sober, and could see that I was truly making an effort to heal and regain my self-esteem. Yet we still had our conflicts, and I tried to explain what it had been like to live with him, to be part of *our* codependent relationship. He was patient and listened, and I believe he truly considered what I was saying and gave it a lot of thought. Jacques has always been open-minded and intelligent enough to know that there are two sides to every story. He impressed me by looking at ours and trying to see things from my perspective. Despite his anger about the affair, which was still significant, he did want to get back together, and so did I. I just wanted things to be different between us. I wanted him to listen to me, and to not minimize and denigrate my accomplishments. I wanted the emotional part of our relationship to be better and more complete. I wanted to feel cared for and needed, and I wanted more touching and intimacy.

I knew that I had a lot of work to do, that our emotional "distance" and inhibitions were my problems as much as his, and perhaps even more on my side. I talked about this a lot with my therapist and continued to work on my many fears, conflicts and struggles. There were my usual feelings of being inadequate and not good enough, and now on top of that I was an unfaithful wife and a failure as a partner. I had many regrets, resentments toward myself, and pain. There were still the lingering questions about my sexuality and why I had had this affair in the first place. Was I gay? I didn't feel gay, but then this strange affair had actually happened and it was impossible to ignore that fact. What was it all about? I was very confused about myself and knew it would take time to sort through this mess and rebuild my self-image and my life. As for Jacques, I wanted him back as a partner and friend, and I really wanted him to *understand me* – my feelings, my pain, my confusion. But mostly I wanted our lives to be good again. I wanted to be in love. With him.

After four months of living at the shop, being sober, working with my therapist and going to AA meetings I was feeling much better about myself and about life in general. Jacques and I had decided to give our relationship another try so I moved back home. Life was improving all around, but we still had much work to do to heal our wounds and rebuild our marriage.

Mike and I were still working hard at the shop and struggling to make ends meet. It had been a difficult first two years, as is typical with all new businesses. But the financial situation was slowly improving and we were moving forward, though sometimes the progress was hard to see. It helped enormously that I wasn't drinking and that I was no longer enmeshed in the relationship with Clara. I was back to my highly productive self and my moods – with the help of the antidepressant and my daily exercise habit – were fairly stable.

But just as things were starting to look up financially Mike sustained a serious back injury while working on a boat. He was finished. He was forced to do nothing, to essentially lie on his back for a month and then take several months of minimal activity to continue his recovery. The business couldn't take the hit – we needed both of us working at capacity in order to make it. We started to fall behind in our bills and struggle to pay the rent. The stress of everything that had happened during the past few years and now this new obstacle – Mike's injury – were too much for us. We decided to call it quits and close the shop.

My personal finances were ruined. I was deeply mired in debt for several reasons. One, I had used my personal credit to finance the business, to purchase equipment, tools and to obtain cash when we needed it. Two, I often used credit to pay for sundry items like gas and groceries, and of course my expensive daily alcohol consumption. And three, because of my drinking I tended to be reckless in every aspect of my behavior, and this included my other spending habits. I often spent money impulsively and with abandon, on small and unnecessary items. It never seemed like a lot at the time, but the small things added up. Over time these expenditures accumulated and, before I knew it, I owed a large chunk of money and was unable to make the payments. In 1998 I filed for bankruptcy. It was the last thing I had ever expected to have to do, but it was the hard choice that we made as a family, and I stuck to it. I went to court alone, faced the judge and attorneys alone and explained to a packed courtroom why I was failing to meet my financial obligations. It was one of the worst days of my life and one of my most shameful. I felt like a complete and total failure.

But time goes on and after that whole episode was finally over I was ready to restart my life once again. Mike had left. After his back healed he moved to North Carolina to take a job working for our uncle, as a mechanic in the family-owned business. I kept working my job as a marine fabricator in order to repay my debts (the bankruptcy entailed a "restructuring" of the debt, so I had re-signed much of it, but with easier repayment terms).

I have been asked why I took on the load of the bankruptcy by myself, even though a good portion of the debt was business-related and therefore should have been shared by Mike as well. The answer to that question is simply that I felt responsible for the failure of the business. Even though we both worked extremely hard, I was the one who drank to excess. I was the one who hired Clara even though we couldn't afford it, and I was the one who allowed myself to become entangled in that relationship. From a financial standpoint, my drinking and the relationship with Clara were damaging to the business because they interfered with my job performance and my ability to make sound decisions. I had been making quite a lot of money before I met her, but once I started spending so much time with her that income dropped. Because Mike and I were always just on the brink of "making it" financially, I believed that that extra amount of money that I would have made had I not been involved with Clara would have made the difference in the survival of our business. So I blamed myself, and beat myself up for it. I reasoned that my assuming the debt load after we dissolved the business was my penance, my punishment for my drinking and the resulting poor decisions that I had made, that ultimately killed the business.

My relationship with Jacques continued to improve while I was sober, and as years passed we rekindled our love for one another and I slowly started to regain his trust. There was still a lot of pain for both of us – and still confusion for me about my sexuality – but these things were much easier to deal with and work through while sober. I found that I had zero attraction to women and as time went on the whole "Clara episode" became more and more surreal. I couldn't imagine how I had managed to become involved in it, and especially with a person "as screwed up as her." It just didn't make any sense to me – it was like it had happened to someone else, not me.

Overall, I was fairly content as a sober person. I was no longer taking the antidepressants. I had made the decision to quit taking the meds myself, partly because they were no longer working well for me (there were bad side effects) but also because I wanted to see if Mike was right, if "all of my problems would go away if I quit drinking." So I tried to keep my mood stable by exercising and maintaining good sleep and eating habits. I did still suffer from insomnia but it wasn't nearly as bad as it had been when I was drinking. And I still suffered from mood swings, but they were also not as frequent and/or as severe as they had been when I was drinking. Everything *did* seem to be improving, both in my home and work life. Financially we were also in much better shape and I had made a good dent in paying off my post-bankruptcy debt. I was no longer going to AA meetings – I had stopped attending them after about a year. I figured I didn't need to go, that I was doing fine on my own, and besides, I had grown bored with hearing the same things over and over again. Life seemed to be on the upswing, and both Jacques and I were happy.

The Middle of The End

In 2001 Jacques landed a full-time job at the University of Michigan, overseeing and working in the Video Studio at the Duderstadt Center on North Campus. At home he had also built a top-notch video capturing and editing system that we personally owned and used for video shoots and editing jobs in addition to sound gigs. It was fun and challenging work and I enjoyed it. There was always something new to discover. The world was full of possibilities for interesting subjects to shoot, new ways to edit, new software to learn, and unlimited avenues for creativity and education. I was no longer working in the marine fabrication trade. Frankly I had become burned out and tired of it and ached to do something different. Getting heavily into video and editing was right up my alley because it provided a constantly challenging learning environment that was both creative and fun.

2001 was also the year that I started drinking again.

I had been sober for over four and a half years. Jacques and I were doing well in our personal relationship, we were again having fun together, our financial situation was stable and my mood was generally good. When I started to feel too "up" or "down" I would do my usual "exercise fix" and this did the job most of the time.

My return to the drinking world started innocently enough, like it does with many alcoholics. We were invited to some friends' house, a couple that we had known for a long time, and they were serving a nice red wine with dinner. I debated with myself for a while and then decided that I would have a glass – just one. After all, I thought, I had been sober for so long, what would be the harm in just one glass of wine? This time I knew I could control it. I didn't *want* to get drunk, I just wanted to have a social glass of wine like everyone else. I told Jacques of this plan and he was dubious, but I assured him that I would only have one glass, and that it couldn't possibly be a problem.

And it wasn't. Not that night, nor was it too much of a problem a month later when I was at a wedding and had *two* glasses of wine. That time I enjoyed an actual buzz – my tolerance was much lower than it had been, of course, because I hadn't been drinking, so two glasses definitely went to my head. Secretly I wanted to have a third glass. I wanted more, but I had promised Jacques I would only have two, so I told myself that I was satisfied and didn't need or want any more. Inside I knew I was lying. I *did* like that buzz, that familiar, wonderful, calming feeling that I loved so much, and I *did* want more. . . in secret, and only to myself. I lied when Jacques asked me how it had been with "just two." I said it was fine, that I had it all under control, and that I thought maybe I could drink "socially" now and then, as long as I kept a tight lid on it.

So the demon alcohol's wheel began turning again, slowly at first, then accelerating until, just like with every other alcoholic, before I knew it I was heading right back to my old patterns of drinking. I did try very hard to control it, however, and to control my behavior. I rationalized that if I could keep myself steady and in a good headspace, and function well at home, and keep up my good work, that I could drink and enjoy an occasional good buzz without upsetting Jacques and having to quit again. It was a sound rationalization. Too bad things don't work that way!

But before I get into the progression – again – of my alcoholism, I need to explain another serious addiction, in addition to exercise, about which I have not yet written. This was my heavy addiction to nicotine. The habit started in my early twenties shortly after I quit swimming, when my whole world was coming apart and crashing all around me. My omission of the nicotine addiction up until this point has nothing to do with its lack of significance. On the contrary, I chose to wait to discuss it in order to give it its own highlighted space. This is because the demon nicotine is every bit as insidious, deadly and evil as the demon alcohol. For me nicotine was a huge crutch, a source of comfort and pleasure, and an enormous elephant on my back. Becoming addicted to it was arguably the dumbest, most idiotic thing I have ever done in my life. I mean that from the bottom of my heart.

The worst thing is that I *knew* it was stupid at the time. And I *hated* it at the time. But I did it anyway. I, with all my anger toward my mother and her smoking, with all my disgust of the smell, the images, the toxic fumes that poisoned everyone around. . . I, with all my self-righteous criticism of people who smoked, actually became a smoker. Yes, it's true. I became a smoker. Then when I decided that smoking was too damaging to my lungs I switched to chewing tobacco, though I still smoked the occasional cigarette at parties or in bars. It baffles me to this day that I started doing that, because I truly, truly hated it. The only thing that makes sense to me is that it was a classic act of rebellion and of feeling like I was taking control of my life. I had been controlled for so long by my rigorous life as a swimmer. When I quit swimming I really wanted and needed to assert my independence, even if doing so meant doing incredibly dumb and reckless things.

Becoming addicted to nicotine truly was dumb. Again, I was one of those people who could "try a drug only once" and become instantly addicted. That's essentially what happened with nicotine. I became addicted almost immediately upon using it, and I had to have it or I would go into fierce withdrawal. I told Jacques about this on our first date – I didn't want him to have any unpleasant surprises – so he knew about my tobacco use, but wanted to be with me anyway. We never had any conflict over it except for the cost. It's an expensive habit and, when coupled with my alcohol consumption, costly to maintain. I tried numerous times to quit but couldn't. My brain and body would just go haywire. I had terrible withdrawal which lasted for months when I would quit cold turkey, and this is not an exaggeration. After a while I no longer got a "buzz" from nicotine, it just helped me to feel normal, and I felt terrible without it. Nicotine helped ease my depressions and keep my mind sharp. It calmed me and relieved my nervousness, my feelings of discontent. It is a stimulant, and my brain became used to it as part of its delicate chemical balance. It is said that nicotine is the hardest drug to quit, harder even than heroin or cocaine, and I believe that from my own personal experience. When Nicorette gum became available over the counter I started "using" that, thinking that it was healthier than tobacco and that it would help me to eventually quit. What happened next is that I ended up with even more of the drug in my system because I would chew one piece after another, every waking hour of my day. There are no regulations with the gum, no places where it isn't allowed. It isn't like chewing tobacco or smoking a cigarette. One can chew the nicotine-laced gum anywhere, anytime, and nobody needs to know about it.

But getting back to drinking and the end of my four year period of sobriety, at first I managed it quite well, as I described earlier. I was able to drink a respectable amount, get a good buzz going, but keep my behavior under control and get my work done. I was again a "highly functioning" alcoholic, and Jacques generally left me alone. I think he had thrown in the towel, so to speak, and just accepted that I was drinking again and there was nothing he could do about it. Plus it gave him an opportunity to also have an occasional drink, which he had not done while I was sober because we never had any alcohol in the house.

So we enjoyed good wine before and during dinner, the occasional excellent margarita(s), and beer around the campfire. We engaged in more social activities, like going to parties and having dinners with friends, because I was now able to attend these functions and appear to drink "responsibly" (though I often brought my own alcohol in a flask and would hit it in secret in the ladies room, or add it surreptitiously to my drink). I had avoided social functions that included alcohol when I was sober because they were too much of a "trigger," and a threat to my sobriety. But now that I was drinking again we were able to have more fun socially, and we both enjoyed it. We also took my friend Alcohol along on our many camping trips and video shooting adventures, which made them even more fun for me. I looked forward to being able to drink at the end of long sweaty days, after a nice camp shower, feeling clean and relaxed by the fire. I had started to shake again in the mornings but I told Jacques this was because of "low sugar" in my blood and that I needed food. Whether he bought that explanation or not I don't know, but he never said anything about it except to comment that "you've got to get your shaking under control or your video is going to look like shit."

My alcohol use was slowly ramping up. I wasn't yet hiding bottles in my closet but I was definitely drinking more as time went on. I was still functioning well and insisting to Jacques that everything was OK, that I had it under control. I drank at home, alone or with him, and again I did most of my drinking after he went to bed so he wouldn't see how much I was consuming. The wheel began to turn faster, as it always does. Once again I was a heavy-drinking alcoholic, and I didn't care. I enjoyed it, and besides, I rationalized to myself, things are going fine. Maybe this time I can manage it, and if I can't, I'll just quit again.

Oh, how we forget the evil workings of alcoholism, how it chips away at our steadfast resolve, working in the background to set the stage for havoc, chaos and destruction! We forget how difficult and nearly impossible it is to finally quit, to finally get a handle on our lives and start to rebuild and heal the damage caused by drink. It's interesting how the mind so quickly forgets pain and suffering. It must be part of our genetic makeup, part of some ancient method of survival that was programmed long ago into our primitive brains. And certainly it's the disease of alcoholism itself that causes us to forget. That's simply how it works for those of us who have it, who are true alcoholics. The disease is always there, will always be there, and will always be lurking nearby, twisted deep into our genetic code, waiting to surface yet again. It is like cancer, and the result of relapse is always the same if the disease is left to take its course: disintegration of the mind and body, degradation and loss of dignity, and eventually, death.

In 2002 Jacques and I started working with a group of people from the Osprey Reintroduction Program of Southern Michigan at Kensington Metropark, near Brighton, Michigan. The program was a joint effort between the Huron-Clinton Metropolitan Authority (a huge park system), the Michigan Department of Natural Resources and the Detroit Zoo. Its goal was to reintroduce the Osprey, a large, fish-eating bird of prey, into Southern Michigan. The Osprey had been eradicated from the southern half of the state by the early 1970s due to loss of habitat and the heavy use of the pesticide DDT, which caused it (and many other bird species) to lay eggs with thin shells that easily broke, thus interfering with their ability to reproduce. DDT use was eventually banned in the United States and many threatened and near-extinct birds, like the California Condor and the Bald Eagle, for example, were able to make a comeback, with assistance from recovery efforts much like the Osprey Reintroduction Program.

Jacques and I became involved with the program in order to produce a documentary about it, to educate the public about the bird and what was being done to restore it to its natural habitat. I secured a job as the Assistant Program Coordinator, working under Coordinator Barb Jensen and Supervising Naturalist Glenn Dent. In so doing I gained access to the inner workings of the program. I was able to have hands-on experience with the young Osprey chicks, feeding and caring for them, and the opportunity to film events that only an insider would be able to see. I loved it. It was an amazing experience for both Jacques and me, as we were able to assist with many aspects of this important effort while filming it, and meet all sorts of interesting people in the process. In the end, after three years of hard work, we produced a feature-length documentary entitled "An Osprey Homecoming," which was broadcast on a local PBS station. Jacques and I both won a Michigan Emmy Award for Best Photography in the Full-Length Program category. We also garnered a Finalist Award at the International Wildlife Film Festival. We were thrilled with the recognition of our efforts, and for the opportunity to learn all about the program and work with such selfless, dedicated people. Producing "An Osprey Homecoming" was another important event in our lives, one in which I am still very honored and proud to have participated.

In 2006 we moved from our home of fifteen years in Whitmore Lake to a cozy old farmhouse in the country. My dad and Pat were so pleased with our find that they loaned us the money to purchase the property outright while we waited for our Whitmore Lake house to sell. Our "new" place is a lovely and quaint hundred-year-old house nestled in a beautiful, heavily wooded valley with a rustic red barn on the property. We love the old-style house, having our own secluded, private wildlife sanctuary, the peace and quiet and the friendly people, our "somewhat" distant neighbors who live in the area. It's the perfect place for an artist to work without distraction, or to rest and recover from whatever ails one. When we moved here I thought it would be a good environment to try, again, to quit my nicotine and alcohol addictions. My use of both drugs was heavy, and I knew I needed to quit, but I was not yet at the point of absolute, total desperation that was necessary (for me, anyway) to take that big step. I was not yet deep in the hole of depressed, alcoholic hell, but I was headed that way – and fast.

In May of 2007 my mother retired after twenty-five years of working for the sports medicine company. She had lived in her house for thirty years, while

Mike and I were growing up and beyond, and was eager to flee Madison for a change of scenery. My mom had been a moderate-to-heavy drinker for many years now, but because of her intense, time-consuming job as Art Director and Advertising Manager her drinking was held mostly in check. She had been a high-functioning alcoholic, getting up early every morning to commute to work and routinely putting in extra hours for which she was not paid. Her work dominated her life, and usually left her mentally and physically drained by the end of the day. When she arrived home at night, exhausted, she would unwind from the day's tensions by working in her immaculate yard, lovingly tending her flowers and garden while sipping gin and tonic. Then, after a couple of large drinks and a light dinner, she would fall into a deep sleep on the couch. Her alcohol consumption remained stable for many years, following that general pattern. But everything changed after she retired.

Without the rigors of her job to structure her life, she began to drink more and earlier in the day (she confided in me later). She made her G&T as usual in her favorite "glass," a large plastic cup with the word "Sport" on it that was half-filled with ice. The drink was often very strong, with just a token splash of tonic, as I noticed when I would occasionally sneak a taste from her "glass," or she would make us both a drink during my visits.

Because of the distance between us I didn't see my mom often. Jacques and I would take one weeklong trip to Madison each year to visit her and the rest of my family, usually at the end of the summer or during one of the holidays. Then in the spring or fall, Mom and I would go on our annual "mother-daughter" camping trip to Lake Superior, a very special vacation to a place that we had been going to since my childhood. Occasionally Jacques or my brother would join us on one of these trips, but most of the time it was just the two of us.

We would each drive north, she through Wisconsin and I through Michigan, to our "secret" rustic campground on the Lake Superior shore. For five to six days we would live at our campsite within earshot of the lapping waves, sleeping in tents and cooking over an open fire. Most of the daylight hours were spent ambling along the rocky shoreline, searching for precious, surf-polished agates and colorful bits of glass hidden amongst the millions of shiny wet stones that glittered in the sunlight. I would enjoy long runs on the firm, wet sand, the gentle sound of the waves soothing my ears and my mom's small, bent-over figure somewhere far in the distance, the vision of her comforting in the solitude of the private beach. Tiny sandpipers with long, spindly legs would skitter in and out of the water ahead of me as I ran, seeming to lead the way as they continued their never-ending quest for insects in the sand. Swimming was out of the question, as the water usually was too cold at those times of year, so daily plunges into the lake served as hasty baths. I would quickly strip off my clothes and wade in, splashing the icy water all over me, then just as quickly dunk under and stumble out naked to soap myself in the sun on the beach. Rinsing off meant another breathtaking icy plunge, but the clean, refreshing end result was always worth the short, somehow pleasurable bit of pain.

Springtime weather in the Upper Peninsula of Michigan is always unpredictable. Sometimes it was glorious, with clear blue skies and warm, soothing offshore breezes. The sun brightened the many shades of light green, yellow and white as the leaves and blossoms emerged from their winter slumber. The rich green and white birch forest that lay beyond this lively, almost neon swath of vegetation formed a lush complement to the deep blue of the lake. Between the water and the forest lay the smooth shoreline with its wide pathway of golden sand that separated the pebbly shore from the woods. The days would be breezy and pleasant, and we would often wear shorts and wade to mid-calf in the cold water while searching for agates and swatting the occasional biting fly.

Other times we weren't so lucky. The days and nights would be raw and bitter, with howling winds whirling under gray, sooty skies, the rain driving sideways on the beach, needling our faces as we tried to keep warm under many layers of fleece and Gore-Tex. On several occasions it even snowed during the trips, making staying warm and sleeping well at night a constant struggle as we snuggled deep into our down sleeping bags, pulling the hoods tightly closed with just a small round opening for breathing.

But regardless of the weather we were determined to have a good time on these adventures and we always did. Mom brought tightly packed coolers and neatly arranged boxes full of good food and always her traditional, delicious homemade potato salad. We joked about how we ate like queens, with great steaks and fire-singed chicken, hamburgers and beer-boiled brats. And of course we always had our faithful alcohol along to ease any discomfort and pave the way for laughter, light-hearted banter, and often deep, serious conversations by the campfire at night.

But we never drank during the day. We both had our rules, after all. Generally we spent the entire day on the beach, starting the routine with a cup of good, rich coffee. This we sipped as we ambled along the campground "loop" that went first down the dirt road to the outhouse and then turned to the lake, with its early morning calm, clear water. After walking a short stretch of beach and making a climb up a sand dune to return to camp, we ate breakfast, which usually consisted of scrambled eggs, toast and pork sausage links cooked over a small fire. After breakfast we packed a light lunch of sandwiches and fruit, lots of water, and headed out for a day of agate hunting.

We walked for miles along the beach and time seemed to stand still. Often we didn't return to camp until the sun was low on the horizon and the lake was calm again, the thermal winds having died and the small waves gently rippling on the shore. The lapping water tickled the endless line of shiny pebbles, sifting the small rocks and making a relaxing tinkling sound as the moving stones tumbled gently back and forth. Late afternoon, with its low, golden light, was the best time for agate hunting, so the return to camp was always slow. Mom usually found more agates than I because sifting through and collecting rocks was all she did during the day, whereas I also spent time running, mountain biking and occasionally windsurfing or paddling some sort of watercraft.

At the end of the day, when we both finally dragged our tired bodies back to camp, we would put down the driftwood and rocks we had gathered and place our precious agates and polished pieces of beach glass – green, white, brown and the occasional rare blue or red – into two separate glass bowls of water, one for hers, and one for mine, set carefully on the weather-worn picnic table. Then we would pour our first drinks. Mom would make hers in her favorite Sport cup – a handful of ice from one of the coolers followed by a hefty slug of gin and splash of tonic. I would usually open a bottle of beer. Then we would sit down on opposite sides of the table and admire each other's treasures, holding them up to the light and "oohing and aahing" at their multicolored translucent stripes, swirls and patterns as we swigged our first drinks of the night.

Looking back on these expeditions it's clear to me that I drank more than my mom. She generally stuck to her gin and tonics and sipped them slowly as the evening wore on. I always started with several bottles of cold, fizzy beer. Nothing tasted so good to me after a long, hot day. These I consumed quickly before dinner, along with chips and salsa or some other salty snack. After the beer came dry red wine both during and after dinner – usually one and a half to two bottles worth when all was said and done. Often, when that wasn't enough and it was very late, I would add a small glass of gin with a handful of ice and splash of tonic, just like the G&Ts my mom made. I always got drunk, though I tried to hide it. Mom often commented about how much I drank, but that was as far as it ever went. I kept my nicotine use a closely guarded secret. I knew she would be appalled and shocked to learn of it, so I chewed my tobacco on nightly "walks to stretch my legs and use the outhouse" or to "go down to look at the lake" or "walk the campground loop to look at the stars." But once I started using Nicorette getting my nicotine fix was no longer a problem. I was always chewing the gum and I don't think anyone ever suspected what it was, or at least if they did, they never said so.

It is hard to describe these trips. Each day seemed timeless and serene yet, in the blink of an eye, we would be dismantling the camp and heading our separate ways. We felt deep nostalgia as we drove away from our campsite, first waving "goodbye" to the beloved lake and later to each other as we reached the main highway turn off. Leaving was always a happy, yet solemn, affair, as we thought about the fun we had had and also remembered a lifetime of memories from this very special and unchanging place.

We made our annual treks to Madison and Lake Superior faithfully and I began to notice that my mom was looking pretty rough. She had gained weight around her middle but the rest of her body was thin. Her face was puffy and her cheeks red with tiny burst blood vessels. I noticed burst vessels on my face as well, and also on my chest, which I knew were a result of my drinking. I worried about my mom and watched her closely. She drank lots of water during the day, and she seemed to eat well during our camping trips, but she didn't look good. She had really slowed down, walking gingerly on the sandy, rock-spattered beach. She just appeared unhealthy in general. This was during the time period shortly before she retired in 2007 and she had already had several emergency trips to the hospital. One was when she fell off a ladder while cleaning leaves from the gutters and broke her leg and foot. Another time she was rushed to the hospital while at work with severe dehydration and dangerously low blood pressure as well as internal stomach bleeding. Soon after her retirement another incident occurred. She fell while pushing a heavily loaded recycling bin and seriously injured her hands and fingers on the cement. I worried about her drinking, that maybe alcohol was causing all of these "accidents" as she called them. She kept telling me not to fret, that she was fine. But I was fretting, and I was starting to put two and two together.

Jacques and I knew that Mom was unhappy in Madison and we were concerned about her living alone now that she had retired. Her first year of retirement was brutal, with the hardest winter on record in Madison. Anticipating a future move, she had already had the entire kitchen and bath remodeled and new carpeting installed throughout the house. Then came the record snows. Snow and ice dams caused the kitchen roof to collapse, which resulted in water streaming down the freshly painted walls and extensive interior and exterior damage. This was a major setback, what with the repairs and ensuing insurance claims that had to be addressed once spring came. Gin and tonic provided energy in helping her cope with the various crises.

I knew Mom was drinking too much – I could tell by her voice when we would talk on the phone. We started discussing her move to Michigan in earnest. She wanted to, but much work remained to be done before she could put the house on the market. She also needed to have yard sales to get rid of as much "stuff" as possible before making the move. All of this took precious time, and as the year passed my mom's condition deteriorated dramatically.

Mom was drinking during the day now, starting in the morning to stop the shakes, and eating very little. Her fainting spells were becoming more frequent as time went on, but she wasn't going to the doctor to get her blood pressure checked or to see if she was dehydrated. Meanwhile she was working hard on her house and yard, doing heavy physical work in the heat, all the while eating minimally and drinking gin.

We skipped our annual spring trip to Lake Superior in 2008 so Mom could come to Michigan instead, to go house-hunting. I was shocked when she arrived, practically stumbling from her car. She was so feeble and so weak that she walked slowly, placing each foot carefully on the uneven ground, and stepping tentatively like an old lady. She had also smashed her thumb loading a massive rock into the car while still at home. She made the drive with her thumb wrapped in bandages, the painful, crushed flesh dark blue-black and seeping blood. I pleaded with her to go to the urgent care clinic immediately but she refused, so we agreed to go the next day for X-Rays and treatment. I was extremely concerned. That night at dinner she drank wine and later gin, but only ate a few bites of food. She told me that she was under so much stress with the impending move and the work still to do that her stomach was in knots, that it was nearly impossible to eat. I told her she would have to eat while at our house or I would not allow her to have any alcohol. The threat aside, she did eat a small amount and was able to drink Gatorade, so her condition improved slightly while she stayed with us.

We went house-hunting and examined many potential homes and condominiums. All the while I watched and worried about Mom's frail condition. She was so physically weak, and she was not the happy, cheerful, positive person that she had always been. She seemed so tired and lackluster, and even though she would say how excited she was to move here, her behavior seemed more like that of grim resignation. We spent several days and looked at many places, and eventually found a condo that she really liked, and decided to buy.

It was a ranch-style condominium, upper level, with high, vaulted ceilings, skylights and many windows. The design was open and spacious with plenty of natural light. In addition to the kitchen, dining and living area it had two large bedrooms and another room for her "painting studio." There was one guest bathroom and a huge master bathroom, complete with a large jacuzzi. It was perfect except for the fact it was on the second floor. Mom was so unsteady on her feet, we were concerned about her falling. Navigating the stairs could be a problem too. But she assured us that it would be fine, and that she loved the place. And besides, she joked like she always did, "Now you won't have to push me down the stairs to get my estate, I'll just fall down by myself." Not funny, I thought to myself. I so wished my mom would stop drinking!

Meanwhile, all the time this was going on, my own drinking had skyrocketed. I was watching my mom with all her stress of moving and her physical decline, and I had such deep, gut-wrenching pain and fear that I was losing her. She was visibly fading away under the grip of her alcoholism and there didn't seem to be a damn thing I could do about it. Of course I had no way to cope with my sadness and fear other than to drink, and drink I did. I had been drinking every night for so long by then that I no longer counted days. Every now and then Jacques would tell me that I should "take a day off." I would reply that I couldn't, that I was addicted and simply could not take a day off. I had awful hangovers and shook terribly in the mornings, and nothing would alleviate this except another "small drink." Jacques didn't know about my secret stash and my morning drinks. He would often say, "Whew, do you ever stink like alcohol!" I assumed he thought it was from the night before. I didn't drink a lot in the morning, and not every day. It was only on the "really bad" days, when I was shaking both inside and out and just couldn't stand it, when I needed that little drink to get me through the day.

I knew that I needed to quit. My moodiness had come back and I was having a hard time controlling my mental state. I continued with my daily exercise but I no longer had nicotine to help stave off depression. In August of 2007 I had decided to give it up, with the aid of the prescription medication Chantix, and it was one of the hardest things I have ever done. Without nicotine I couldn't read, couldn't concentrate and was essentially useless from a cognitive standpoint for several months. My mood was depressed some of the time but I was mostly hypomanic. I spent hours and hours every day cutting grass, running, biking, swimming and anything else I could do physically to quell that hyper feeling and the physiological agony of withdrawal. My mind would spin and spin. I was so wound up all the time I felt like I would explode. I drank to help ease the pain, but withdrawal was terrible for me and it lasted a long time. It took about eight months of complete abstinence from nicotine before I felt "normal" and finally was able to tell myself, "I think, *maybe*, I can do this."

I started seriously thinking about quitting alcohol as I watched my mom's decline, which really hit me hard when I saw her that spring of 2008, the time she came to look for a place to live. But I knew that I wouldn't be able to quit while all the moving and transitioning was in progress. It was an extremely stressful time period for me too. I figured I would get my mom squared away, help her move and then somehow get her into treatment. After she was taken care of, I would go into treatment myself, maybe after New Year's. It seemed like a good plan at the time.

As much as I loved my mom, I dreaded her coming to live near us. I saw her condition and envisioned her being weak and helpless, and getting worse. I saw myself going over there daily to help her with small tasks, doing chores and other things that would be a headache and a hassle. I pictured many "fainting episodes" and trips to the hospital. I imagined calling and getting no answer, rushing over to find her at the bottom of the stairs, unconscious or dead. The idea of her coming to live near us often made me cringe, and I would literally shake myself like a wet dog to try to erase that creepy, shivering feeling from my body.

During the summer and early autumn of 2008, while my mom was struggling in Madison to prepare for the move, I was working hard on a video shooting and editing project for Arts on Earth, an academic unit at the University of Michigan. We were building a multi-faceted collaborative arts piece created by faculty and students from several departments at the university. The project was called *Mapping the River*, and centered around the Huron River, its beginnings, its history, its life and its environmental degradation. The end result would be a multimedia performance consisting of three large projected screens of high definition video, dance and poetry readings with a live chamber orchestra, and drum and percussion instruments performing during the show. It was a very complex and integrated piece, and difficult to design and produce because there were often conflicts between the various collaborating faculty members about how it should be created. Essentially, there was not one Director but five, and it made my job extremely difficult.

My role in the project was to shoot all the HD video and to design and edit the video segments that would be projected onto the three large screens during the show. The projected images were an integral part of the overall performance and an enormous challenge to create, not just from an artistic standpoint but from a technical standpoint as well. It was a lengthy project that started with filming in May and continued into November, when the final performances would be held. Once all of the shooting was finished and the editing started I struggled to keep my sanity and maintain my professionalism in the face of conflicting views and opinions from the various faculty members. We were constantly building things up and then tearing them down, creating segments of beautiful, intricately designed video only to trash them and start over with something completely different. It was an intense and stressful job that took hundreds of hours of frustrating, hair-pulling editing, and lots of patience.

As the show deadline drew near I was working around the clock for days in the editing suite to finish and render out the three final, forty-five minute segments of HD video that would be played in synchronization during the show. Adding to my enormous stress over the time pressure was the fact that the computers kept crashing midway through the final outputs, and I would have to repeat the rendering process all over again as the hours ticked by. On the last day, when I finally left the editing suite at four o'clock in the morning the day of the show, I had given up and officially "quit." I was beyond despair, and was totally physically and emotionally spent. The computers kept crashing and I had no idea why. I was unable to output the files and feared there would be no video – which was such a major element of the project – for the show. I left an explanatory note for Jacques, who ran the Video Studio, and wrote that unless he and the other technicians could solve the problem, there would be no show. I drank wine as I cried all the way home, just nine hours to show time. I hoped like hell they would be able to figure out what was wrong, and there would still be time for the computers to crunch the numbers and render out the files. Fortunately, and much to my indescribable relief, they solved the problem. The last file was ready to go with less than one hour to show time, the "magic of the eleventh hour," as is known in the performance world.

I looked terrible and probably reeked of wine, but I wore my nice suit, applied my makeup and returned to the studio just in time to watch the first afternoon performance. It came off without a hitch, and was magical. I watched the show with pride and pleasure, both exhausted and deeply relieved. Afterwards I staggered home and fell into bed, not an ounce of gas left. It was the first night that I hadn't drunk in a long, long time, and I slept like the dead.

While I was working with the Arts on Earth project my mom was sweltering in the summer heat, having yard sales, overseeing repairs on the house and dealing with financing while on deadline for the realtor to start showing the "neat" premises. The move was scheduled to occur at the end of September. She was really struggling with the enormity of the seemingly insurmountable tasks, but I was not aware of that. When we would talk on the phone she would say that she was very busy with the work, but that everything was going fine. Everything was *not* going fine, but she didn't tell me, I suspect because she didn't want me to worry and be distracted from my own work.

I knew she was drinking heavily, and this was confirmed when she made her last trip to Michigan in August to sign the documents that made the purchase of her condo official. I arrived at the airport to find my mother clinging to the pipe of a road sign, sweating profusely, looking wan and exhausted and barely able to stand on her own. Apparently the airline had put her in a wheelchair to transport her to the passenger pick-up area, where she had been waiting for me in the late summer heat. I got her into the car and begged her to let me take her to the hospital. I knew she was dehydrated and probably not eating, living on Gatorade, gin and tonic. She refused adamantly to go so, yet again, we managed in a few days to get her rehydrated and eating bits of food. Her condition improved but she was still weak and unsteady on her feet as I took her to the airport and sent her back to Madison. The next time I would see my mom would be almost two months later, at the end of September when I would go to Madison to help with the actual move and bring her – finally – to Michigan.

~~~

I was deeply engrossed with Arts on Earth when Mom called in near hysterics. The time had come – it was the end of September, several days before I was scheduled to help with the move. She was panicked and desperate. The movers were coming in a few days and she was not ready. All the stress and strain of the past year, coupled with her heavy drinking, had finally gotten to her and she had cracked. She cried to me on the phone that she just couldn't do any more, that she was overwhelmed and just couldn't cope, and could I please, please come a few days early and help. My mom never asked me for help; she was always the one who *I* went to when there was a problem. Of course, I said, I would come immediately.

    I dropped everything I was doing, packed hastily and got into the car for the seven-hour drive to Madison. Jacques said he would clear his schedule and be available if I needed his assistance there, that I was to call anytime and he would come too. We both knew that something serious was happening. My mom kept calling while I drove, asking where I was and when I would arrive, slurring her words as she spoke and sounding drunk. My stomach was in knots the entire trip. I was so nervous and afraid of what I would find when I got to my mom's house that I spent hours on the phone as I drove, talking to

Jacques and my friend Sue, who reassured me that things would be OK and that I would be strong enough to handle whatever came my way. As usual, about an hour from "home" I pulled into a gas station and bought a six-pack. I still tried to follow my "one hour from destination" rule. The cold beer tasted so good, and slowly the knots in my stomach released, the tension in my neck and shoulders began to dissipate and the stress in my body eased away. I felt that comfortable warmth that I knew so well begin to spread through me. As I rounded the last curve on the freeway heading into Madison I opened beer number four. Fifteen minutes later I pulled into Mom's driveway.

The house, a two-story "salt-box" with light beige vinyl siding, and its detached garage, looked nice in the evening light, as though it had recently been power-washed. The small front and large back yard were neatly trimmed and immaculate as usual. Mom was still an avid gardener with an amazing artistic eye. Everywhere one looked it was splendid, a visual extravaganza with the contrasting colors of plants in the ground, bushes, the climbing vines on trellises and the potted flowers on stands that created lovely multi-tiered areas and gardens. It smelled good too – fresh, clean air with a tinge of floral sweetness. Next to the steps to the back porch, her favorite "room," was a large, colorful rock garden, created from beautiful lake-polished stones of various sizes, each one lovingly selected and carried during our many trips to Lake Superior. I was surprised at the excellent condition of the yard. Suspecting how run down my mom was, I marveled that she was physically able to do so much work, in addition to all the interior work that she had been doing.

As I got out of the car she didn't get up to greet me as she usually did, but rather stayed sitting at the picnic table in the screened porch looking out at the large back yard as she snuffed out her cigarette.

"Heeelloooo," she sang as I walked up the steps.

She smiled broadly at me as I opened the side door and walked into the small porch. It was clean and tidy, which again surprised me. The floor and ceiling had been repainted and everything was in its place, orderly as usual.

Several packed boxes were stacked against the wall by the house. I took a few steps and gave her a half-hug while she sat at the table. Her plastic Sport cup was in front of her next to an open newspaper and the just snuffed-out cigarette, which still emitted a small wisp of smoke from the over-filled ashtray. She reeked of alcohol and I observed that the cup was almost full. I sat down. She started talking about the neighbors' dog, about how cute and sweet he was. She rambled on as I listened and she reached for her cigarettes. She was clearly very drunk. I excused myself to use the bathroom, got up and went into the house.

The inside was also very neat, but it didn't look at all ready for the movers, who were coming in three days. There were a couple of partially filled boxes in the living room, and some in her bedroom, but otherwise the rest of the house looked like it always did, except it was more sparse because she had sold many items. Upstairs were a few packed boxes in my old room and some in the other bedroom. I sighed. It wasn't a complete disaster, but there was an awful, awful lot of work to do.

I grabbed a beer from the refrigerator and returned to the porch, but Mom was not there. I found her sitting in the grass in the neighbors' yard, talking loudly with them and playing with the small dog. She didn't seem to notice or care that I was there; she didn't even comment on my presence to the neighbors. We said our hellos and chatted briefly, then I told Mom that she needed to come back to the porch so we could talk. I had to help her stand, and then I stood very close to her as she slowly, carefully wobbled across the yard back to her house. She looked so weak – she walked like a drunken, ninety-year old lady. My fears mounted with every passing minute. I felt an ominous sense of despair and dread. How was I ever going to get through this?

We made it back to the picnic table on the porch and tried to talk about the move. She wasn't making any sense and was rambling nearly incoherently. It was very strange – I had never seen her like this, even though I had seen her fairly drunk on various occasions before. But she had always been lucid, even when intoxicated. This time we couldn't even carry on a conversation. It was like all the connections between brain and mouth were severed and only gibberish was able to come out. I wondered if maybe she was about to have a stroke, or had already had one. Or maybe she had recently fallen and hit her head. That seemed more likely. I begged, *pleaded* with her to let me take her to the hospital but she refused. "No, no, no," she said, shaking her head with exaggeration, "no hospital." Suddenly a clear sentence emerged through the babbling. "We have to get ready for the move. I am leaving Madison on Friday, period." It seemed to be getting better then, her speech, as though the neurons in her brain were suddenly recharging and starting to fire in the right directions. It was odd to watch this transformation from complete incoherence to lucidity. In a few minutes she seemed fine, back to her normal self. I was terrified and didn't know what to do. I called Jacques.

"Call 911," he said.

"But I can't now. She seems perfectly fine." She was sitting outside at the table doing her crossword puzzle and smoking.

"If I call now they'll just come and find a drunk woman, and she'll be pissed," I replied.

"Well," he said, "then you're going to just have to wait until something happens, and it sounds like something will, and soon. You are going to have to steel yourself for the worst. Call me anytime, and I can come if you want."

"No," I said, "I can handle it. I'll check in with you later."

I made myself dinner and tried to get my mother to eat but she wouldn't. I placed my dinner and glass of red wine at the end of the picnic table as it grew dark. She had moved to her other "smoking spot" on the porch, a steel chair with a thin cushion next to the wall where there was a long, low shelf and a small TV set. I had secretly retrieved my palm-sized video camera from my bag and had it next to me on the table.

Mom was barely able to walk. To get up and make it to the bathroom she had to hold onto furniture along the way or lean with one hand against the wall. In the kitchen she slid on her butt across the linoleum floor. I followed her from the porch into the kitchen with my camera, filming her sliding toward the cabinet and her supply of gin.

"No cameras," she said, drunkenly.

"I'm filming you. We need to go to the hospital," I said as I looked down at her, intent on the image in the view screen. I put my foot against the cabinet door. She was so weak I knew she wouldn't be able to open it, and I was so angry I had double strength.

"Let me have my gin! I need my gin, goddammit!" she screamed frantically.

We argued about the gin and about going to the hospital, all the while with me filming.

"Do you want to die? Is that what this is about?!"

"No. I. . ." She started to cry. "Everything is just so. . . pointless. There's nothing. . . nothing left," she sobbed.

Never had I seen my mother like this, *ever*. I put the camera on the counter and stopped recording, and bent down to give her a hug. Her pain flowed through me like a wave, or maybe it was just my own pain. I couldn't stand it another moment, just couldn't bear to watch her suffering like this. I opened the cabinet and took out the bottle of gin, and fixed her a drink. I helped her back to her spot by the porch wall and refilled my glass of wine. I placed the camera on the table and aimed it at my glass, and the squat, round candle that glowed and flickered behind it. A fitting scene, I thought as I hit the record button again. I really thought my mom was going to die that night.

So I asked questions and we started talking. We talked about things that had happened in the past. Good things. We talked about our many trips to Lake Superior, and all the fun we had had, all the adventures. We remembered the ceremonial blue glass bottle that we tossed in the waves at the far beach every year, to "seed" the beach with little broken bits of polished blue glass for future collecting. We talked about the time I had gone windsurfing and ended up several miles offshore when the wind died like a stone. I had to paddle the rig back the entire way, in fifty degree water, while watching her figure, with her hands on her hips, grow larger as I approached the deserted beach. Boy, was she ever pissed! We laughed at that one. We talked about my swimming career and how it had ended. I cried and she gave me advice and told me again that I just had to "let it go." We talked about my dad and the divorce, my childhood, the good times with Mike. I told her of all the crazy things we used to do that she didn't know about. She said she knew, but I thought she was fibbing. She told me stories about when she was in grad school, and about things that had happened with her friends and on various trips out west. She told me more about her one true love and her eventual broken heart, and I told her, again, about my own devastating heartbreak. Pain and loss. Happiness, sadness, hope, despair. I told her about my terrible depressions and how much I suffered. She had had no idea, and said so.

We talked about everything, while my camera listened. I recorded our conversation for me and only me, so I would have a good memory of my mom, sort of like an audio photo album. Well into the wee hours we reminisced, laughed and cried. She sat in her chair and drank her gin, and I leaned against the porch wall, my back to the yard and the quiet night sounds, in my usual spot at the picnic table bench. It was surreal. The whole scene was so *normal* now, with us talking and having such a deep, bonding conversation. She was totally lucid again, and didn't seem drunk to me at all. Perhaps it was because I was drunk, I'm not sure. But my memory of that night is clear, and it turned out to be one of the most fulfilling discussions I had had with my mom in a long time.

Finally I had to say goodnight. I left her smoking on the porch, gazing at the mute TV set. We hugged, and I staggered off to bed, exhausted to the core of my soul. I took one last gulp of wine and set my empty glass in the sink. I carried my small camera upstairs to my room. Evidence, I thought to myself. Now I have *proof*. Now I can prove that she needs help! Now somebody will watch the video, will finally do something and she will be *forced* to get help! I hugged the little camera and felt pleased with myself. Tomorrow I would figure out what to do with the footage of her in the kitchen, and I would make sure that something would be done. I just had to do *something*.

The next morning came too soon and I was awakened by my mom's overly cheerful voice shouting up the stairs. "Good morning! Time to get up!! We have *work* to do!" I groaned as I rolled over, feeling like a bus had driven through my head. "What time is it?" I looked at my watch. Eight-thirty. Ugh, too early, I thought. We had talked until well past two. I slowly got dressed and made my way downstairs, groggy and hungover. I didn't eat breakfast in those days but Mom insisted on feeding me coffee cake. It was all I could do to not gag but I managed to choke it down. I tried to get her to have some but she refused. "I'll eat later," she said. I didn't bother asking her if she had been drinking already. Despite my hangover and the fact that I probably stunk of alcohol myself, I could smell the unmistakable aroma of fresh booze. I stifled my anger and also felt something else – guilt. How many times had I had that "little morning drink" to stop the shakes or ease a hangover? Why was I so angry at her for doing the same thing that I had done so many times? I didn't understand it, but it didn't matter. I was suffering that morning but I resolved to not have that "little drink." I would rise above it. I would be "better" than her. But God, I was so angry! She was self-destructing and I was forced to watch.

I busied myself packing while Mom sat on the back porch, smoking and doing her crossword puzzle, with the ever-present Sport cup in front of her. Every now and then she would come in and check on me, and give some directive or another. She was getting more drunk, and I was getting more worried. She was so unsteady – I couldn't understand how she kept going in this condition and didn't just keel right over. But I knew that was going to happen. I just had a premonition that today was the day, that at some point, sometime, she was going to have another "fainting spell," pass out and fall. I deliberately stayed close by in the house, just in case. And sure enough, toward the middle of the afternoon it happened. I was working in the front corner of the house in her studio, packing boxes of notebooks, sketch pads, every imaginable type of art supply, computer equipment, paintings and so forth. I heard the door to the back porch open and then suddenly a big *Whomp!* that literally shook the whole house. I ran to the kitchen.

There she was, stretched out on her back, her arms at her sides. Her eyes were closed and she was breathing, but slowly. "Are you OK?" I took her hand. No response. "Mother!" *Shit!* My heart was pounding in my chest as I picked up the phone and dialed 911.

It seemed an eternity but finally EMS arrived – two fire trucks, an ambulance and a police car. Meanwhile my mom was starting to come to. I prayed that she would still be unconscious when they came in. I wanted them to take her away. Desperately I wanted *help*. Suddenly the house was full of emergency personnel. They put a neck brace on her and were carefully strapping her to a stretcher when she awoke. "I'm going to get you for this, Christi, goddammit!" she said, her head immobilized and her teeth clenched. I was shaking from the moment I had dialed the phone, and one of the fire fighters noticed this.

"Don't worry," she said, "she won't remember saying that, and probably won't remember any of this part anyway."

I thanked her. She told me I looked like I needed to take a walk or do something to calm down, to decompress. I must have looked like shit, working all day in my grubby clothes, unshowered, and now shaking, the tears streaming from my eyes like a child. I thanked her again. Finally, after all the questions were answered and hasty notes taken, they took Mom away to the hospital. I sat down on the living room couch and cried and cried.

Next I called Jacques and Mike to tell them what had happened. It turned out that Mom had a concussion and slight bleeding on her brain, so they were keeping her in the ICU overnight. I went to the hospital for a brief visit and she was *happy*. I was furious. She kept saying how glad she was that someone was taking care of her, and how much she needed TLC. I fumed as I walked up to the Head Nurse. "How long will she be staying here?" I asked. "It's tough to say at this point," she replied, "but probably several days at most." *What?* I thought, incredulous. How could they possibly release a person in her condition who had just sustained a concussion, who had bleeding on her brain, who could barely walk, in "several days?" I was outraged. I told the nurse of our plans to leave on the ferry for Michigan on Friday. It was now Wednesday morning, and the movers were coming Thursday afternoon. There is no way that woman is going to be ready to travel by Friday, I thought, nor do I want her to! I wanted her to stay in the hospital. I wanted her healed and well. I so desperately wanted her to get *help*.

The Head Nurse came from behind the desk in the Nurses' Office and put her arm around my back as she led me to a quiet spot in the waiting area. We sat down in two upholstered chairs, facing each other. She looked at me squarely, with concern in her eyes despite her tense, overworked face.

"Look," she said, "we can't keep her here against her will unless it's medically necessary, and in a few days we will probably have to release her." She paused. "I don't think you have any idea what you have gotten yourself into. Your life, from now until the unforeseeable future, is going to be extremely difficult."

I nodded as she looked at me intently. "I think I'm starting to get the picture," I said.

"Maybe. Have you heard of Al-Anon? Good. I strongly, *strongly* recommend that you get involved with Al-Anon as soon as you get back to Michigan. You are really going to need the support."

I thanked her as she got up and briskly walked away. I sank into the chair.

Al-Anon. A support group for friends and family members of alcoholics and drug addicts. Yep. Like that's going to solve any of my problems.

I returned to Mom's house and took a brief inventory of every room. My watch said it was just after four o'clock – I had exactly twenty-one hours before the movers would arrive, and damn near everything in the house needed to be wrapped and packed in boxes, some items carefully, like dishes and glasses, and some not. God, I wonder if I can do this? I thought to myself. Well. . . better roll up my sleeves and get to work! I opened a beer, took a big slug and went to get my camera. I had decided to document my journey, my heroic trip to Madison to rescue my mother. I hit "record" and did a quick "before" shot of every room. Then I placed the camera on the shelf in the studio to "watch" me as I resumed packing from where I had left off.

I worked like a deranged person, as hard and fast as I could go. I packed everything in the studio first, because it contained the most items and the most things that needed to be carefully wrapped. Then I moved to the kitchen, the "second worst" on my list. Then on to the upstairs bedrooms, closets and cabinets. All the time I narrated the video as I shot before and after footage, and even turned the camera on myself to record my feelings as I was working, how I felt about my mom's condition and about our planned trip to Michigan. The hours were racing by.

Suddenly it was after nine o'clock and I realized I hadn't eaten since the light breakfast almost twelve hours earlier. God, I thought, I'm doing exactly what she does. I'm drinking and not eating. My stomach was in knots too. *I get it, I get it, but I have to rise above.* I forced myself to take a break and eat a quick dinner, washing it down with several more glasses of wine. Fueled by the food and alcohol, I set to work again with a vengeance. I drank wine as I worked, taking gulps in between boxes from a big water glass (a wine glass was far too small, of course). Later I switched to gin and tonic, using a Sport cup just like the one my mom used. It was the perfect size for a good, hefty drink, and easy to carry from room to room without spilling.

It had been a long time since my drinking had any "romance" to it, except for during the occasional celebratory dinner with friends. Gone were the days of slowly swirling a fine wine in a crystal glass, sniffing and analyzing its subtle aromas before taking that first small, tentative sip, then letting it roll around the palate with head slightly tilted back and eyes closed, savoring its delicate flavor. Bah! I bought the big bottles, the 1.5 liter "doubles" of dry red wine, for my "daily maintenance" drinking. Sometimes I bought it by the box because it was cheap. There was no need to "analyze" it, swirl it, sniff it, or do anything other than drink it. Sure, I liked the good, expensive wines better, but I was content to drink the cheap stuff on a daily basis. And I just drank it, like juice. No candles, no soft clinking of glasses between me and my handsome lover, no gazing of eyes and smiling, sensual faces. It was a utilitarian activity that served a utilitarian purpose: to get drunk. Drinking whiskey was the same. Yes, I enjoyed it in a pretty, beveled glass with clinking ice, but much of the time I drank it straight from the bottle, a quick gulp or two from my secret stash in the closet. I loved it while I was doing it, I hated it the next morning. And so it went those days, and so it went that night. The alcohol kept me going, it kept the dull, tedious chore from being too boring and it gave me the stamina to keep working, until three o'clock, when I finally dragged myself to bed and collapsed.

The next morning I awoke at seven, made coffee, drank my orange juice and went right back to work. A bottle of beer made me wretch but it eased my throbbing headache. I picked up the camera and took a walk through the house, with its stacks of neatly labeled boxes waiting for the movers. I had done well but there was still much more to do. The camera turned toward myself, I talked again about my experience and about my fears – of my mom leaving the hospital, of the trip, of what lay ahead. In my mind I was just like Katie Couric: sweetly beautiful, calm and clinical in my statement of the facts during my unbiased interview of myself and my accurate assessment of this tough situation. I was collected, confident and cool, both the reporter and the survivor of some horrible, traumatic accident. In my imagination I was working hard for the good cause of moving my ailing mother to Michigan, to be close to us so we could care for her. I was both the heroine and the martyr.

So Christi the heroic daughter greeted the movers when they arrived at noon on Thursday and filmed them emptying her childhood home of all its possessions and loading them neatly into a big, steel-sided truck. They were fast and efficient. They finished wrapping and boxing what I was unable to get to and cleared out the entire house, including the basement and garage, in about two hours. And then, just as quickly as they arrived, they left. Poof! Just like that, the first half of my life was packed in a truck and headed to the highway. Remaining were some food and cooking utensils, a few items in the refrigerator including my beer and wine, my travel belongings and two air mattresses with bedding for my mom and me (to sleep on when she got out of the hospital). I wandered around from room to room, exhausted. The place was desolate and lonely without the furniture, the artwork, the books, the plants and all the interesting bric-a-brac collected over the years. Depression began to settle around me like a cold, dense fog and I had to get out. I climbed into the car and drove to the hospital.

Somehow, some way, my mother had convinced the doctors and nurses that she was fit enough to be released. Somehow, no doubt through her sheer, strong, desperate will power, she had passed all the tests: getting up out of a chair, walking unassisted down the hallway, going to the bathroom, etc. When I arrived she was in the process of being discharged. I was appalled and fuming, but there was absolutely nothing I could do. I tried. I talked to the Head Nurse, a different one this time, and strongly asserted that my mom was not well yet, that I didn't think she could possibly be ready to travel. The nurse was sympathetic but unmoved. Mom passed the tests, after all. She wanted to go and that was the end of it. All I got was the advice to bring her back if she started getting a headache and to have her checked as soon as we arrived in Michigan. I gave up, resigned. Mom wanted so badly to be on that ferry the next day and finally make the move that nothing on Earth was going to stop her. I caved. Even in her weakened state she beat me, she steamrollered over me and my furious resolve like she always had. I was exhausted. I just couldn't take the arguing anymore, the pressure. I couldn't stand my anger at her, my frustration with the hospital staff, my feelings of utter, total helplessness. Even my damning video was of no use. Nobody wanted to see it. *That doesn't matter*, the Head Nurse had said. *If she wants to continue to drink herself to death there is absolutely nothing you, or I, or anyone can do about it. Please, go to Al-Anon when you get to Michigan, please. And good luck to you. I really mean that.*

The next morning we boarded the ferry in Milwaukee, my mom leaning heavily on a yeoman's arm as we walked slowly from the parking deck to the passenger area. I settled her in a comfortable chair and went up to the top deck to watch the Wisconsin shore and Milwaukee's skyline recede as the ship coasted smoothly from the harbor. As soon as it reached the harbor's mouth the captain gave the order to open up the throttle and I turned around to grab the railing. The sleek, fast boat quickly lifted up on plane and cut neatly through the waves toward Michigan, leaving two long, white, foaming wakes behind it. The wind on the upper deck was cold. It blasted through me as I held fast to the railing, looking down at the dark water streaming by. It felt good to be up there, alone on the deck now, clinging tight in that stiff, frigid wind. *Keep hanging on,* I thought, *keep hanging on.*

The End of The End

I dreaded Christmas. It seemed that bad things always happened over the holidays. Too much anticipation, too much shopping, too many people, too much stress. I had had too many bad holidays in my life, but this one was definitely the worst. My mom and Jacques' dad were both dying and I had no way to dull the pain. A month earlier, just before Thanksgiving, Jacques' dad had been diagnosed with a fast-growing, malignant form of brain cancer called a glioblastoma. He had a tumor the size of a baseball in the middle of his brain. There was no treatment, and they gave him only several months to live. It would be a slow decline, they told us. His bodily functions would cease to operate one by one, and he would become less cognizant and less able to do things, while he quietly waited to die. The decision was made to bring him home where he could still have his martinis and be surrounded by his family and beloved dogs.

It was December ninth when I went to Mom's condo to bring her food and tried – again – to get her to eat. She had been sitting on the couch working on a crossword puzzle, her legs curled under her and her favorite plastic cup of gin and tonic half full on the small wooden coffee table. She said she wasn't hungry as she took a sip from the cup. I looked at her and the cup with fury, disdain, and disgust: disgust for her, and disgust for myself. I had had it! I had really, truly, finally had *enough!* I was sick of watching her die, and I was sick of my own hypocrisy.

After the move Mom had promised me that she would quit drinking, and she did for a while. But then, slowly and innocently, she started again. It didn't take long before she was right back to where she had left off. She was drunk every day now, and again wasn't eating. I kept hearing about Jacques' damn Christmas lasagna, his traditional special recipe, and how she couldn't wait for Christmas so she could eat it. *Sure, I thought to myself.*

The condo was in a state of fixed entropy, and nothing was happening. Partially unpacked boxes sat on the floor and on chairs, left there from the move. Paintings were leaning against the walls. On the kitchen table was a stack of mail, much of it unopened, note pads, pens and newspapers. It was all very neat and tidy; it was simply untouched, waiting, as though someone was in the process of moving in or moving out. "I need to pay my bills and start my taxes," Mom would say. But nothing was getting done. The stack of mail remained intact. I laughed when she told me, heavily slurring her words, that she still had to go get her new driver's license. *Right, I said, go ahead on in there, staggering and stinking of gin and ask for a driver's license!* I was supremely pissed. She could barely walk and we couldn't even have a simple conversation. I felt guilty thinking it, but part of me just wished she would die, to end this horrible suffering for both of us.

"I've made a decision," I told her as she put down the cup and gazed at me unsteadily through glassy, red-rimmed eyes. "There's not a goddamn thing I can do about your alcoholism but I can do something about mine. I've decided to go into treatment and quit drinking, and I think you should too."

That night I stayed up late drinking wine until I was thoroughly drunk, and finally went to sleep around two o'clock. I woke up early the next morning, December tenth, and drove to the north side of Ann Arbor to the University of Michigan Rachel Upjohn Depression Center. There, down a long hallway lined with artwork that I barely noticed, was the door to the UM Addiction Treatment Services (UMATS). I had been there the previous day for an evaluation, an hour-long interview that consisted of questions and mostly me talking and crying the entire time. The therapist who interviewed me strongly suggested that I not wait, that I start their Intensive Outpatient Program the next day. She said she was concerned that if I delayed I wouldn't do it, that I would back out. I thought so too, and so there I was, the very next day, ready to start the treatment program.

I was terrified, depressed and felt horrible. Between alcohol withdrawal, my raging hangover and my fear, my hands were shaking so badly I could barely hold my water bottle. I was so anxious – my mind was spinning, like a wild animal caught in a cage, circling round and round and trying frantically to find a way out. The nurse was patient and kind, as were the doctors and therapists. And I felt so utterly defeated, so exhausted, so completely resigned to the fact that I needed help and that this may well be my absolute, last ditch hope. With total desperation I reached for these people, these strangers, as a drowning woman reaches for that last, low-hanging branch. I knew without even the slightest shade of doubt that I couldn't do this alone, that I absolutely could not quit drinking by myself. I surrendered completely and I stayed that morning, and started to work the program. I stayed – and my sobriety date remains December tenth, 2008.

But detoxing from alcohol is neither easy nor fun, not that anyone would expect it to be. I had a persistent headache, a "pressure," that felt like my head was in a vise. I was extremely anxious and couldn't think – my mind just seemed to spin, and I had difficulty putting thoughts together. I was nauseous and my hands shook. Sometimes the shaking was only a slight tremor but other times it was rather violent, for example when I was particularly nervous, which was frequent. During the first week of treatment at UMATS I could hardly hold my coffee for the shaking, and the cheap, "institutional" brew often made me gag. I was prescribed phenobarbital to prevent seizure (which can occur when one abruptly quits using alcohol or some other drugs) and that did help to alleviate some of the symptoms of withdrawal, mostly the shaking and the headache.

Because my alcohol use was so heavy the detox process took a while, in fact it was nearly a week before the shaking stopped and I was able to think more clearly. But detoxing is only the beginning. Even after the immediate discomfort is over the brain needs time to heal from so much chemical disruption. For me, even though I started to feel much better physically within a week or so, it took months before I felt close to "normal" from a cognitive standpoint. Much like my experience with nicotine, the withdrawal and physical recovery from alcohol was a long and arduous ordeal that had its share of ups and downs.

My bipolar disorder complicated matters. Many alcoholics and drug addicts also suffer from anxiety, depression, bipolar disorder or other psychiatric illnesses so dual-diagnosis is not uncommon. It took time to find the right combination of medications to treat my disorder and other lingering problems – chronic pain, for one. This was a slow and frustrating process because it often took several weeks, depending on the medication, to see positive results, and waiting to feel good again seemed interminable.

But despite my impatient nature I did wait and with support from the UMATS team, the other "patients" and my husband I managed to get through the rough spots. The first few months of my sobriety were definitely the hardest. Remembering that early experience is one method of coping that I have used many times in the past when I have had an urge to drink. It was such an intensely painful time period, both from a physical and a psychological standpoint. The fear of having to repeat it is a healthy fear, and the experience of detox and early sobriety one that I never want to repeat.

~~~

Meanwhile, the "neighbor lady" in the condos knew my mom was not well, and why, though we never spoke out loud about Mom's drinking problem. The two women had been getting to know each other and got along fairly well. I saw Mary once outside of her condo as I pulled into Mom's driveway. We said our hellos and she asked how my mom was doing.

"Not well," I said, "and I'm about at my wits' end. Do you know anything about Meals on Wheels?"

"Well," she said slowly, looking at me intently, "I know that she's not eating any of your food, why would she eat theirs?"

By mid-December my mother could barely walk and was often crawling on the floor in her carpeted upper-level condo. To get up and down the stairs she would slide on her butt to keep from falling. After she drove (yes, drove) to the nearby market to get her gin she would lean heavily on the shopping cart to stay upright as she trudged slowly through the aisles. Everywhere she went she wore the same worn dark blue parka and royal blue knit wool cap, white sneakers and pink sweat pants that were too short, and hung loosely on her emaciated frame. Her "smoking clothes." When I would come to visit she was almost always downstairs next to the front door, sitting on a white steel chair in that same outfit and smoking a cigarette. She looked like a homeless person.

On Christmas Day, at noon, I had called Mom to see how she was doing. I dialed the number with dread, as I always did those days. What if she doesn't answer? What if she's – I steeled myself as the phone rang and rang until the answering machine finally picked up.

"*Hi, this is. . .*" click, clunk, shuffle, clunk.

"Heellooo!" she said in her usual sing-song voice. "Meeerrry Christmas!! Meeeeerrrrryy Chrriiiiissttmaaaas!"

"Hello, Dearie," I said, trying to sound upbeat. "Merry Christmas to you too. How are you?"

"Oh, fine, fine. When are you coming? I need to take a shower. Is the lasagna in the oven yet? I wanna play Scrabble!"

I rolled my eyes.

"Yes, yes, one thing at a time. I'm going to come get you in about an hour, OK?"

I knew we weren't going to play Scrabble. I knew she wouldn't eat any of the lasagna. But I played along anyway, not knowing what else to do.

"An hour? That's too soon. I need to take a shower. . ."

"Well get going, will you? I will be there in an hour. Then we'll come here and play Scrabble while the lasagna bakes, OK?"

That fateful Christmas day I arrived at her place at one o'clock and there she sat on her chair by the door, leaning with one elbow on her knee and the other hand holding a cigarette. She didn't smile at me as I drove up, and I didn't smile either. I couldn't remember the last time I had smiled, or laughed. We said hello and I helped her crawl upstairs. She hadn't showered and was clearly not ready to go. When we got to the top of the stairs she got up on her knees and started to unzip her coat. Suddenly she lost her balance and fell backwards, her knees twisting sideways as she hit the floor, her head bouncing off the thickly padded carpet.

"OK, that's it," I said, my anger starting to build. "I'm taking you to the hospital. Don't even try to argue with me. That is *it!*"

I could feel the anger turning to rage, and something else: a deep, gnawing fear. I quashed the emotions down as I always did. "Do NOT feel!" I told myself sternly. "Just get the job done. Focus on the work. Get the job done. Focus. . ." My hands started to shake as I helped her sit up. I could smell the gin.

"Don't bother taking off your coat. We're going right now."

I expected her to argue but to my surprise she didn't.

"OK," she said wearily. "I think I need my blood pressure checked. They'll do it for free, you know. You just walk in and they check your blood pressure. But we have to play Scrabble. And I want that lasagna, goddammit!"

I called Jacques so he could come help me get her down the stairs and into the car.

"Hold off putting the lasagna in the oven," I said quietly, my ear pressed tightly against the receiver as I turned away from my mom. "I think this is going to be a while."

Later that evening Jacques and I sat together on the couch, feeling each others' warmth as we quietly watched the fire burning in our wood stove. Mom was safely in a bed in the intensive care unit. I was a wrung-out rag. I sank into the couch and pressed against Jacques as every cell in my body slowly let go, the stress leaching out and away. We weren't talking much; we didn't need to. Jacques and I shared a special bond that only deep grief and the impending loss of a loved one can define. We both expected to mourn the deaths of our parents together.

The next morning, much to our utter shock, we discovered that my mother had agreed to go to detox and into treatment. She had been resisting this for so long – for the past year I had tried in vain to get her to do it. I wondered what it was that had made her change her mind this time. *Oh, thank God*, I thought. The psychiatric team at the hospital had contacted Brighton Hospital and there was an opening. They arranged for her to be admitted and we were to come get her as soon as she was discharged.

So I was just over two weeks sober myself as Jacques and I drove to Mom's condo that gray, misty morning after Christmas. We packed a small bag of essentials for her trip to Brighton and headed to the ER to pick her up. Along the way I prayed a silent, urgent plea to a God I didn't know: *Please, please, please help us*. Mom was waiting outside the ER doors in a wheelchair, dressed as usual in her blue and pink "smoking clothes" and puffing on a cigarette, the smoke curling upward in a slow blue spiral. Jacques helped her from the chair and into the back seat.

The End of The End

The intake processing at Brighton Hospital was busy as was the reception room. Many people had been waiting to get through the holiday. I could imagine the conversations:

"If Jimmy can just make it through Christmas. . ."

"Theresa, you have *got* to keep it together for the holiday. All the family is coming and I will *not* have you ruin it again!"

The day after Christmas, and especially New Year's Day, are busy times at treatment centers, and this was no exception. We stood in the cold entranceway while an intake nurse, safe behind a wall of thick glass, instructed us to stand by the locked glass door and wait for another nurse to come get us.

Finally we were ushered into a small waiting room that had a high, vaulted ceiling and rows of upholstered chairs, which reminded me somewhat of an airport lobby. There was a narrow counter on one side with a half-full coffee pot, styrofoam cups and various coffee fixings on it. Artwork hung on the other side of the room. Tall windows on another side opened to a view of the surrounding woods, with its dark, wet trees and scrubby underbrush drooping over a thin mat of melting, mud-flecked snow.

The rain continued to fall in a light mist from the low-hanging leaden sky and everywhere was a pervasive feeling of gloom. The room was dark and monochromatic, the colors seeping out through the tall windows as the grey dampness pressed in. We wheeled my mother's chair into the middle of the room and waited with the others to be called out for interviews. When it was our turn my mom was sent in first to talk with a doctor privately. Later I was called to discuss her situation and hear what her treatment would entail. I was told that the facility could handle her serious health conditions and withdrawal from alcohol. I was concerned because my own withdrawal had been so bad, I knew hers would be too, and she was in much worse shape physically than I had been. But they assured me they would take good care of her and that I would be allowed to visit later in the week. In the meantime there was no communication allowed, in or out, so we had to leave her there and trust that all would be well.

I wheeled her back to the waiting room, where Jacques was sitting reading a magazine. Oddly, there were only a couple of other people still scattered about. We were instructed to leave my mom in the waiting room and go, and a nurse would come to get her.

I'll never forget leaving her there, in that dim gloomy room. She sat rigid in her wheelchair, still bundled in her old blue parka, the blue cap pulled over her ears with a few matted wisps of blond hair peeking out. Her pink sweatpants rode halfway up her calves, exposing short white socks and swollen ankles. Stone-faced and unsmiling, she sat gazing at us through tired, steely eyes. Her skin was gray, her face deeply lined and pinched at the brow, the loose, sagging skin showing the contours of her bony facial structure. Her face resembled that of a mummy: still, dry and corpselike. But the eyes. The eyes were fiercely alive and staring, small black pupils surrounded by dark green irises, the whites the color of blood-stained urine. Red-rimmed and glassy, the eyes gazed out at us silently through the deathly mask, watching, waiting. I approached her slowly to give a hug goodbye. She returned it stiffly. This is not my mother, I thought as I turned away, my eyes welling with tears. This is not my mother.

Wonder Woman

My mom has always been my hero, my mentor. Throughout my life I have had such deep respect and veneration for her: her incredible work ethic and many accomplishments, her generosity, her happy, positive attitude, her honesty and upstanding character, her devotion and dedication to Mike and me, her love of nature and art, her love of life. I could write a longer list of things about my mom that I admire and all the positive traits that she has. Even when we weren't getting along when I was in high school I placed my mom on a tall pedestal. This made it particularly horrible to see what alcohol did to her, how it wreaked havoc on her mind and body and seemed to suck the very life right out of her soul. To watch her disintegrate and be completely helpless to do anything about it was the absolute worst hell I have ever experienced.

I remember one afternoon in late November. It was a few weeks before I quit drinking and Mom was starting to get bad again. She was at our house pulling various items out of a plastic bag that she had brought. She was always giving us things – vegetables and fruit, newspapers, photos, funny letters from her sister, things we could use around the house that she purchased at garage sales, things for the yard. This time, toward the end of the giving session, she pulled out a small, nicely wrapped gift for me. I slowly opened it, my heart heavy in my chest, because I knew what it was. "This is because you were such a life saver during the move from Madison," she said. "You're my hero, and I'm passing the torch to you." I pulled off the wrapping paper and there was the clear, rectangular paperweight with its orange lettering. "Wonder Woman Works Here."

I held back my tears. My mom was again in an accelerating decline, and – denial aside – she must have known it, at least on some level. Maybe she feared the severity of her drinking as much I had always feared mine? Perhaps she was in as much pain and agony as I was, knowing she was deep in the grip of alcoholism and stuck in its downward spiral? Maybe she, too, felt helpless and alone, like I so often had? I had never considered this before, had never considered that maybe she, also, knew the inner truth about herself and her drinking and felt *bad* about it. I hadn't thought about her feelings and I felt guilty about that. And then there I was. . . Wonder Woman? I felt funny taking back the gift, and somewhat dishonest. I felt dishonest for two reasons: one, I was also drinking heavily and knew I was on the same road as she, and two, just a few days earlier I had finally gathered the courage to watch the video I had shot in Madison during the move.

It slugged me between the eyes. What I saw was not the image of the strong, valiant daughter riding in on a grand white horse, beautiful, calm and composed, arriving home to rescue her ailing mother. The footage I shot with the camera turned on myself showed an exhausted, fear-ridden, tense, stressed-to-the-max, frantic middle-aged woman coming apart at the seams. My hair was a mess, my eyes red and puffy with dark circles underneath. I was wearing grungy gray sweat pants and a wrinkled white T-shirt. I spoke rapidly when I narrated, so fast at times that it didn't make sense, like words were processed faster in my brain than they were able to come out in speech. Sometimes the footage of the rooms, when I panned around, was shaky, obviously because my hands and body were quaking. My skin tone was bluish-gray, which may have simply been due to the indoor light and an incorrect white balance setting, but it was very unflattering nonetheless. In a nutshell, I looked terrible – drawn and tired, stressed and tense. I looked and sounded nothing like Katie Couric. The worst part was watching how frantic I was as I madly packed and moved spastically from room to room. I may have been heroic in the act of getting all of the work done, but it sure wasn't pretty. The camera never lies.

So when my mom gave me the paperweight that held so much meaning for us, so much history, and represented such grit, determination, toughness and strength of will, I had mixed feelings. On the one hand it was a very meaningful gesture for her to recognize and acknowledge how much my efforts had meant. But on the other, in "passing the torch" to me, I wondered, was she giving up? I felt sadness as I accepted it, and placed it carefully on my desk, where it still sits. Every day I see it, and every day it makes me think of my mom. But these are good thoughts now, happy thoughts. Our story wasn't over yet in *The Passing of the Wonder Woman Torch*, not by a long shot, but it *did* eventually get better. A lot better.

~~~

January was a hard month for us. Often one has to go through intense pain in order to emerge stronger on the other side. I wasn't used to experiencing pain without the comfort of alcohol so I cried almost constantly in therapy and during our group sessions at UMATS, where I was still in treatment at the Rachel Upjohn Center. I found out later that some of the other patients called me "Christi the Crier," but I didn't know that at the time. I had been going there, to UMATS, for nearly four weeks now and things were slowly improving. Normally the Intensive Outpatient Treatment Program (IOP) is four weeks long, but because I had started before the holidays and they all fell on weekdays that year I ended up attending IOP for six weeks.

Early every weekday morning I drove to the north side of Ann Arbor to attend the four-hour program. It started with a group session, where we discussed our current situations and how we felt about them, and received feedback from the counselors and other patients. Then, after a short break, there was an educational session, where we learned more about addiction, relationships, codependency, what the various drugs do to the body physically, the psychological aspects of addiction, how addiction affects relationships and those around us and so forth. After another short break the second group session began which consisted of more talking and feedback from the participants. It was interesting meeting the other "alkies and addicts," as I called them, and hearing their stories. The details were different, but in essence all our stories were basically the same, and we had a lot in common. After a while I began to enjoy going to IOP. I liked the structure of arising early every day and getting started. It was such a pleasure to wake up without a hangover, to enjoy the taste of my coffee and not have that awful stench of old alcohol in my breath and in my mouth.

    I was still naturally nervous and shy, so at first it was difficult to open up and discuss painful topics in front of strangers. But as time went on I became more comfortable with the others and I even made some casual friendships, which was a nice surprise. My mood improved too as I slowly eased out of depression. After decades of suffering I had been correctly diagnosed and was being treated with medication for bipolar disorder and related problems, like anxiety and insomnia. I felt indescribable relief in being under such competent care and finally, *finally* having these problems addressed. Between the excellent medical attention and my patient, responsive caregivers I gained tremendous overall confidence in my recovery program.

    But even with that growing confidence I continued to cry during the therapy sessions because I was forced to talk about things that were very tough, both with my current situation and about events that had happened in the past. The point of the talk therapy, of course, was to get these painful topics out in the open and discuss them, so one could begin learning new ways of coping with difficult emotions and situations rather than continuing in unhealthy behavior patterns. In my case I had avoided pain by smothering it, either by sheer force of will, by exercising excessively or by drinking. I had used alcohol to numb my feelings and go *around* situations rather than experience and go *through* them, so negativity – anger, resentment, disappointment – was always festering and rotting deep inside me, and every now and then it would bubble to the surface and cause pain, fear or other negative emotion. I hadn't known how else to cope with that except to use my old, tried and tested methods. So in order to quit drinking and stay sober it was essential that I learn new behavior patterns, new ways to think about and work through these difficult emotions so that I could address them, rather than stifle them.

It was very hard. It's difficult to quit an addiction to begin with because the physiological aspects – how the brain and body react to the substance chemically – are so enmeshed with the psychological – how the addictive behaviors have become entangled with every part of one's life. Quitting is even more of a challenge when there is chaos and drama all around you, or if there is a lack of support for the person trying to recover, be it at home or with other important relationships.

Situations on our home front were intense while I was first getting sober. My father-in-law was in hospice care at home and was close to death. My husband was holding himself together well, but the strain of his anguish was obvious to me, and that put stress on me as well. My mom was in the ICU at a hospital in Novi. She had been sent there by ambulance from Brighton Hospital after four days in the treatment center because her condition had deteriorated to the point where they were not equipped to handle it. Her liver was essentially failing.

I went to visit her several times while she was in the hospital. Not every day – it was a long drive from our house and it was hard on me mentally. My counselors and the others in my group had advised against going "too often" because the strain of it was a threat to my sobriety. In order to stay sober one has to put one's sobriety before all else, as priority number one, because if sobriety is *not* the first priority, then it generally doesn't last and all else falls apart again. It was difficult for me to do this because when it came to my mother I was used to putting her needs and wants before my own. And as much as I loved her, I still was so very, very angry. Sometimes when I was in group and talking about her decline, and all the suffering I had both witnessed and endured, I literally would start shaking and crying with rage. How could she leave me like this? We had so much unfinished business! Still so much to talk about, and to work through! I just couldn't fathom life without her, but I also was having a terrible time handling life with her, seeing her in this totally enfeebled and physically decrepit condition.

Nobody – my counselors especially – thought she was going to live. Maybe she herself did, but I certainly didn't. I was so angry at having to grieve her death and she wasn't even dead yet. And death from alcoholism is such a horrible thing to endure, so awful to watch. It's often a long, slow way to go, and quite painful as organs shut down and bodily functions cease to operate. Watching a once brilliant person's mind wither is an awful thing. For a couple of months during my mom's hospital stay and after she was discharged it seemed all we could ever talk about was eating and shitting. There was no meaningful conversation – she just wasn't there mentally and her thoughts were focused on getting better. To me it had seemed like a long, long time since my mom had been "there." Between the time period *before* she quit drinking, when she was in such bad shape from the alcohol, and the time *after* she quit, when toxins from her cirrhosis and related Ascites (described below) were affecting her mind, it had a been a lengthy span of time. Being around her was so emotionally and physically draining for me that I badly wanted it to end.

Mom was released from the hospital about the same time that I finished with IOP treatment, during the second week of January. The parts of her liver that were not damaged beyond repair were starting to recover, and her condition was improving. She was far from being out of the woods and was still very ill, but it gave us a glimmer of hope that she might somehow survive this. The following week Jacques' father died from his brain cancer. I hadn't seen Jacques much during that final week. Every day after work he would go to "the farm" to help with his dad as usual, and he had started to spend the nights there, sleeping in a small bed next to his dad's hospital bed, in case he was needed and also because he wanted to be there when his father passed away. When the time finally came his passing was gentle, and, according to the hospice nurse, "as good as it could be." We were all very sad, but relieved that the awful ordeal was over.

As for me, I was spending a portion of the day at UMATS going to one of the group meetings, as part of my daily "maintenance therapy." The UMATS program is geared toward easing patients into the twelve-step program of Alcoholics Anonymous, so part of the discussions were always about AA meetings and whether we had attended any. I was reluctant to go to AA and resisted it fiercely. I had tried it once, I argued, and didn't really like it. The counselors and other patients kept urging me to go, to give it a try again. They thought that my previous experience was unusual and that I hadn't tried hard enough to find meetings that I liked. I listened to all of this, but still I resisted.

Meanwhile my mother was back at her condo slowly recovering. She was suffering terribly from Ascites, a painful condition that occurs when one has cirrhosis of the liver, severe liver disease, cancer or other significant medical problems. Ascites is an accumulation of fluid primarily in the abdominal cavity and can bring with it an assortment of problems. In my mom's case she had abdominal swelling as well as significant swelling in her legs, ankles and feet. She also suffered from chronic fatigue and weight loss. Sometimes when I would come to visit I would be shocked to find her lying on the couch under a pile of blankets with just her emaciated pale face showing. One time I found her sleeping like this and thought she was dead, her face was so drawn and her pallor so grayish-yellow. When she stood she looked like an odd caricature of herself, like someone had squeezed all her bodily liquids from the top down. She looked like a pregnant Michelin Man with skinny arms and a tiny head. It was awful to watch her suffer, and the Ascites definitely affected her cognizance. To treat it, she was taking high doses of diuretics to expel the fluid, so she was constantly running to the bathroom. In addition to that, she had to go to the hospital once to be "drained." Literally, and without the benefit of pain-killers (her weakened liver couldn't handle that), a tube was punched into her abdomen and the excess fluid drained out. This situation lasted for months and was very trying on me – I can only imagine how horrible it was for her, and my heart aches to think about it.

Ever so slowly my mom got better and we became more hopeful. Jacques and I would joke that she was "way too stubborn and headstrong to let herself die after all she'd been through." The doctors told us that it was possible – if she was careful with her diet and never drank alcohol again – that the undamaged parts of her liver could regenerate and make a full recovery, and she could potentially still have a lot of years left in her. I was relieved but also afraid. We had been through so much, and now we were both sober. The pain of watching her nearly die was so overwhelming for me – someday I will have to do this again, I knew. I honestly didn't think I could. And part of me was still enraged at her. She was my hero, after all. How could she let herself fall so hard? How could she have the *nerve* to be anything less than what I had come to expect from her? Now, as a sober person, I had to truly deal with my own emotions – the pain, the rage, the fear of losing her, the guilt I felt so many times during this ordeal when I had wished she would die. And I had lots of buried "old baggage" as well that I had to address: my lost love and the agony of that relationship, the pain and anger at myself for quitting swimming before my senior year, my anger at my parents for getting divorced, my anger and confusion about the affair with Clara. I still cried in group when I discussed these feelings, my sadness pouring out from deep down inside like a dark river. It seemed to me that I had more "emotional bullshit" than anyone else, but maybe that was just my perception. I certainly cried a lot more than most of the other participants, and for that I often felt very embarrassed.

My mom had no interest in going into treatment for her alcoholism and didn't want to talk about what had happened at all. She is very "old school" that way, and wished to keep her health matters private.

She would sometimes say to me, "I hope you don't talk about me at your group meetings."

"Well *of course* I talk about you," I would reply.

How could I not? Her deterioration and near death from alcoholism, that I had watched for so long, was a huge factor in my decision to get sober myself. And she had always played such a major role in my life, as a mentor, a model, a sometimes adversary and a friend. Now that we were both sober we had to learn to relate to each other as sober people, as mature adults. In essence, we had to start building a relationship all over again, seeing each other clearly now for the first time in many, many years. I needed help with this because during my whole life I had felt "second" to my mom and "beneath" her, even as a grown woman in my early forties. Her need to control, her perfectionism and her domineering nature had always annoyed me, and often had made me very angry. I had to understand that I could not control her or her behavior, and that in order for us to have a pleasant relationship I was going to have to accept her as she was. But there's a fine line between *accepting* that someone is domineering and controlling and *allowing* that person to dominate and control oneself. Being a heavy drinker for so long, I hadn't learned how to set appropriate boundaries and I often allowed myself to be used, trampled upon and dominated by others. To stay sober I had to change this "doormat behavior" by learning who I was and what my boundaries were going to be. It seems so simple, but for me it was confusing and difficult. For one thing I was still trying to figure out who I was, now, as a sober person. I was all mixed up inside about my self-image and identity. Who was I, really, now that the fog of alcohol no longer surrounded me, blunting my senses and my vision? I didn't know, and I relied on my counselors and the people in my group for advice and support as I worked my way through this complex topic.

By April Mom's condition had improved dramatically. She was still very, very thin, but the swelling from Ascites had gone down and she was up and around and able to do things, although she moved slowly and weakly, like a much older person. I was also doing well. I had been sober for over four months and felt great physically. My bipolar disorder, anxiety and insomnia were being treated with medication and my moods for the most part were stable and good. And finally, after so many years of suffering, I was able to enjoy night after night of precious, deep, restful sleep. There is nothing so pleasurable as the release from pain, and that is how the ability to sleep felt to me and still does. Sleep was such a precious gift as a result of my sobriety. There were many more gifts that were to come from being sober too, as I found out later. But there was also work to do. I had always known that nothing that is great comes easy, at least not for me. Happiness in sobriety and life has been my biggest challenge.

After four months of being sober and still going to group therapy at UMATS I was told that it was time to leave and that I had to head out and face the world. I knew that my sobriety was tenuous, and I knew I had to do something, something more, now that I was to be "on my own." I agreed to give AA another shot. What the hell? I thought. I have to do *something*.

Hope and Faith

I believe in God. I believe in miracles. There are some people, perhaps some who knew me "back then," who will feel uncomfortable with those statements. Has Christi become a religious freak now, they might wonder? And there are some who will read this and think, "Oh, here we go. Another 'athlete-substance-abuser-finds-religion-gets-sober' book." For the record, I was a semi-doubter, a half-hearted agnostic, for much of my life. When I began my recovery from alcoholism I didn't want to hear about religion or God and was very headstrong about it. If I went to a group therapy session and people started talking about God I sometimes even got up and left, so strong was my unease and distaste for that type of discussion.

My family was not religious, so we didn't hear much about God growing up. We celebrated religious holidays and attended ceremonies (weddings, funerals) with reverence and respect, but belief and/or talk of God was not part of our daily lives. I always had a sense that there was something bigger "out there," that there were good forces and evil forces. My mother often talked of nature as a spiritual force, and that one might consider Mother Nature a god, or perhaps there were many gods in Nature (a pantheistic view). As for me, I liked the idea of good forces and bad forces, and that one could "tap in" to either force as they chose. How to tap into those forces at will was the question, though. Obviously I wanted to be connected with the good forces, and sometimes I felt that I was very much "in tune" with them. But an interactive God? One to whom you could talk and pray? One from whom you could receive answers, guidance and help? This I wasn't sure about. It just seemed sort of far-fetched, and I had a hard time believing in that idea. I understood the concept of faith, but I hadn't taken the "leap," as it were. If someone were to ask, I would answer that I considered myself an agnostic (i.e., one who doubts the existence of God).

It took some work and energy for me to take the "leap of faith" and start truly believing in a responsive and interactive God. I began to closely examine my history and my various beliefs at different stages in my life. Ridiculous as it seemed to me at first, I began to pray on a daily basis, asking not for "things," but rather for understanding, for the willingness to be open-minded, and for faith itself. I recalled many things that had happened in the past – some were serious, life-threatening events – where I had prayed to God with all my heart and had received undeniable, unexpected help, help that saved me from serious injury or death. I remembered the time when I stood atop that parking structure looking down, just before my senior year at UM, fully intending to end my life. Was that all-surrounding voice that so gently yet firmly told me to *"Just walk away"* the voice of God? I recalled other close calls with suicide, when I was so mired in depression, so utterly consumed with despair and hopelessness, that I had come close to "ending it all." Why hadn't I gone through with it? Did God have something to do with that as well? And then there were all my prayers before I got sober, times when I was so desperate that I begged God for help: help for me to get sober, help for my mom to get sober, help for us to get through our awful situation and, later, help for her not to die. On reflection I found numerous events in my life that had turned out one way when they could have turned out dramatically different, and in all of those cases I had prayed with pure, desperate, heartfelt need. For some time I still rebelled against the idea of an interactive God and I tried to attribute these various events to "chance" or "luck." But after much consideration and soul-searching I found that my logical mind just couldn't swallow that idea. I had to believe in something divine, a "Higher Power," and so I did. It was the only thing that made sense to me.

My conversion from an agnostic to a believer has been extremely important in my life and in my recovery from alcoholism. This is not to say that one must have faith in a Higher Power in order to recover. Certainly there are many people in recovery who do not and are successful. I am only speaking for myself. And for me, faith has given me comfort in knowing that I am never alone and that I can put my complete trust in God, because I truly believe that nothing happens in God's world by mistake. That sentence in itself covers an awful lot of scenarios and situations, if one really thinks about it. Also important for me is my belief that only a Power greater than myself could have restored me to sanity. My drinking was truly insane. I couldn't control it and I couldn't stop it. I kept repeating the same crazy behaviors and finding the same negative consequences of my actions over and over again. God knows I tried, so many times, to quit on my own, and I – as successful and strong-willed as I am – simply could not do it. It wasn't until I gave up, stopped fighting, and *surrendered myself* to a Higher Power that I was able to finally quit. But the acts of surrendering and quitting, significant as they are, are only the first steps. The question is, can one *stay* sober? Can one live a sober life and be happy, joyous and free? Being "happy, joyous and free" is one of The Promises of working the twelve steps of Alcoholics Anonymous. But is it really possible?

I am going to be blunt and honest in answering those questions for myself. "Can one stay sober?" Yes. So far, with a lot of support from my family and the fellowship of AA, medical treatment for my bipolar disorder and my faith in God, I have been able to stay sober since December of 2008. Truthfully, it has not been an easy path. My early sobriety was very difficult. It took time to find the correct medications and I still endured periods where I suffered from anxiety, depression and/or extreme mood changes. There were confusing emotions and buried pain to work through as well and, without alcohol to soothe me, I had to actually *feel* all of this pain and emotion. It sometimes seemed unbearable, like there was no end in sight, but I did get through it. I was also learning new coping mechanisms, new ways to handle stress and new ways to relate to the important people in my life, like my husband and my family. It was an emotionally draining and often trying time period and there were several instances where I almost gave in, where I almost relapsed and went back to the dark hell of alcohol. It is during times like these where the skills one learns in recovery can be lifesavers.

I continued to exercise on a daily basis and during my early sobriety this was especially helpful. Often when I was struggling with anxiety or depression a short, brisk walk – even just twenty or thirty minutes – would alleviate the symptoms and help me get "out of my head" enough to make it through the day. Sometimes, on particularly difficult days, I would head out several times to walk, to help me refocus on the positive. I still enjoy bike riding and swimming, taking long hikes in the woods and other physical activities. These activities are of utmost importance to my staying sober and happy. It's such a pleasure to be able to swim and to do it as well as I do. Swimming is so sacred to me. The feeling I get after a good swim is that of calmness, serenity and relaxed pleasure, a looseness throughout my body that I can't achieve in any other way. I suppose it is much like yoga or other stretching-intensive exercise. Swimming is one of the means by which I connect with my Higher Power, a way in which I can become "in tune" with the positive energy that I believe surrounds and flows through us. It gives me a feeling of physical and mental freedom, and I look forward to it as one of the best parts of the day.

So the next question, "can one live a sober life and be happy, joyous and free?" So far, at the time of this writing, I have been sober for well over four years. I have to honestly say that it has been a hell of a journey, and my life as a sober person has not always been happy, joyous and free. But I also have to say that my life is a whole lot better, most of the time, than it was while I was drinking. Gone are the days of horrific hangovers, of sleeping until two o'clock in the afternoon, of blackouts and drunk driving, of shame, guilt, remorse and regret. I wake up in the morning and I know where the car is. My coffee tastes great and my head isn't pounding. My hands no longer shake and I no longer feel nauseous for the first half of every day. I admit that I miss some of the fun I had, the crazy reckless things I used to do, the drinking I did with friends and the outrageous good times we had. But on the whole, my life is much better. Happy, joyous and free? Some of the time, yes, but not all of the time. I have to remind myself now and then that we strive for progress, not perfection, and that *any* progress toward a goal is a good thing. Not every day is going to be a great day, and I have learned that that's okay.

I was extremely nervous when I went to my first AA meeting. I have terrible social anxiety and it was pure torture to walk into that hospital cafeteria full of people I didn't know, fully aware that I was going to be singled out at some point and asked to say my name in front of everyone. I felt that all eyes were upon me as I slowly made my way to a table and sat down. And sure enough, there does come a point in the preliminaries of a meeting where newcomers are asked to identify themselves by saying their names and, if they want to, that they are an alcoholic, or an addict, or both. Like many people do, I started to cry after I introduced myself, partly because of my nervousness but also because of the sheer enormity of it. I had actually gone to an AA meeting and stated, in front of a group of strangers, that I was an alcoholic and was there, of course, because I couldn't stay sober on my own and needed help. It's funny looking back how traumatic that first meeting was for me. It was such a monumental act to decide to go, and I had dreaded it for so long. Now I can't imagine *not* going to meetings, and I try to go every day if possible. I just enjoy them so much, and get such pleasure from being a member of the fellowship.

So what exactly is this "fellowship?" What we are is a group of people who normally would not mix. We come from all walks of life; we represent all ages, backgrounds and all socioeconomic classes. We have come together because we share a common bond – alcohol and/or drug abuse – and we need each other in order to stay sober. It's that simple.

And it really does work. By attending meetings we learn from others how to cope with situations. We learn new tools and strategies to use when life becomes difficult, or unbearable. We make acquaintances and friends, and have a place to go and "hang out" with others when we feel lonely or isolated. There is much fun and laughter, joking and banter before and after meetings, and often small groups will go out after a meeting to have coffee or eat together. There is camaraderie and acceptance of one another. We are like soldiers back from war, who share an intimate bond that only another "comrade-in-arms" can truly understand. I honestly don't know what I would do without my evening AA meetings. I love seeing my AA friends regularly and enjoy the social aspect of the fellowship. Without it I think I would be a very lonely person, and the odds of my staying sober would be slim.

Long ago my brother claimed that "all of my problems would go away if I quit drinking." I am still in the process of testing that assertion. Certainly a lot of my problems have gone away. But life is what it is and there will always be at least a few problems, occasional tough challenges, difficult times and sad events. At some point in everyone's life there will be heartache and loss. But it's how we deal with these occurrences that matters. Are we going to go back to using drugs or alcohol to smother pain, fear, hardship and suffering, or are we going to work through our difficulties using new coping strategies, new tools and new behaviors in order to continue on the path to improving our lives?

Throughout this book I have written about swimming and the huge impact it has had on my life, from an early age. I spoke of how much I initially hated it, but so desperately wanted to become a part of the "Good Swimmer" club, and finally succeeded. Later I brashly stated that I think swimming at the serious-to-elite level is a dangerous sport, both from a physical and a psychological standpoint. I wrote about my physical injuries and the pain that I endure daily as a result of years and years of intense training. I stated that I, and others that I know, have emotional scars and various psychological problems that I believe can be attributed to the sport. I also wrote about the positive consequences of being a competitive swimmer: the self-confidence and poise it gave me plus the friendships and camaraderie, the positive body and self-image, the incredible work ethic, the ability to focus, to set and achieve goals, among other things.

So what are the emotional scars? For me swimming was like a drug and I loved it. I was addicted to the daily grind, the stress and pressure of both practice and competition, the great feeling I had after a grueling, exhausting workout and the sense of accomplishment after practice or a successful competition. But the sport – despite the friendships – was isolating for me. It allowed me to stifle my adolescent feelings and smother my fear and pain. It allowed me to be alone with myself and my unguided, self-absorbed and introspective thoughts too much, I think. In that respect it was very much like my alcohol use: isolating, numbing, stifling, self-serving. The sport encouraged growth in certain ways – confidence, poise, self-esteem, work ethic, goal-setting – but quelled it in others, i.e., how to express and deal with negative emotions, like pain, fear, and in my case, questions about my body image and sexuality. Often the amount of work crossed the line into abusive and I *liked* that. I *thrived* on it. But it was mentally unhealthy because it set the standard for me that hard work was always about pushing to the extreme, regardless of pain and/or physical cost. For me there was no moderation, no balance. I was either going "all out" in something or not doing it. It was not a comfortable way to live, and I still struggle with how to find balance and moderation in my life. This, I believe, is an emotional scar that is a direct result of swimming, a behavior pattern learned and encouraged during my swimming career.

My bipolar disorder is another example of imbalance. I have often wondered if the extreme training caused the disorder, or, if I already had it, did the training exacerbate it? There were a lot of "extremes" occurring during my time as a competitive swimmer and I truly believe that, cumulatively, they were very unhealthy: significant chemical and hormonal influences in the developing brain and body, physical injuries and pain from overuse, extreme overeating, extreme drinking. Did these bodily extremes contribute to my bipolar disorder, e.g., my depression, my "normal" state of hypomania and the occasional bouts with mania? How could such severe biochemical disruptions in a young person, whose body and brain are not fully developed until age twenty-five, *not* cause some sort of irregularity? I'm no scientist and am only speculating here. But based on my own experience it seems logical that "extreme living" is both a symptom of an underlying problem and can likewise cause other problems, perhaps even mood disorders like anxiety and bipolar disorder.

Then there is alcohol and drug abuse. It was so rampant in every team in which I swam – it was just a "part of it." We worked hard, we partied hard. Drinking was another acceptable and encouraged form of extreme behavior that the sport allowed. Sure, there were a few people on all my various teams who did not consume alcohol, but by and large it was the norm to drink, and I believe it still is. I know that some young people will emerge from this unscathed, but then there will be others, like me, who will turn into full-blown alcoholics and will endure all the pain and suffering that this life brings with it.

Back to my brother: did "all" of my problems go away when I quit drinking? No. I am still working on areas of my life and am still in the process of healing. However, so many things have improved because I am sober. I am now able to talk about the end of my swimming career without crying and feeling the anguish of deep regret. I have come to accept what happened and have forgiven myself for my perceived weaknesses and failures. Mostly I'm at peace, and can look back at my career with pride and satisfaction, rather than sadness and remorse.

My mother and I have built a new relationship that is loving, positive and respectful of each other. Miraculously she survived her brush with death and her liver made a complete recovery. She has not had a drink since that fateful Christmas Day in 2008 and is back to her happy, positive, busy, feisty self. On my end I have accepted my mom as she is, have embraced certain aspects of her lifestyle and incorporated them into my own, and have rejected others. I do not feel dominated and controlled by her, but rather I feel assertive and strong and able to be true to myself. Because she survived we have had the opportunity to talk about past events that were painful for us and resolve conflicts. It is truly a miracle and the greatest blessing to have my mother back in my life, with both of us sober.

My relationship with my husband has improved too. We no longer engage in negative, codependent behavior. We are respectful of one another's needs, accept each other for who we are and are not controlling. It did take some time and work for our relationship to evolve into the positive one that it is now, but the energy we put into it was well spent. I am empowered by my sobriety and Jacques seems to like the upgraded version of me. Life in our home is calm, peaceful and pleasant. We discuss issues of contention rationally and without anger, and almost never argue. He is my best friend again, and this is another priceless gift of sobriety.

As for my sexuality issues I still cringe in my heart when I think of how it felt to be called a "freak," "weirdo," "dyke," "fag," "lesbo," "sir," or "whatever." But most, though not all the time, I am comfortable with myself, how I look and how I feel inside. I am not attracted to women, but am also not ashamed that I was. I believe that my attractions and my affair were natural parts of a learning process that I (after so much verbal abuse for many years and the resulting confusion from it) needed to go through in order to better understand who I am. The ability to think this through and find resolution with it has also been a result of my sobriety. I couldn't have addressed the sexuality issue while I was drinking because part of why I drank was to bury it, which of course didn't work. It still bothers me and makes me uncomfortable sometimes to be called "sir," but that is happening less and less as I get older, and it no longer angers me.

My self-image and identity remain closely tied to my body image and my view of myself as an athlete. I realize that my challenge lies in altering this view to that of an "aging athlete," because that is the reality. I also understand the need to view myself from many angles and not just the athletic side, which is quickly evolving into something quite different from my perception and experience of my physical self when I was thirty. I am slowly learning to accept what has happened to my body and recognize other aspects of myself that make me a well-rounded person. This is a healthy form of growth, though it is often difficult because it again requires introspection and thorough self-examination. I still sometimes feel that nagging sense that I am not "good enough." It is a negative perception of my Self, and one that I am constantly working to change.

In sobriety I have learned that it is critical for me to have acceptance, faith and hope. I must have acceptance of myself and acceptance of circumstances external to myself in order to have serenity. This means that I need to understand that I am able to control only myself and my actions. Everyone and most everything else are beyond my control and, in my mind, are in God's hands. The concept of not being in control of the whole show and "turning it over" to God has been very liberating for me, and has given me freedom from a certain bondage, the heavy yoke of self-slavery (the exhausting work of trying to control situations that are not to my liking). My faith in God has enabled me to "let go" of this need to control and to "let God" do the work.

What has worked for me, and what has kept me sober, is a multi-faceted approach to my recovery. One, I have a solid conviction that there is a Higher Power, that I call God. I believe that God restored me to sanity and now gives me a daily reprieve from the compulsion to drink. Also, because of my faith, I have confidence that things will work out, if I just put my trust in God. Two,

Hope and Faith

I am fortunate to have people who provide support and help me on a regular basis: my husband, my family, my doctor who manages my medications and my therapist at UMATS, my AA sponsor, and my friends. Three, I now have tools and strategies for living that I have learned by working my recovery program. And four, by attending AA meetings regularly I have access to the experience, strength and hope of the many good people that I have met through the fellowship, and an active social life as well.

Finally, I have hope. There must always be hope, if even only a faint glimmer. I have experienced deep despair, crushing depression and feelings of uselessness and hopelessness. I have spent my share of time in the bottom of the well, the "jumping off place," as we say in AA. On several occasions I came close to ending my life, but obviously did not. Always, even in my darkest moments, somewhere way back in the shadow of my private hell there was a thread of hope. I do not know how to explain feeling hopeless and suicidal while at the same time seeing a thread of hope. That is something that I must attribute to the existence of an interactive, responsive Higher Power. How else to explain it?

Hope and faith are now my foundation for living and I have benefitted greatly from this. I no longer feel that nagging, gnawing fear deep within, or the "hole" in my Self that I have described earlier in this book. Faith has given me confidence and courage; hope has given me strength and a positive outlook on life. I even experience serenity, which in the past I doubted would be possible. I believe that being sober is the key to my being successful in all aspects of my life. And I firmly believe that acceptance, faith and hope are critical elements in the quest to be happy, joyous and free. I am deeply grateful for my sobriety, and for every day that I am alive and well and have the opportunity to be useful – and to be Me.

Epilogue

On Friday, July 13, 2012 Jacques' sister Daryl died from a heroin overdose. That same morning she was released from prison following a three-month incarceration for breaking her parole, for using drugs. Several hours after being freed Daryl shot up for the last time in a McDonald's restroom near interstate 94. Employees had to break down the door to find her body. Daryl and I were not close, but I did care for her, and I always felt empathy when it came to her and her drug problem. She was a sweet, gentle person who *did* really want to quit using, but she was just so caught up in the swirling black hole of drugs and all the drama of that lifestyle that she could never find a way out. Daryl was 54, the average age of death of an alcoholic or drug addict. In addition to Jacques and their mother, Daryl left behind a husband, two adult children and a granddaughter.

Addiction is such a serious and complex disease. I believe that an effective way to fight it and to stay sober is to apply a multi-faceted approach – to hit it from every angle by treating the psychological as well as the biological components. This means focusing on emotional issues such as loneliness, fear, isolationism, negative habitual behavior patterns and problems with relationships. These can be addressed through therapy with a psychologist and/or talk therapy with a group, for example Alcoholics Anonymous. For those who suffer from additional medical problems like bipolar disorder, depression, anxiety, insomnia and so forth there are effective treatments available that target those specific problems. There are also medicines that alleviate cravings for alcohol and other drugs. Research is ongoing and science has come a long way in understanding the disease of addiction and how it affects the body and brain, both physically (structurally) and psychologically.

My recovery plan includes treating my bipolar disorder, chronic pain, anxiety and insomnia with medication, and I am certain that feeling *well* helps tremendously with my ability to stay sober. Therapy and participation in AA are also very important and necessary ingredients, as is my spiritual development. While it has not been an easy path, I now have confidence in my recovery, and hope – hope for a happy and productive future. My message to the reader who may have an addiction problem is this: *never lose hope and never give up looking for a solution.* Chances are good that there is a solution out there, but it is up to you to find it and stick with it. You and only you can decide to climb out of River B. But there *is* help available to you, and there *is* hope. I am proof of that.

When Daryl died I cried for days. My AA sponsor bluntly said, "well, better her than you," to try to comfort me. It didn't. But I came to see that she was right, and I'm sure that that is one reason why Daryl's death touched me so deeply, why it hurt so much. *It could've been me.* Actually, it could've been any one of *us*, meaning we alcoholics and addicts. We walk such a fine line as it is – the odds of staying sober are statistically low for us. It takes daily diligence to stay sober and is often very tough, for some more than for others. We often have to "play the tape through to the end" when we are considering drinking or using again. We have to see – again – what the future holds when we are enmeshed in that lifestyle. We must know in our hearts and minds that in the blink of an eye, a turn of the car key, a dose too big, another bad decision, that everything can go away in an instant, that all can change, forever.

I have tried to be honest throughout this work, and I have also tried to be kind. My mom once told me, "When one has a child it doesn't come with an instruction manual." My family had and still has troubles like everyone's does, but we are loving, good-hearted, generous people who truly care about each other and others. And forgiveness is such an essential component of staying sober. Over time I have forgiven my family for their mistakes, and they have forgiven me for mine. Most significantly we love each other, and I know that they are supportive of my sobriety. For that I am eternally grateful.

Appendix A: Source Notes

CHAPTER 16: MARRIAGE AND CODEPENDENCE

Page 189   Rama Rao, M.D.,
"Overcoming Codependency"
www.radiologychannel.com